LIBELLUS

LIBELLUS

ADDRESSED TO LEO X, SUPREME PONTIFF

by

Blessed Paolo Giustiniani
&
Pietro Querini

Hermits of Camaldoli

LATIN & ENGLISH EDITED & TRANSLATED, WITH NOTES TO THE LATIN, BY

Stephen M. Beall

INTRODUCTION, WITH NOTES TO THE ENGLISH, BY

John J. Schmitt

MARQUETTE
UNIVERSITY
PRESS

REFORMATION TEXTS WITH TRANSLATION (1350–1650)

VOLUME 14

KENNETH HAGEN, GENERAL EDITOR

THEOLOGY AND PIETY, VOL. 6

IAN CHRISTOPHER LEVY, SERIES EDITOR

© 2016 Marquette University Press
Milwaukee, Wisconsin 53201-3141
All rights reserved.
www.marquette.edu/mupress/

LIBRARY OF CONGRESS CATALOGING-IN-PUBLICATION DATA

Names: Giustiniani, Paolo, 1476-1528, author. | Quirini, Pietro, 1479-1514, author. | Beall, Stephen, editor, translator. | Schmitt, John J., editor, writer of introduction. | Giustiniani, Paolo, 1476-1528. Libellus ad Leonem X. | Giustiniani, Paolo, 1476-1528. Libellus ad Leonem X. English.
Title: Libellus : Addressed To Leo X, Supreme Pontiff / By Blessed Paolo Giustiniani & Pietro Quirini, Hermits Of Camaldoli ; Latin & English Edited & Translated, With Notes To The Latin, By Stephen M. Beall ; Introduction, With Notes To The English, By John J. Schmitt.
Description: Milwaukee, Wisconsin : Marquette University Press, 2016. | Series: Reformation texts with translation (1350/1650) ; volume 14 | Series: Theology and piety, ; vol. 6 | English and Latin. | Includes bibliographical references and index.
Identifiers: LCCN 2016039906 | ISBN 9780874627152 (pbk. : alk. paper)
Subjects: LCSH: Church renewal—Catholic Church—Early works to 1800. | Jews—Conversion to Christianity—Early works to 1800. | Missions to Jews—Early works to 1800. | Missions to Muslims—Early works to 1800. | Catholic Church—Relations—Eastern churches—Early works to 1800. | Eastern churches—Relations—Catholic Church—Early works to 1800. | Catholic Church—History—16th century. | Leo IX, Pope, 1475-1521.
Classification: LCC BX1315 .G58 2016 | DDC 262.001/7—dc23
LC record available at https://urldefense.proofpoint.com/v2/url?u=https-3A__lccn.loc.gov_2016039906&d=DQIFAg&c=S1d2Gs1Y1NQV8Lx35_Qi5FnTH2uYWyh_OhOS94IqYCo&r=hokKgJ4JxWGN8r507i6qR6wpZ-D_MmlVVO57591llHQ&m=IXCm023fkrsn4n-sStcPeTPrZ2S5ESQsRfPMk7W7wEk&s=GEJG63oHMnr-P8zov7_9uUG-EhW3QgaeLNBymovNdHw&e=

♾ The paper used in this publication meets the minimum requirements of the American National Standard for Information Sciences— Permanence of Paper for Printed Library Materials, ANSI Z39.48-1992.

Association of American
University Presses

MARQUETTE UNIVERSITY PRESS
MILWAUKEE

The Association of Jesuit University Presses

CONTENTS

DEDICATIONS

For my wife, Judith: quantum in te crescit amor,
tantum crescit pulchritudo (St. Augustine)

Stephen

For my wife Bobbie

John

PREFACE

The history of this publication of the Libellus begins with Fr. Basil Corriere, ErCam, of Holy Family Hermitage, Ohio, who spoke with me about Paul Giustiniani and the Libellus. I later read, in *Camaldolese Extraordinary*, that despite Pope Leo X's neglect of this "little book," Giustiniani some years afterwards was still convinced of the concerns that he and Peter Querini had discussed and which he put in writing. I was struck by the fact that it was never translated into English or any other language (with a neglected Italian translation in 1995 which I learned of later).

The idea took a leap forward when Fr. Ugo Fossa, OSBCam, Camaldoli, Italy, gave me, in the library of Camaldoli, a photocopy of the only manuscript of the Libellus

I asked Dr. Stephen Beall if he would be interested in being its translator. I am grateful that he accepted the offer and that he has produced a graceful translation. The work progressed with Dr. Katherine Milco reading and recording the manuscript and Dr. Constance Nielsen putting the text of the *Annales* into a computer file. Lee Sytsma, PhD Cand., provided a bilingual format.

Some of the references to biblical texts have been noted. Giustiniani would have referred to biblical passages by the names and numbering of the Vulgate. This book uses the Revised Standard Version for the names of the books and the verses. The abbreviations for the biblical books are those used in the *Catholic Biblical Quarterly*. Dates use the inclusive designation B.C.E. (Before the Common Era) and C.E. (Common Era) rather than B.C. and A.D.

The word Pope is used in the Introduction and notes, but not in the translation of the text. Giustiniani did not use it. In addition, the adherents of the religion of Islam are called Muslim, and not by the now offensive word Mohammadan.

The spelling of Giustiniani's colleague on the title page is Quirini, while in the Introduction and notes it is Querini. This reflects the variation in orthography that he used himself.

The abbreviation Er.Cam., or simply E.C., stands for Eremita Camaldolensis, Camaldolese Hermit.

My sincere gratitude is extended to all who helped in the production of this volume. These include those mentioned above and especially Dr. Ian Levy, the editor of the Series, and Dr. Andrew Tallon, the director of Marquette University Press. The librarians of Marquette Library have been most helpful, especially Rose Trupiano.

SPECIAL NOTICE & ACKNOWLEDGMENT IN GRATITUDE FOR USE OF THE COVER ICON

The following description of this unique icon was written by Reverend Richard G. Cannuli, O.S.A., for the golden jubilee of Holy Family Hermitage, September 8, 2009.

The Hermitage coat of arms appears in the upper center.

On the right stands Saint Romuald (952-1027), the founder of Camaldolese Order, who holds in his left hand a ladder that recalls the Jacob-like vision that preceded his foundation of Camaldoli; in the same hand he holds a crook which rests in the stream of the Spirit, while his extended right hand passes on the eremitic tradition.

On the left side stands the Camaldolese reformer, Blessed Paul Giustiniani (1476-1528). His left hand is extended to receive from St. Romuald "a double portion of his spirit" (cf. 2 Kings 2:9).

In the words of Saint Bruno-Boniface, "The father of rational hermits, who live according to a law" the scroll in Blessed Paul Giustiniani's right hand pays tribute to his predecessor, thus fulfilling the precept of St. Paul (Romans 12:10), "in honor preferring one another."

Holy Family Hermitage
Camaldolese Hermits
1501 Fairplay Road
Bloomingdale, OH
43910-7971

INTRODUCTION

*L*ibellus ad Leonem Decimum is a long letter addressed in 1513 to the new pope Leo X. The authors of the document were two Camaldolese monks, Paolo Giustiniani and Pietro Querini, convinced that the Church needed imminent reform. There had been many and multiple calls for church reform for centuries, and they would continue. The Libellus predates the Theses of Martin Luther by three years. The Libellus was written almost one hundred years after Jan Hus (1369-1415) was executed for his reforming position. The monks' call for reform agreed in principle with some points in the previous reformers' understanding of the problems and their solutions. But their orientation was fully in support of the core of traditional doctrine and of the supremacy of the bishop of Rome and the steadfast tradition of previous councils.

Northern Italy was still aware of the execution of the reformer Giralomo Savonarola (1452-1498) in Florence. He had appealed to the secular powers to call a council that would depose the Borgia Pope Alexander VI. This pope is often taken as the depths of unworthy men who held the position. Savonarola decried a corrupt papacy and lack of asceticism in the members of religious orders and in the laity. In addition he predicted an imminent judgment and the end of the world because of this corruption. He did not address himself very much to the lack of education among the priests in the church. The misguided faithful were at the mercy of men who entered the service of the church with inadequate preparation. Some applicants became clergy in order to gain wealth and to create careers in a church which was in need of great reform. A successful ecclesiastical careerist could accumulate many benefices (positions that brought income) and, as that cleric rose above the lower ranks, he could use incompetent substitutes as priests in place of his own pastoral care.

Moreover, the church in its leaders had begun selling spiritual goods and indulgences for the sake of financing wars and the building of elaborate places of worship. Prelates lived in luxury with little, if any, thought of repentance or piety. The corruption of the papacy itself was well known and decried. Church leadership was often bought, even at the highest levels.

The people in the pews were subject to preachers who explained the Bible and the faith in ways that did not really follow the main tradition of the church. Fears about an imminent end of the world were among the troubling elements of the time. Superstitions abounded among the common people that should have been corrected by informed leaders. The undertrained clergy, the corruption at high levels within the hierarchy, the lack of knowledge of the Bible, the rampant superstition among the faithful, and the need for the whole human race to understand and accept the Gospel of Christ rightly were the concern of many who recognized the need for reform.

Nonetheless, the early fifteenth century began to enjoy the news of the discovery of new lands and new peoples in the western parts of the world. And to the east of Europe, a different religion was on the rise and gaining more followers and more land. This spread of Islam was interpreted as an intolerable threat to Europe and the Christians living there. Constantinople, which has been regarded as the second Rome, had fallen in 1453 to the Ottoman Turks. In turn, Muslims were evicted from the united Kingdoms of Aragon and Castile in 1502 (ten years after the Jews had experienced exile from Spain). But knowledge of the armies of the Arabs and the Turks increasingly brought fears to Europe and its Christian inhabitants.

The successor of Alexander VI (1341-1503, pope from August 1492- August 1503), Julius II (1443-1513, pope from November 1503 to February 1513) did little as pope to reform the church in its head and members. Julius's preoccupations centered on politics and military activity, even to the point of mounting his own horse to lead an army. There was a bit of irony in his condemnation of nepotism and of the purchasing of the papacy because these were two means by which he himself had attained the papacy. In 1508, Julius joined the League of Cambria (France, Germany, and Spain), and they defeated the republic of Venice. Julius, however, had further interests in the arts, and he commissioned the plan for a new basilica of St. Peter in Rome and engaged Michelangelo to paint the ceiling of the Sistine chapel. His enemies included King Louis XII of France and Emperor Maximilian I, who assembled some cardinals in Pisa for a council to dethrone Julius. But in 1512, to fulfill promises he had made, he himself called a council that would meet in Rome (which would become

Lateran V). He attended four sessions beginning 1512. He could not attend the fifth session in February 1513 because of sickness, and he died within a week.

The first five sessions of the Lateran V accomplished the condemnation of the group who had participated in the unauthorized council that was called in Pisa (which intended to unseat Julius II, an effort supported by French king Louis XII and the emperor Maximilian) and the abrogation of the Pragmatic Sanction of Bourges. That sanction both proclaimed the authority of a council over a pope and declared that the French political leaders could appoint bishops without consulting the pope. Cardinal Giovanni De' Medici was elected pope March 19, 1513, and took the name of Leo X. He was crowned ten days later.

This seemed like an auspicious new beginning. Perhaps with a new pope, a very young one, the general council then in session would be the best hope for the needed revitalization of the life of the church.

The authors of the Libellus were two Camaldolese hermits, Vincenzo Querini and Tommaso Giustiniani. Both were from aristocratic families and knew Giovanni De' Medici, who had become Pope Leo X, well enough to make clear to him the needs of the church as they saw them and which, they felt, cried out for attention.

The authors were Venetians of upper nobility who had studied together at the University of Padua. Querini chose the pursuit of further education, while Giustiniani chose the pursuit of holiness. Although Querini defended his doctoral dissertation before several cardinals in 1502 and earned praise for bringing together the teachings of Plato and Aristotle, it was Giustiniani who became a very prolific writer. While much of his vast writing remains in manuscript, various treatises and devotional works have appeared in print.

After university studies, Giustiniani lived in Venice and with others, including Gasparo Contarini, a future cardinal, formed a fellowship of spiritual and intellectual development. The group thrived under the leadership of Giustiniani. Soon Querini was appointed to the diplomatic corps of the republic of Venice. Eventually Giustiniani made a pilgrimage to the Holy Land. Both observed the variety of peoples and the condition of the church in the various places they visited: Querini in the courts of Burgundy, England, Spain and Strasbourg, and Giustiniani in the lands of the Eastern Christians and the lands of Muslim peoples. Both were well equipped to observe and comment on the condition of the human race in the old world and in the recently discovered lands across seas.

Tommaso Giustiniani entered the monastery of Camaldoli in Tuscany in 1510, receiving the habit on Christmas day and taking the name of Paolo/Paul. He was joined there by Vincenzo Querini the following year who took the name Pietro/Peter. Both soon set out to reform the order, restoring greater fervor to all the monks and obtaining the independence of the hermits, who lived in independent cells, from the control of the cenobites who lived in community further down the mountain of Camaldoli. The reform of the order was achieved with the required approval of the new pope, Leo X. With this reform of the order accomplished successfully, the two turned their attention to the universal church.

Their ideas took the form of a long letter to Leo X. The main ideas of the Libellus may have been worked out in early 1513, and the writing probably occurred during the months of June and July. The probability is that Giustiniani wrote the entire piece after thorough discussion with Querini, although Giustiniani in this document refers to himself only once and to his pilgrimage to the Holy Land. (Bowd, pp. 136-137) Thus the following comments and the notes in this volume refer to the author in the singular.

How this document was received in Rome, either by those around Leo X or by the Pope himself, is not known. There was no response from Leo X, and no description of his reaction.

Nor is there any evidence that Querini, while he served in the court of Leo X, ever asked him whether he had seen the document. His access to the Pope was restricted. One conversation is reported among Leo X, Cardinal Bembo and Querini on April 15, 1514. Querini died in September 1514, before he could receive the honor of cardinalate, which was the rumor that had circulated about Leo X's intention.

There are recorded, however, Giustiniani's later comments about the Libellus. In response to a colleague's request for a copy of it some twelve years later, Giustiniani replied in a letter, which remained unfinished, to his fellow Camaldolese hermit, Galeazzo Gabrielli (in religion, Peter of Fano). Giustiniani wrote that he fears there might be weaknesses in its writing, but not in its analyses of the corruption of the church and the needs of the world. At his age and condition of health, he was not up to corrections. He did think that his desires expressed in the document still applied.

I agree with you and others that it would be necessary to correct it. But do not imagine that at my age, grown cold in body and spirit, I could apply myself to see if there are some errors in the Latin or if some non-Latin words have crept in. The one thing I want you to know is that I made every effort in this writing to set forth the ideal and the desire that I felt then in my soul, since I had no other aim in writing, as I believe I said in the preface, than to put before Pope Leo what I was daily asking the Lord God in my prayers. . . . I do not think that it is out of place to desire the conversion of the Jews and of idolaters to the faith, the conversion of the Muslims, the reunion of all Christian peoples with the Roman Church, and worldwide reform, and these are the main topics treated. This is just what I felt I had to submit to Pope Leo X for his consideration. At the beginning of his elevation to the pontifical throne, I hoped for reform in the world as did many others, who were as mistaken as I was. . . . . . Moreover, I believe someone like Lord Peter Bembo would counsel no other correction than casting it into the fire. ... To sum up, my style in this treatise is monastic, as one of my friends says, and that is all I can say.[1]

Both Giustiniani and Querini had given thorough thought to the conditions which the western church was experiencing. They were moved by an encompassing care and an intense love of the church to produce this document. It seems unfortunate that their intense motivation did not rub off effectively and in the same way onto the members of the Venice group from years before, for some of them rose to influential positions in the church.

After the writing of the Libellus, Giustiniani went on to found a group of hermits apart from the monastery and hermitage of Camaldoli. The group later became the Camaldolese Hermits of Monte Corona. He continued to have contact with various church officials. He founded many eremitical houses in different parts of Italy. He fled Rome during the sack of Rome, which began in 1527. He died at the age of 52 on Mount Soracte on June 28, 1528.

Perhaps the first influence of the Libellus can be seen in the Concilium de emendanda ecclesia (1537). This report, commissioned by Pope Paul III, was written by a group of scholarly church leaders, headed by Gasparo Contarini. The influence of the Libellus occurs through the commission's president, who had been part of the

---

1   Camaldolese Extraordinary, pp. 192-193 (in the French, Un humaniste eremite , pp. 129-130).

Venice group with Querini and its leader Giustiniani. The document recommends and fully endorses only the internal church reforms of the Libellus; it does not discuss the ideas of evangelization of the new world or the conversions of Jews and Muslims.

The first biography of Giustiniani was written by a monk who is referred to as Luke of Spain. He treats at some length the life of Paul. In the late seventeenth century, John of Treviso wrote perhaps a fuller life of Paul using some of Paul's own writings. This work of John of Treviso remains only in manuscript.[2]

In 1729, Agostino Romano Fiori, wrote a *Vita Del Paolo Giustiniani*. He does not discuss any of Giustiniani's works at length. After the narrative of his life, Fiori lists many topics and headings that Giustiniani wrote about. He includes, no doubt referring to what is now known as the Libellus, a writing he called *de officio pontificis ad Leonem*, among the first four important ones.[3] This title must refer to the Libellus because the Libellus does focus on the needs of all humanity as they rest on the shoulders of the Supreme Pontiff. A few other scholars have mentioned this alternate title.

The *Annales Camaldulenses* is a compilation of documents of the Camaldolese order. The compilation was made by Johannes-Benedictus Mittarelli and Anselmus Costadoni, abbots of Camaldoli. They had not been members of Giustiniani's own group, the Camaldolese Hermits of Monte Corona, who follow a more eremitical observance of the Camaldolese tradition. Giustiniani's works and other Coronese materials are in Volume 9, the supplemental Addenda. It may be that Mittarelli and Costadoni gave the work its name of Libellus, using that on the title page of the work.

In the twentieth century, a variety of scholars analyzed and commented on the Libellus. In 1926, Joseph Schnitzer wrote a study of the abbot of Camaldoli under whom Paul Giustiniani had entered the hermitage and became a Camaldolese, namely, Peter Delfin. Schnitzler treats Querini and Giustiniani and their work in 22 pages, describing the content of their memorial to Leo X without using the title for it in the *Annales*.

The renowned German church historian Hubert Jedin published *A History of the Council of Trent*. Jedin had carefully read the work of

---

2   Leclercq, in *Camaldolese Extraordinary*, p.30.
3   On the copy of this book digitized by Goggle, at page 431 there is a hand-written note which reads "in folio."

Giustiniani and Querini. He speaks of the "grandeur of their plan." Worth quoting are these words, "It is no exaggeration to say that the reform programme of the two Camaldolese monks preoccupied the Church for more than a century (trans. Ernest Graf; 1: 129 and 130).

In 1962, the Italian scholar Silvio Tramontin published a thorough study on the Libellus. In 26 pages he gives a fairly complete report. The title of the article may be misleading: the Libellus was not written explicitly for the council, but addressed to the Pope.

In response to Pope John XXIII calling a general council, the German theologian Hans Küng wrote a book, *The Council, Reform and Reunion*, which mentions the two authors twice by name but not the title of the work, or specifically what the work involves. He did name the authors as "spokesmen of radical reform" presenting "bold recommendations" (pp. 71 and 82).

At the Second Vatican Council itself, 1962-1965, the Libellus was not quoted directly. But key items which the Libellus had proposed were finally addressed. The liturgy should be in the language of the people so that they might really profit from participation in it. The hierarchy of the church must be responsible in serving the needs of the faithful. The call toward holiness must be clear to all in the church.

The Canadian canonist Lawrence G. Wrenn wrote, in 1981, a very insightful and enjoyable report on the Libellus. He entitled it "Giuistiniani and Quirini: A Reflection on Church Reform." The article is probably the most lively presentation of the Libellus's highlights in English. He presents both the strengths and weaknesses of the sixteenth century writing. Wrenn admits that he was led to the document by the brief reference to it by Hans Küng. He also quotes the German church historian Hubert Jedin, as quoted above.

The first published translation of the Libellus in a modern language appeared in 1995. This Italian translation was entitled *Lettera al Papa: Libellus ad Leonem X*. The work seems not to have been reviewed.

In 2001 the Libellus was recommended by unnamed Catholic authorities in the *Directory on Popular Piety and the Liturgy: Principles and Guidelines*. Because of this recognition by a Roman congregation of the significance of the Libellus, a full citation is appropriate.

> Among those most concerned for the reform of the Church at the beginning of the sixteenth century, mention must be made of two Camaldolese monks, Paolo Giustiniani and Pietro Querini, authors of the famous Libellus ad Leonem X which set out important

principles for the revitalization of the Liturgy as to open its treasures to the entire People of God. They advocated biblical instruction for the clergy and religious, the adoption of the vernacular in
the celebration of the divine mysteries and the reform of the litur-
gical books. They also advocated the elimination of spurious elements deriving from erroneous popular piety, and the promotion
of catechesis so as to make the faithful aware of the importance of
the Liturgy.

Stephen Bowd has studied Querini, his life, spirituality and his drive
to reform. Bowd offers many and invaluable reflections on the Libellus.
He has researched the life and activity of one of the Camaldolese be-
hind the Libellus. This masterful work and its author helped in many
ways in the production of this volume.

There have been various other studies in recent years on the Libellus
on different topics and from various angles. Giuseppi Alberigo published at least two articles on the Libellus and the reforms that it called
for.

Eugenio Massa has done the most work on Giustiniani, both cata-
loguing the manuscripts of his voluminous writings and analyzing the
content of his thought. Massa has published often on Giustiniani, in
different contexts and from differing perspectives. Various topics in
the Libellus are treated at length in Eugenio Massa, *Una Cristianità
nell' alba del Rinascimento.*

More recently a new Italian translation has appeared in *Un Eremita
al Servizio della Chiesa* (*Il* Libellus ad Leonem X *e altri opuscoli*): *Scritti
del Beato Paolo Giustiniani 3* (trans. Lorenzo Barletta, E.C.; Milan:
San Paolo, 2012). The footnotes of that volume are far beyond any
work on the Libellus thus far. All ideas are given their historical beginnings and development. The references are mostly to sources that
could be found in a Camaldolese hermitage library, often, out-dated
reference books and older compilations of church documents. This
work is an incredible service to scholarship on the Libellus. It is an
essential tool for its future study. It would be an aid for wider scholarship on the Libellus for someone to translate into English and update
these excellent notes.

Three conferences were held, Bologna (2010), Nijmegen (2011),
and Bologna (2012), on the general topic of Catholic identity in the
sixteenth century. The third meeting used the Libellus as an important
dividing line in intellectual-religious history; "Pluralism and Identity

Formation in the Catholic World: from 'Libellus ad Leonem' (1513) to the Council of Trent." *Franciscan Studies* 71 (2013) contains some papers read at the conference.

Some articles in the volume focus on the Libellus itself. Umberto Mazzone in "Libellus ad Leonem X: Note in margine all'edizione e alla storiographica le edizione del testo," first takes on the specific problem regarding the manuscript used in the printed edition of the Libellus in the *Annales*. It traces history of the confusion over the specific manuscript used in the *Annales*. That confusion began already in the seventeenth century. It was continued in 1995 when Bianchi stated that the manuscript used was MS 1110. The editors, however, had used MS Muriano 1071. The same article continues and traces the various studies on the Libellus, some of which are noted above.

There is a study of how Paul Giustiniani's ideas in the Libellus influenced the contemplative reform of the Franciscan movement at the time, namely the development of the Capuchins. Ludovic Viallet shows how the Libellus fits in with the movement toward great attention to the written rules of the different orders. It does not mention the interesting fact that Giustiniani gave refuge to three observant persecuted Franciscan friars in one of his reformed hermitages, an event which led to the foundation of the Capuchins.

Another article at the conference traces the development of an issue that was of special importance of the authors of the Libellus. Superstition is an offense against the sovereignty of God. Vincenzo Lavenia traces the major events and actions against so-called witches and their Sabbaths. The authors report on various papal documents and various actions against witchcraft and other superstitious practices in different parts of Europe during the time between the Libellus (1513) and the Council of Trent (1545-1563), and often referring back to the Libellus.

My own fascination with the publication in English began in September 2001. While on a pilgrimage to Camaldolese houses in Italy, I was in the library of the monastery of Camaldoli. Father Ugo, the librarian at the time, gave me a copy of manuscript 1071. While Dr. Katherine Milco was working on the photocopy, she realized that parts of the copy were not clear enough to read. Father Ugo graciously, with newer equipment, sent a much improved copy. Those gifts from him were the beginning and foundation of this project. We send our heartfelt thanks to him.

Most recently, James Kroemer, a Marquette University Ph.D. in Medieval Studies, who has taught as adjunct at Marquette, wrote and read papers on the Libellus at many congresses. His topics began with comparing Giustiniani's Libellus with the thought of Martin Luther on the principles of biblical interpretation. They continue with focus on the Jews, on the Muslims, on reform, and on the perceived Turkish threat.

Words cannot express my appreciation to Fr. Basil (in Ohio) and Fr. Winfried (in Italy) and other members of the Camaldolese Hermits of Monte Corona who gave me encouragement, support and sources for my work.

BIBLIOGRAPHY

Alberigo, Giuseppe, "Sul *Libellus ad Leonem X* degli eremiti camaldolesi : Vincenzo Querini et Paolo Giustiniani," *Humanisme et Église en Italie et en France méridionale (XVᵉ siècle – milieu du XVIᵉ)* (ed. Patrick Gilli; Rome: École française de Rome, 2004), 349-359

Alberigo, Giuseppe, "The Reform of the Episcopate in the *Libellus* to Leo X by the Camaldolese Hermits Vincenzo Querini and Tommaso Giustiniani," *Reforming the Church before Modernity: Patterns, Problems and Approaches* (ed. Christopher Bellitto and Louis Hamilton; Burlington, VT, 2005), 139-152

Barletta, E.C., Lorenzo, trans. *Un Eremita al Servizio della Chiesa (Il Libellus ad Leonem X e altri opuscoli): Scritti del Beato Paolo Giustiniani 3* (Milan: San Paolo, 2012)

Bowd, Stephen D. *Reform before the Reformation: Vincenzo Querini and the Religious Renaissance in Italy* (Studies in Medieval and Reformation Thought LXXXVII) Boston: Brill, 2002.

Congregation for Divine Worship and the Discipline of the Sacraments, *The Directory on Popular Piety and the Liturgy: Principles and Guidelines* (published in English by Congregatio pro Sacramentis et Cultu Divino; Vatican City, 2001; North American ed., Boston: Pauline Books & Media, 2002)

Fiori, Agostino Romano, *Vita del B.P. Giustiniani, institutore della congregatione de' PP. Eremiti Camaldolesi di Romualdo, detta di Monte Corona* (Rome: Antonio de' Rossi, 1729). On Google Books.

Giustiniani, Paolo, *Un Eremita al Servizio della Chiesa (Il Libellus ad Leonem X e altri opuscoli): "Scritti del Beato Paolo Giustiniani 3"* (trans. Lorenzo Barletta, E.C.; Milan: San Paolo, 2012).

Giustiniani, Paolo, *Lettera al Papa: Libellus ad Leonem X*, trans., Geminiano Bianchini; Modena: Artioli, 1995.

Jedin, Hubert, *A History of the Council of Trent 1.* (trans. Ernest Graf) St. Louis: B. Herder Book Co., 1957 (German orig., *Geschichte des Konzils von Trient* [4 vols., Freiberg: Herder, 1951-1975)

Küng, Hans, *The Council, Reform and Reunion* (New York: Sheed and Ward, 1961; German orig., *Konzil und Weidervereiningung*, 3d ed.; Freiburg: Herder, 1961)

Lavenia, Vincenzo, "La Lotta alle superstizioni: Obiettivi e discussioni dal Libellus al Concilio di Trento," *Franciscan Studies* 71 (2013), 163-181

Leclercq ,Jean, and Giustiniani, Paul, *Camaldolese Extraordinary: The Life, Doctrine and Rule of Blessed Paul Giustiniani* (Eds., Camaldolese Hermits of Monte Corona), Ercam Editions: Bloomingdale, Ohio, 2003. This volume contains an English translation of Leclercq's *Un Humaniste Eremite: le Bienheureux Paul Giustiniani* (Rome: Edizioni Camaldoli, 1951) and his *Seul avec Dieu: La Vie Érémitique*, 1961, which had already been published in English, *Alone with God* (New York, Farrar, Straus and Cudahy, 1961).

Lucas Hispanico, Franciscus *La Historica Romoaldina: Overo Eremitica dell'ordine Camaldolese di Monte Corona* (Venice: Misserini, 1590; photographic reprint, Roma Edizioni di Storia e letteratura, 2005, with a new introduction "La Historia Romoaldina et la Figura di Paolo Giustinini" by Eugenio Massa.)

Mazzone, Umberto, "Libellus ad Leonem X: Note in margine all'edizione e alla storiographica. Le edizione del testo," *Franciscan Studies* 71 (2013), 19-32

Massa, Eugenio, *Una Cristianità nell'alba del Rinascimento: Paolo Giustinani e il "Libellus ad Leonem X" (1513)* (Genova: Marietti, 2005)

Mittarelli, Johannes-Benedictus and Anselmus Costadoni, *Annales Camaldulenses Ordinis Sancti Benedicti* (9 vols., Venice, 1755-1773; repr., 9 vols. Farnborough, England, 1970), col. 612-719.

Schnitzer, Joseph, *Peter Delfin, General des Camaldulenserordens, 1445-1525; ein Beitrag zur Geschichte der Kirchensreform Alexanders VI. und Savonarolas* (Munich: Reinhardt: 1926).

Tramontin, Silvio, "Un programma di riforma della Chiesa per il Concilio Lateranense V: il Libelllus ad Leonom X dei veneziani Paolo Giustiniani e Pietro Quirini," in *Venezia e I Concili* (ed. Antonion Niero; Venice: Seminario patriarcale, 1962), 67-93

Viallet, Ludovic, "Social Control, Regular Observance and Identity of a Religious Order: A Franciscan Interpretation of the Libellus ad Leonem," *Franciscan Studies* 71 (2013), 33-51

Wrenn, Lawrence G. "Giuistiniani and Quirini: A Reflection on Church Reform," *Studia Canonica: Revue Canadienne de Droit Canonique* 15 (1981), 481-496

A NOTE ON THE TEXT AND
TRANSLATION

The Latin text is a revision of the *editio princeps*, which appeared in Volume 9 of the *Annales Camaldulenses* (ed. J.B. Mittarelli and A. Costadoni, Venice, 1775). The editors state that they used a single manuscript in the library of S. Michele di Murano, bearing the number 1110. This library has been dispersed, but a MS numbered 1071 in the library of Camaldoli has been identified as the Annalists' exemplar (see E. Mazzone in *Franciscan Studies* 71 [2013], 19-32). It contains a number of significant variants from the printed text, not all of which are indicated in this edition. Regrettably, E. Massa passed away before he could realize his plan of a new critical text.

The present text follows the punctuation and capitalization of the *Annales* edition. For ease of comprehension, I have made the spelling conform to contemporary Ecclesiastical Latin usage. I have also emended the text in several places where the sense clearly requires it. All emendations, along with the relevant testimony of the *Annales* edition (ED) and the MS, are indicated in footnotes.

After completing the draft of this edition in July, 2014, I obtained a copy of the Italian translation of Fra Lorenzo Barletta, EC: *Un Eremita al servizio della chiesa*, (Il Libellus ad Leonem X e altri opucoli): Scritti del Beato Paolo Giustiniani 3 (Milano: San Paolo, 2012). In his notes, Fra Lorenzo proposes a number of emendations of the *Annales* text, which I have included in my footnotes. He was evidently not able to consult the MS.

While the style of the *Libellus* is clear and lively, its long, undulating sentences present a challenge to the English translator. Likewise, the Latin edition appears for the most part as continuous text, with a minimum of breaks and other signposts to mark transitions in the argument. This can create a fatiguing experience for the modern reader. Thus, I have often rendered the Latin with more numerous and less complex English sentences and have introduced additional paragraph breaks. At the same time, I have tried to preserve the essential qualities of the Latin style. The *Annales* edition was presented in numbered columns, two to a page; the original numbers appear in square brackets in this edition, in both the Latin and English texts.

The project of translating the *Libellus* into English was initiated by my colleague, Dr. John Schmitt. Dr. Schmitt obtained excellent photographs of the Camaldoli MS from Fr. Ugo Fossa. Dr. Constance Nielsen transcribed the Latin text of the *editio princeps*, and Dr. Katherine Milco prepared a working collation of the MS. Mr. Lee Sytsma prepared the original electronic files of this bilingual edition.

Blessed Paolo Giustiniani
&
Pietro Querini
Hermits of Camaldoli

LIBELLUS

B. Pauli Iustiniani

et Petri Quirini

Eremitarum Camaldulensium

LIBELLUS

AD LEONEM X

PONTIFICEM MAXIMUM

Blessed Paolo Giustiniani

and

Pietro Quirini

Hermits of Camaldoli

LIBELLUS

ADDRESSED TO

LEO X

SUPREME PONTIFF

[612] SUSCIPE Beatissime Pater Leo Decime Pontifex Maxime
Libellum, quem Tibi humiles Sanctitatis Tuae Servi Petrus, et Paulus
Eremitae offerunt. Neque enim aliud in admirabili hac exaltatione
Tua, magnaque totius Orbis laetitia in eorum erga Te fidei, ac obser-
vantiae testimonium habuerunt, quod offerrent.

Hunc, si ad multas, maximasque occupationes Tuas respexeris,
immensum fortasse volumen existimabis: Si vero ad ea, de quibus
sermonem fecimus, animum intenderis, pro rerum magnitudine, ac
diversitate brevem, ieiunamque Orationem censueris. In eo autem,
Pater Beatissime, si quae facere iam aliquot annos Pontifices consueverunt, a Iesu Christo, quod minime credimus, probabuntur, inania
deliramenta, aniles fabulas, aegrotantium somnia reperies. Si vero,
quae legitimum Pontificem, qualem Te esse non ambigimus, facere
oporteat potius, quam quod alii fecerint, considerare volueris, multa
fortasse utilia, quaedam etiam invenies necessaria, si Tibi a Domino
demandatum munus, non solum nominis excellentia, et personae
dignitate, sed operis quoque consumatione implere desideras. Qua-
mplurima autem in eo vana, atque minus opportune dicta esse nos
ipsi suspicamur: quoniam in multiloquio peccata deesse non solent;
satis tamen desiderio nostro fecisse credimus, si more eorum feceri-
mus, qui metalla effodiunt. Cum enim purum aurum, et argentum ex
terrae visceribus eruere nunquam valeant, multum vilioris materiae
extrahunt, quod tamen, cum malleis conterendum, igniumque flam-
mis examinandum committunt, pretiosi aliquid metalli suscipiunt.
Nobis certe eorum exemplo multum erit, si haec ipsa, quae permixta,
ac confusa hoc Libello continentur, malleo profundissimae cogitatio-
nis Tuae contrita, igneque singularis Sapientiae Tuae examinata,

[612] Accept, most blessed Father, Leo X, Supreme Pontiff, this "little book," which your humble servants, the hermits Peter and Paul, present to you. For on the occasion of your wonderful elevation to the papacy, amid the rejoicing of the entire world, they have nothing else to offer as a testimony of their faith and obedience.

Perhaps the size of this volume, if you think of your many great occupations, will seem too great; but if you consider the matters about which we are speaking and their diversity and importance, our essay will seem brief and ungenerous by comparison. Moreover, Holy Father, if the actions that Pontiffs for some years now have seen fit to perform are really approved by Christ—and we do not believe this for a minute—you will find in this book empty ravings, old wives' tales, and the dreams of ailing men. But if you are willing to consider what a true Pontiff, such as we assume you to be, should do, rather than what others have done, you may find much that is useful and even necessary—if indeed you desire to fulfill your God-given role not only with nominal excellence and personal distinction, but with actual accomplishment as well. That this book contains many pointless or inappropriate statements, we too are prepared to acknowledge; for in much talking there is usually no lack of faults (Prov 10:19).[1] Nevertheless, we think we shall be satisfied if we act like those who dig for precious metals. Since they are never able to remove gold or silver in its pure state from the bowels of the earth, they extract a great deal of baser material; but when they take the latter and pound it with hammers and prove it with fire, they do obtain some valuable metal. Following their example, we will do well if the confused and mixed contents of this book are first beaten with the hammer of your more profound reflection and tested by the fire of your singular wisdom, and prove to have some pure metal—

---

1 This is also quoted in the Rule of St. Benedict, chapter 6. Benedict of Nursia wrote the rule in the sixth century, and the Camaldolese Order follows this rule for community life.

[613] purum aliquid, si non auri aut argenti, vilioris saltem metalli habuisse probabuntur.

Rogamus vero Amplitudinis Tuae Pietatem, ut non rudem loquendi modum, non qualiter, sed quae potius diximus, considerare velit; immo non quae diximus, sed quae dicere voluimus, attendat. Nobis etenim Clementissime Pater, posteaquam Monasticam, et Eremiticam vitam in Apennini summitate professi sumus, christiane vivendi potior cura fuit semper, quam latine, aut eloquenter scribendi, et ad mentis etiam Tuae perspicacissimae rerum omnium cognitionem rhetoricis uti artibus minus congruum existimavimus. Quod enim res ipsae Tibi persuadere non poterunt, nulla certe satis erit eloquentiae vis ad persuadendum. Semper enim, sicut ad imperitiores, ac tardiores animos commovendos multum eloquentiam valere existimavimus: ita ad sapientiorum, ac prudentiorum corda flectenda nudas res ipsas, simplicique sermone prolatas plus posse, quam ullum verborum delectum, aut Orationis ornatum iudicamus. Sentiunt, qui sapientiores sunt, quibuscumque verbis proferantur, cuiusnam res ipsae momenti sint, et rerum potius soliditate, quam verborum inanitate moventur. Neque etiam quinam illi sint, qui haec ad Te scribere benignitatis Tuae abundantia freti, non timuerunt, Sapentiam Tuam intueri oportet: sed Divinae potius Sapientiae profunditatem considerare, quae vilissimis plerumque instrumentis ea operari soleat, quae prodesse etiam Sapientissimis possint. Ad aures autem Tuas haec pervenire ille fortasse Dominus voluit, qui nihil ad rem pertinere arbitratus est, a quibusnam, aut quam latine dicerentur. Quare Beatissime Pontifex non quales nos sumus, aut qualiter loquamur, sed quae dicimus potius, et quo pervenire[1] eadem possint, Sapientia Tua metiatur. Nostrae vero temeritati, ac rusticitati Pietas illa Tua, quae in hac exaltatione sua nemini

---

1   quo pervenire: a quo pervenire MS, quo provenire ED

[613] if not gold or silver, at least some baser element.

We implore Your Holiness, however, to overlook our uncouth manner of speaking—in other words, to consider what we say, rather than how we say it. Or rather, consider not what we have said, but what we meant to say. For after making our profession of the monastic and eremitical life in the Apennine hills, kindly Father, we have been more concerned with living the Christian life than with writing correct and elegant Latin, and we also deemed it inappropriate to apply the rhetorical arts to your all-embracing and penetrating intelligence. If the facts themselves are unable to persuade you, surely no amount of eloquence will suffice; and just as we have always thought that eloquence has great power to move less educated and less agile minds, we also believe that the hearts of wiser and more prudent men are more powerfully influenced by the bare facts, simply expressed, than by choice vocabulary or rhetorical ornament. Wiser men instinctively know the importance of the issues at hand, no matter how they are expressed, and they are influenced more by solid facts than by empty words. Moreover, Your Holiness should not be troubled about the identity of the men who, relying on your abundant kindness, have the temerity to write you this letter. Rather, consider the depth of the Divine Wisdom, which often employs the basest instruments for the benefit of the wisest men. Perhaps God wills that these words should come to your ears, and it makes no difference to him who says them and how correctly they are phrased. Therefore, most blessed Pontiff, let your wisdom measure not what sort of people we are or how we speak, but rather what we say and the results it may achieve. Let not your kindness, which since your elevation has denied clemency to no one

[614] Clementiam denegavit, veniam dare non recuset. Neque enim venia indignos nos arbitrari poteris, si quae a Deo O. M. assiduis precibus, multisque lacrimis diu noctuque petere non cessamus, eadem ad Te, qui eius in Terra vices geris, semel scribere ausi sumus, cum maxime Te precibus eorum omnium, qui consolationem Israel expectant, a Domino datum Pontificem, atque Pastorem non dubitemus.

Sex in Partes dividitur Libellus.

Prima. Pontificis Potestatem, eiusque officium ostendit.

Secunda. Iudaeos, et Idololatras ad Fidem vocandos suadet.

Tertia. Mahumetanos aut convertendos, aut in pugnam vincendos proponit.

Quarta. Septem Christianorum Nationes, quae a Romana Ecclesia sunt divisae, Capiti uniendas dicit.

Quinta. De Christianorum omnium, qui Romano oboediunt Pontifici, reformatione agit.

Sexta. Temporale Ecclesiae Imperium per universas Infidelium Regiones augendum hortatur.

[614], refuse to indulge our temerity and rudeness. Indeed you will not think us unworthy of pardon if we have dared to write once to you, God's vicar on earth, about the very things for which we always implore God with assiduous prayers and copious tears, both day and night; for we are certain that the Lord has given you to us as Pontiff and Shepherd in answer to the prayers of all who await the consolation of Israel (Luke 2:25).

Our *Libellus* is divided into six parts:

The First shows the power of the Pontiff and his office.

The Second urges that Jews and Pagans be brought to the Faith.

The Third proposes that Muslims be either converted or conquered in battle.

The Fourth states that the seven Christian nations that are divided from the Roman Church should be joined to their Head.

The Fifth treats of the reformation of all who obey the Roman Pontiff.

The Sixth urges that the temporal power of the Church be increased throughout the territories of the Infidels.

Nos, Beatissime Pater, qui ex manibus tuis Religionis nostrae repa-
rationem suscepturi ex Camaldulensis Eremi secreto,[2] Te, Iulianoque
Fratre tuo vocante, ad Florentinae Civitatis frequentiam laeti his
proximis diebus descenderamus: nunc intimae exultationis, atque
exuberantis laetitiae pleni, his Beatitudinem tuam scriptis adire,
magnaque animi iubilatione ante Te procidentes in Beatorum Pedum
tuorum oscula proruere non dubitamus, non huius modo nostri
pusilli gregis, sed totius iam Christianae Religionis restaurationem
expetentes, atque illam a Te per viscera Misericordiae Iesu Christi
votis omnibus efflagitantes. Te enim ad hoc opus peragendum, praeter hominum expectationem, a Domino electum, atque ad sublimem
Pontificalis dignitatis apicem elevatum existimamus. Viderat quippe
Summus ille rerum omnium Moderator, qua alacritate, quo recto
animi affectu Religionem semper coluisses. Et nuperrime demandatum Tibi a Iulio, qui tunc Pontificem agebat, reformandae Religionis
nostrae munus susceperas: et qui animi desiderium, piumque eius
affectum pro opere computare solet, non passus est Te diutius his
rebus minimis occupari, neque expectare voluit, ut opere impleres,
quae mente conceperas: Sed ex ipsa sola

---

2 Eremi secreto MS: Eremi ED

[Part I]

In these recent days, blessed Father, at your invitation and that of
your brother Julian,[2] we joyfully came down from our hermitage at
Camaldoli to the city of Florence, to receive from your hands the
renewal of our holy Order.[3] Now we come to you in writing, filled
with inward exultation and overflowing joy, and in our jubilation
we do not hesitate to fall and kiss your blessed feet and to seek
the renewal not only of our weak little flock, but also of the entire
Christian religion, imploring you moreover through the tender mercy
of Jesus Christ. It is to achieve this task, we believe, that you were
chosen by God and raised, beyond all expectation, to the high office
of Supreme Pontiff; for the Great Governor of the world had seen
your enthusiasm and correct attitude toward the religious life. You
had, moreover, recently undertaken the task of reforming our Order,
which was entrusted to you by the late Supreme Pontiff Julius. God,
who is accustomed to count the desire and pious intention of the soul
as accomplishment itself, did not allow you to be any longer occupied
with small matters, nor was he willing to wait for you to fulfill what
you had planned. Rather, concluding from your intention

---

2   This is Giuliano de' Medici, who later became Duke of Nemours.
3   The Camaldolese order traditionally began with St. Romuald in 1012.

[615] animi intentione satis de Te experimenti suscepisse ratus,
maiora Tibi, immo maxima committere non dubitavit. Te enim ideo
toti Christianae Reipublicae praeposuit, et Sacrosanctae nostrae Religionis Pontificem Summum instituit, ut qui post multa, maximaque
in omnes Monasticos Ordines beneficia, novissime prolapsam P. N.
Romualdi domunculam restaurandam, parvum, Amplitudinique
tuae impar negotium, magno Religionis zelo succensus suscipere non
recusaveras, dignissimo iam iam, tuaeque Sapientiae congruo munere
universalem ipsam Religionum omnium Matrem, labentem Christi Ecclesiam reparare, atque in pristinum suae clartitatis decorem
reducere inciperes.

Non enim ad hanc Summam Amplitudinis Dignitatem, ac maximam
omnium, quae sub Caelo sunt, potestatem, ideo Te ille humanarum
omnium rerum Dispensator Optimus evexit, ut inani Pontificis
nomine, aut mundanae gloriae vanitate contentus, luxu, otio, atque
ignavia, quae a Te semper aliena fuere, in Terris vitam duceres; sed ea
potius ratione universum Terrarum orbem tuo moderamini, imperi-
oque subiecit, ut per industriam, sollicitudinem, ac sapientiam tuam
ad instar Caelestis Regni una humanarum omnium Creaturarum
Christo Domino servientium Respublica constitueretur in Terra.
Cum enim nullus omnino in universo terrarum orbe hominum sit,
qui a Divinae Maiestatis Potestate se alienum esse ulla ratione valeat
suspicari, Tuque in Terris immensae illius Maiestatis vices geras,
manifestissime fit, totum humanum genus, omnes scilicet gentes,
populos, nationes, quae sub Caelo sunt, tuae subditas esse potestati,
tuisque nutibus regenda humana omnia, atque tuo arbitrio moderanda. Ideo enim ad Evangelium omnibus Creaturis in universo
orbe praedicandum Apostolos suos Dominus mittebat; ideo illos
non solum in Ierusalem, Iudaea, et Samaria; sed usque ad ultimum
Terrae sibi testes futuros praedicebat, ut qui Apostolicae functionis
onus susciperent, facile intellegere possent, illius supremae Dignitatis
munus esse non parvam aliquam Terrae particulam, non quasdam
hominum conditiones, sed Orbem ipsum universum, totumque prorsus humanum genus regere, ac moderari: Non ut terreno Imperio
aucta sublimiori loco Apostolica Sedes constituatur, quam de sola
humilitate D. N. Iesu Christi vestigiis inhaerentem gloriari decet; sed
magis, ut omnium humanarum Creaturarum Domina effecta, ille,
qui ad sedendum in ipsa a Domino eligitur, eos,

[615] that he had tested you sufficiently, he did not hesitate to entrust to you greater things—indeed, the greatest things of all. For he put you in charge of the entire Christian Commonwealth and made you the Supreme Pontiff of our Holy Religion, so that one who had not refused, after so many great kindnesses toward all the monastic orders, to undertake with zeal the restoration of the recently collapsed house of Our Father Romuald—a small task, unworthy of your greatness—might now begin a work most commensurate with your wisdom: to repair the universal Mother of all religious orders, the unsteady Church of Christ, and to restore her to her original glory.

Thus the Great Dispenser of all human affairs did not raise you to this lofty dignity and to the greatest power under heaven that you might live content with the empty title of Pontiff and the vanity of worldly glory in luxury, idleness, and worthlessness—things that have always been alien to you. Rather he has subjected the entire world to your command and government, so that through your industry, care, and wisdom a single Commonwealth of human beings serving Christ our Lord may be established on earth, on the model of the Kingdom of Heaven. For since there is no one in the entire world of men who can think that he is exempt from the power of the divine majesty, and since you take the place of this immense majesty on earth, it is obvious that the entire human race, all peoples, races, and nations under heaven, are subject to your power, and that all human affairs should be ruled by your assent and governed by your will. It was for this that the Lord sent his apostles to preach the Gospel to all creation throughout the world, and predicted that they would be his witnesses not only in Jerusalem, Judea, and Samaria, but even to the uttermost part of the earth (Acts 1:8). In this way, those who undertook the burden of Apostolic service might come to understand that the burden of that supreme Dignity is to rule and govern not some small parcel of land and certain classes of people, but the entire world and the entire human race. God's purpose was not to augment the Apostolic See with worldly power and to establish it in a higher place, for it should glory only in humility, following in the footsteps of our Lord Jesus Christ. Rather, the Lord desires that when this See has been established as teacher of all human beings, the man chosen to occupy it will use the example of his life to win over those

[616] qui nondum Fidem Christi, in qua sola salus est, susceperunt,
ad illam suscipiendam, vitae exemplo invitare, beneficiis allicere,
atque attrahere possit. Illos vero, qui semel Fidei Veritate suscepta,
aut perversorum hominum fallaciis[3] decepti, aut propriis voluptati-
bus allecti ab ea discessisse videntur, opportunis, congruisque artibus
ad Fidei ipsius Veritatem cognoscendam, sectandamque pie cogere
valeat.

Hoc enim Pontificis Maximi munus esse, si re ipsa non tantum nomine Pontifex sit futurus, neminem sanae mentis dubitare existimamus.
Qui vero de Pontificis Potestate disputare audent, nequaquam nobis
sani iudicii esse videntur. Quippe, quoniam si id solum animadvertere
non neglegerent, cuiusnam vices Pontifex in Terris gerere ab omnibus
censeatur, facile omnem in illo plenitudinem Potestatis perciperent,
quem Summi, Maximi, Omnipotentissimique Dei omnium Auctoris,
atque Moderatoris Vicarium esse apertissime confitentur. Nam insul-
sum sane est claudendi, aperiendique Caelorum Regna potestatem ab
ipso Caelorum, Terrarumque Domino Pontifici traditam non negare,
et adhuc de plenissima supra universum genus humanum Pontificis
potestate dubitare; praesertim cum toties in Evangelio Dominicos
greges pascendos, regendosque illi traditos, atque commissos le-
gamus, certissimeque cognoscamus nullum in hoc Terrarum ambitu
hominum esse, qui inter illius Pastoris Optimi oves computari non
debeat, qui pro universorum hominum salute, Dei Filius cum esset,
carnem assumere, et in ea mortem subire non dubitavit.

Qui vero aliarum Ecclesiarum Antistites Romano Pontifici Potestatis, aut Dignitatis excellentia aequare contendunt, non minus, immo
multo etiam magis aberrare iudicandi sunt; quoniam non frustra,
aut casu factum existimare debemus, qui Petro potius, quam alicui
aliorum Apostolorum traditas Regni Caelorum claves legimus: quod
illi, et non alteri dictum sit: Tu es Petrus, et super hanc petram aedi-
ficabo Ecclesiam meam; quod discessurus ab Apostolorum praesentia
Dominus Petro potius, quam alteri, ter etiam repetito sermone, oves,
agnosque suos pascendos committeret; quod de Petri potius, quam
de ceterorum Fide dixerit Dominus: Rogavi pro Te, ut non deficiat
Fides tua: et tu aliquando conversus confirma Fratres tuos. Nonnisi
magno Sancti Spiritus ministerio factum, quod Evangelistae testimonio, dum Apostoli numerandi sunt, Petri nomen non solum ante
alios ponitur,

---

3   fallaciis: fallacis MS, fallacia ED

[616] who have not received the Faith of Christ, in which alone salvation consists, and to attract them by good deeds. Moreover, he desires that those who once accepted the true Faith, but were deceived by the perversity of men or seduced by their own desires and have apparently withdrawn from it, may be gently compelled by this man through timely and suitable devices to acknowledge this truth and follow it.

That this is the task of the Supreme Pontiff, if he will be such in fact and not merely in name, no sane man can doubt. Those, however, who presume to question his power do not, in our view, possess sound judgment. For if they bothered to consider whose place he is believed to take in this world, they would easily see that the fullness of power resides in the one they openly profess to be the Vicar of the Highest and Greatest, Almighty God, the Author and Governor of all. Now, it is certainly foolish to admit, on the one hand, that the Lord, the Creator of heaven and earth, has given to the Pontiff the power of opening and closing the kingdom of heaven, and to doubt, on the other, that the Pontiff has complete power over the entire human race. Indeed, we often read in the Gospels that the Lord has entrusted to him the care and feeding of his flock, and we also know that every man throughout the world must be counted among the sheep of the Good Shepherd, who did not hesitate, though he was the Son of God, to assume flesh and endure death for the salvation of all.

Those, however, who try to equate the bishops of other churches with the Roman Pontiff in power and dignity should be regarded as no less, or rather even more in error. For we should not suppose that it was by chance or in vain that the keys to the kingdom of heaven were entrusted to Peter rather than to any of the other apostles, and that to him rather than another it was said, "You are Peter, and upon this rock I will build my Church" (Matt 16:18), and that when the Lord was about to depart from the apostles' presence he gave to Peter, and not to another, the care of his sheep and lambs in a threefold mandate, and that it was concerning Peter's faith rather than that of the others that the Lord said, "I have prayed for you, that your faith may not fail; and do you, being once converted, confirm your brethren" (Luke 22:32). It is only by the ministry of the Holy Spirit that, when the apostles are mentioned in the Gospels, Peter is not only named before the others, but is always named first,

[617] sed primus omnino nominatur, primus utique et dignitate, et
potestate, tantaque excellentiae sublimitate, ut nullus in Terris illi
aequari possit. Quemadmodum enim unus in Caelis est omnium
Dominus Iesus Christus, ita unum in Terris, qui eius vices gerat,
reliquit Petrum, Petrique legitimum successorem. Quod videntes
antiquiores illi Sanctissimi Patres ad Sacras Synodos universales congregati, apertissimis Definitionibus declaravere, omnium Ecclesiarum
Caput Romanam Beatorum Apostolorum Petri et Pauli Sanguine
consecratam Ecclesiam esse. Cum itaque omni dubio procul subli-
missima haec Beatissimi Petri Sedes, in qua nunc Tu Sanctissime
Pater a Domino mirabili electione collocatus es, sit omnium, quae in
Universo sunt, Ecclesiarum Caput, et Domina, cum nihil omnino de
plenitudine Apostolicae potestatis dilatandum sit, evidentissime col-
ligere possumus, tuae nunc Beatitatis munus esse, universum Terrarum orbem, ac omne hominum genus regere, et moderari, nullamque
penitus esse Orbis partem, neque humanarum creaturarum aliquam,
quae tuis Imperiis parere, tuisque nutibus obtemperare non habeat.
Te enim vere hodie constituit Dominus super gentes, et Regna, super
gentes scilicet universas, quae sub Caelo sunt, et super omnia Regna
Mundi huius, ut tuo arbitrio evellas et destruas disperdas et dissipes,
et aedifices et plantes.

Verum Tu certe omnibus melius sentis, Pater Beatissime, qualis
Tibi a Domino commissa provincia fuerit; non enim angustissimae
huius Italiae modo, aut etiam non satis latae Europae solum, sed
longe etiam ampliora, potentioraque Africae, Asiaeque, totius scilicet
Universi Regna, et Imperia omnia tuae subiecit potestati, tuaeque
fidei commisit. Triplicem namque Capiti tuo coronam imposuit, ut
Universum ipsum, quod in tres partes dividitur, tuis imperiis sub-
iectum non ambigeres. Non Italorum modo hominum, non eorum
Christianorum, qui aptiorem hanc Orbis partem, Europam scilicet
ipsam incolunt; sed et cum his eorum etiam omnium, qui, licet propter Regionum distantiam nobis minus sint noti, sub Christi tamen
nomine viventes multis, amplissimisque Regnis maximas universi
orbis Provincias, Asiam fere totam, et habitabiles Africae Regiones
occupant, Cura, Salusque Tibi commissa est. Quid enim Christiano
utcumque nomine censeri potest, quod Christi Vicario commissum,
subiectumque non esse intellegatur; sed et praeter

LATIN TEXT WITH ENGLISH TRANSLATION

[617] being first in every respect: in dignity, in power, and in excellence, such that no one on earth can be compared to him. For just as there is one Lord in heaven, Jesus Christ, so too the Lord left one man on earth to take his place: Peter, and Peter's legitimate successor. Seeing this, the Holy Fathers of ancient times, when they met in holy synods of the Universal Church, clearly defined the doctrine that the Roman Church, consecrated by the blood of the blessed apostles Peter and Paul, is the head of all churches.[4] And so, since there is no doubt that this sublime See of Blessed Peter, in which you, Holy Father, have now been placed by your wonderful election, is the head and mistress of all the churches in the world, and since there is no scope for dissenting from the fullness of apostolic power, we may conclude on most evident grounds that it is Your Holiness' duty to rule and govern the whole world and the entire human race, and that there is no part of the world nor any human being that is not obliged to obey your commands and act upon your wishes. For God has "truly set you this day over the nations and kingdoms"—that is, over all nations under heaven and all the kingdoms of this world—"to root up and pull down, to waste and to destroy, to build and to plant" as you see fit (Jer 1:10).

But surely you more than anyone else, Holy Father, appreciate the authority committed to you; for the Lord has entrusted to your power and good faith not only this small region of Italy, nor the narrow expanse of Europe alone, but also the much wider and more powerful domains of Africa, Asia, and the entire world. He has put upon your head a triple crown, so that you may not doubt that the world, which is divided into three parts, is subject to your commands. Thus God has entrusted to you the care and salvation not only of Italians or of those Christians who occupy the more accessible part of the world—that is, Europe—but also of all people who, owing to their distance, are less known to us but live under the name of Christ in many substantial realms and who occupy the greatest regions of the earth—that is, practically all of Asia and the habitable parts of Africa. For what can be counted as Christian that is not also subject and entrusted to the Vicar of Christ? In addition to

---

4   Council of Chalcedon (451), canon 28.

[618] Christianas omnes gentes, etiam illas, populos, et nationes, quae cum Christum aliquando cognovissent, Haereticorum, perversorumque hominum fallaciis deceptae, aversae a Christi Fide impios alios vivendi ritus, falsaque nefandae alterius Religionis Dogmata susceperunt: quales illi omnes sunt, qui spurcissimi, et impiissimi hominis Mahumeti contaminatissimam, omniumque Haereticorum infectam venenis Haeresim sequuntur, et cum his illos etiam, qui perversa cordis duritia, obdurataque contra veritatem cervice, nunquam Christianae Fidei iugum suscipere voluerunt, tuae subiectos potestati, tuae commissos fidei, et diligentiae, ille esse voluit, qui cum omnium Dominus sit, omnes vult homines salvos fieri, ut Tibi eius in Terris vices gerenti, humanarum omnium penitus creaturarum salus sit cordi, ut commissum Tibi hominum genus suprema hac omnium potestate, maximaque illa animi tui Sapientia ita regeres, ut[4] per tranquillissimam in Terris pacem ad aeternae Beatitudinis felicitatem, omnes pariter homines perduceres.

Hoc, Beatissime Pater, proprium, praecipuumque Pontificis munus esse, tuam non ambigere Beatitudinem credimus. Ecclesiam Sanctam Dei Tibi commissam esse omnes intellegunt; veram autem Ecclesiam Dei, non terrenae habitationis civitates, aut manufacta aedificia, sed hominum Congregationem esse te latere non debet. Inde enim iam usu suscepto vocabulo, ii Sacrorum Domorum parietes et tecta Ecclesiae[5] Dei nuncupantur, quod in eis fidelium animarum multitudo, quae vera Ecclesia est, congregetur. Deus enim non in manufactis inhabitat, sed Templum Sanctum Dei, Pauli Apostoli testimonio, homines ipsi sunt; tu vero Templi vivi istius antistes, tu sublimitate Dignitatis, auctoritatisque constitutus, ideo omni maiori cura, studio ac diligentia, quaecumque in eo turpia, aut indecora sunt, emendare, et quaecumque illi desunt, vera, Deoque digna ornamenta adiicere debes; quoniam Christo Domino, cui soli inservire Tibi cura omnis esse debet, pretiosius, cariusque est, unum hoc vivis ex lapidibus constructum Templum, quam quaecumque magnificentissimis ex parietibus, sublimibusque tectis, pretiosissimisque ornamentis manufacta templa, quae Deo unquam in universo dicata fuere. Nullus enim Te ipso apertius nosse debuit, quod non universalium modo Creaturarum, sed unius cuiuscumque Animae salus pretiosior sit in conspectu Domini Nostri Iesu Christi, quam omnia

---

4   ut: et MS, ED
5   Ecclesiae: Ecclesia MS, ED

[618] all the Christian nations, there are also the peoples and nations that once knew Christ but have been deceived by the lies of heretics and wayward men and have been turned from the Faith of Christ to adopt other, impious practices and the false teachings of a different religion. For such are all who follow the heresy of that disgusting and impious character Muhammad, which is infected with the venom of all heresies. There are also those who, from a wicked hardness of heart and with necks stiffened against the truth, have never been willing to take up the yoke of the Christian faith. These, too, have been subjected to your power and entrusted to your faithfulness and diligence by the will of the Lord, who, being the Lord of all, desires that all men be saved, so that you who take his place on earth may be concerned for the salvation of all human beings, and that you may rule the entire human race, which has been placed in your keeping, by means of this supreme power and your excellent wisdom in such a way as to bring all men through the tranquility of peace on earth to the joy of eternal beatitude.

This, Holy Father, is the proper and principal task of the Pontiff, as you no doubt realize. That the holy Church of God has been entrusted to you, everyone understands; but it should not escape you that the true Church of God does not consist of earthly cities or buildings, but is a congregation of men. Indeed, the walls and roofs of sacred buildings are commonly called "churches of God" precisely because many faithful souls, who are the true Church, are gathered within them. God does not dwell in houses made by hands, but the temple of God, as St. Paul testifies (Eph 2:21-2), are men themselves. You, the priest of this living temple, placed at the summit of dignity and authority, should correct with all diligence, care, and zeal whatever is foul or unseemly there, and add such true and godly ornaments as may be lacking. This one temple built of living stones is more precious to Christ our Lord, whose service alone should be your entire concern, than all the churches with magnificent walls, lofty roofs, and precious ornaments that have ever been dedicated to him. No one should know better than you that the salvation not only of all creatures, but of each and every soul is more precious in the sight of our Lord Jesus Christ than all

[619] universi orbis huius Regna ipsa, et Imperia. Quippe cum Te
non lateat ipsum pro hominum salute acerbissimam Crucis mortem subire voluisse, tantamque erga humani generis Creaturas eius
dilectionem, caritatemque esse, ut nullus adeo in universo humilis,
abiectusque sit, pro cuius solius salute, si opus esset, non se iterum
libentissime Cruci, mortique traderet; Mundi autem Regna omnia
ostendentem, imperiaque pollicentem neque audire sustinuit, sed et
graviter increpans, eum a se discedere iussit, penitusque abiecit. Quae
quidem Spiritu Sancto dictante scripta sunt, ut ad nostram Doctrinam singula quaeque trahentes, facile intellegere possimus, illis,
qui Christo placere student, aeternaeque ab eo retributionis munera
expectant, uniuscuiusque animae salutem, magis quam multarum
Civitatum Imperia curae esse debere. Illa enim et sempiterna est, et a
Divinitatis participatione non aliena; hae autem, quaecumque fuerint
Civitates, atque etiam terrena Imperia, si ad aeternitatem conferas,
momento citius dilabuntur et pereunt, nec stabiliora videntur habere
fundamenta, quam ea tabernacula Pastorum, quae mane posita cum
sint, vespere destruuntur. Transeunte enim, vento citius, Mundi
huius figura, quid in eo stabile, aut non momentaneum esse potest?
Haec autem eadem Regna ipsa, et Imperia, etiamsi diutius permane-
rent, nonne si cum humani animi dignitate, cum ea, cuius est capax,
Divinitate conferre incipias, omni pulvere viliora sunt existimanda?
Ex hac vero, Beatissime Pater, supputatione ea exoritur summa, tuae
scilicet amplitudinis munus esse, si Christi vestigia imitari, eiusque
beneplacitis in hac ab eo Tibi tradita potestate inhaerere volueris,
non Civitates, et Castra Terrenae huius Ecclesiae potestati subiicere;
sed tuis manibus Christo Domino puros commissarum tibi ovium
animos offerre, ut illa citius perficiatur Ecclesia, quae in Caelis vivis,
aeternisque construitur ex lapidibus.

Cum itaque Summi Pontificis cura, minima quidem circa Terreni Imperii dilatationem, maxima vero circa humanarum omnium
Creaturarum salutem versanda sit: iam alta sublimis mentis tuae
consideratione Te prospexisse credimus, Universam hanc omnium
in Terris degentium multitudinem, cui Tu et praeesse, et non minus
prodesse debes, ex diversa, multiplicique hominum varietate constare.
Non eadem est omnibus Religio, non Fides, mores, non aequa conditio; Te enim id, quod omnibus fere notum est, latere non potest,

[619] the kingdoms and empires of this world. You are well aware
that for the salvation of men he was willing to endure the bitter death
of the cross, and that his love and charity toward the human race is
such that there is no one so humble and abject that Christ would not
willingly offer himself to the cross and death a second time, if it were
necessary, to save that person alone. He likewise paid no heed to the
one who showed him all the kingdoms of the world and promised
him all power, but with harsh rebukes the Lord rejected him and
sent him away (Matt 4:1-11; Luke 4:1-13). These things have been
written at the dictation of the Holy Spirit so that we, applying them
singly to our own edification, may easily understand that anyone
who wishes to please Christ and who expects an eternal reward from
him must be more concerned with the salvation of each and every
soul than with power over many cities. For salvation is eternal and
participates in divinity, but cities and even earthly empires, when
you compare them with eternity, fall and perish more quickly than
a moment. Indeed, their foundations seem no more stable than the
tents of shepherds, which are pitched in the morning and folded in
the evening. Since the fashion of this world passes away more quickly
than the wind (1 Cor 7:31), what in this world can be stable and
not of a moment's duration? Should not these same kingdoms and
empires, even if they endure longer, be regarded as less valuable than
dust when compared with the dignity of the human soul and the
divinity of which the soul is capable? When all of this is summed
up, Holy Father, it is your responsibility, if you wish to follow in
the footsteps of Christ and to do his will with the power he has
given you, not to subject cities and forts to the power of this earthly
Church, but with your own hands to offer to Christ the Lord the
pure souls of the sheep entrusted to you, so that the Church, which
is constructed in Heaven from living and eternal stones, may be
completed all the more quickly (1 Pet 2:5).

And so, since the Supreme Pontiff should be concerned least of
all with the extension of his earthly power and most of all with
the salvation of all human beings, we trust that you have already
perceived, in your mind's lofty meditation, that this entire multitude
of the earth's inhabitants, which you should both govern and benefit,
consists of a great diversity of people. They do not all have the same
religion, faith, customs, and state of life; for surely Your Holiness can
see what everybody knows,

[620] hac huius saeculi tempestate sic se genus humanum universum habere, ut quantum ad Fidei veritatem attinet, quadruplici[6] possit diversitate distingui; quidam etenim ita extra Christianae Ecclesiae pietatem penitus sunt, ut intra eam nunquam fuisse cognoscantur: alii autem, eo quod extra rectam Ecclesiae Fidem nunc penitus sunt, cum superioribus quidem computari possent, sed propterea diversi ab illis existimantur, quoniam intra ipsius Christianae Ecclesiae ambitum aliquando fuisse intelleguntur: multo vero plures et illi existunt, qui ita Christianae Veritatis quaedam suscipere, quaedam autem non suscipere videntur; ut nullus omnino, praeter Beatitudinem tuam, si intra Ecclesiam, aut extra illam sint, aperte valeat definire. His tribus hominum conditionibus quartum illud adiicitur, quod genus electum, regale Sacerdotium, gens Sancta, populus aquisitionis, Beati Petri Apostoli voce appellatur. Hi sunt, qui intra castissimum Christianae Ecclesiae gremium, ceu intra piissimae Matris sinum carissimi filii continentur.

Sentis, Beatissime Pater, magnam in Terris esse hominum diversitatem, neminem tamen aut a dignitatis tuae potestate liberum, aut a tuae pietatis cura alienum esse, sentire Te credimus; quoniam quale amplissimi officii munus sit, ille Te admonere saepius potuit, qui ad Apostolatus Dignitatem a Domino vocatus, dicebat: Graecis, et Barbaris, sapientibus et insipientibus debitor sum, nullarum[7] certe gentium, quamquam Infidelium a se curam alienam indicans. Quod apertius etiam significare volens, alibi aiebat: Cum liber essem ex omnibus, omnium me servum feci, ut plures lucrifacerem; Iudaeis scilicet, tamquam Iudaeus; his qui sub lege sunt, tamquam sub lege; his qui sine lege[8] sunt, tamquam sine lege; infirmis tamquam infirmus, et denique omnibus omnia factus sum, ut omnes lucrifacerem. Et vere, cum non huius solius, sed omnium Apostolorum, et Apostolicorum virorum maximam semper curam fuisse cognoscas, ex universarum gentium diversitate, unam Christi Ecclesiam congregare, Tu Principis Apostolorum locum tenens dubitare non potes, ad tuae amplitudinis Maiestatem attinere: sic omnium humanarum creaturarum curam suscipere, ut nulla adeo barbara, adeo infidelis, et a Christianae pietatis veritate aliena gens sit, cui Tu, Christi amore, inservire non habeas, ut ex ea, quoscumque poteris, Christo lucrifacias. Si enim, ut antiquiora non recenseamus, Infidelium a se alienam curam

---

6   quadruplici: qua duplici MS, triplici ED
7   nullarum MS: larum ED
8   sine lege: secundum legem MS, ED

[620] that in the tempest of this world the human race, as far as the truth of the Faith is concerned, can be divided into four classes. Some are so far removed from the observance of the Christian Church that they were obviously never within it. Others, who are now very much outside the true faith, could be counted with the former, but are regarded differently because they were formerly within the sphere of the Christian Church. More numerous are those who appear to accept certain elements of Christian truth and not to accept others, so that practically no one, besides Yourself, can determine whether they are inside the Church or outside her. To these three classes of men is added a fourth, which the blessed Apostle Peter calls "a chosen generation, a kingly priesthood, a holy nation, a purchased people" (1 Pet 2:9). These are held in the chaste bosom of the Christian Church, like dear sons in the lap of a kindly mother.

You see, most Holy Father, that while there is a great diversity of men on earth, no one is free from the power of your office or outside your benevolent concern. You will often be reminded of the kind of responsibility that attends this noble office by the one who, being called by the Lord to the rank of Apostle, said "To the Greeks and to the barbarians, to the wise and the unwise, I am a debtor" (Rom 1:14), indicating that he was not exempt from care for any race, even if it was pagan. And when he wished to signify this even more clearly, he said elsewhere, "For whereas I was free as to all, I made myself the servant of all, that I might gain the more. And I became to the Jews a Jew, that I might gain the Jews; to those who are under the law, as if I were under the law; to those who were without the law, as if I were without the law. To the weak I became weak, that I might gain the weak. I became all things to all men, that I might save all" (1 Cor 9:19-22). And indeed, it has always been the chief concern not only of this apostle, but of all apostles and apostolic men, to bring together from the diversity of all peoples one Church of Christ. Thus you, who hold the place of the Prince of the Apostles, know that it is your duty to undertake the care of all human beings in such a way that you serve all peoples, no matter how barbarous, unbelieving, and removed from the truth of Christianity they may be, for the love of Christ, and to gain as many souls as possible for him. For if the Blessed Pontiff Gregory, not to speak of more ancient precedents, had regarded the care of infidels as none of his business

[621] Beatus ille Pontifex Gregorius existimasset, quomodo fidelis nunc Anglia Christum coleret?

Cum his igitur tribus hominum conditionibus, qui non penitus intra Ecclesiae pietatem sunt, non minus, immo et multo magis fortasse, quam illis, qui intra pium Ecclesiae gremium continentur, si Apostolicae Dignitatis munus implere cogitas, Te debitorem esse intelleges, magna illa animi Tui Sapientia ac Pietate. Quomodo his hominum conditionibus prodesse possis, iam considerare Te credimus, et totam mentis tuae intentionem circa haec versari censemus. Quare Beatitudini tuae non grave futurum existimamus, si de his ad amplitudinis tuae maiestatem nos quaedam altius repetita scribere audebimus: non quod ea, quae scripturi sumus, profundissimam illam tuam rerum cognitionem subterfugere posse ullo modo iudicemus; sed quod in hac exaltationis tuae magna totius orbis laetitia nos has imperitas voces continere nullo modo potuimus.

[Part II]

SI igitur primo ad eam hominum conditionem, qui omnino extra Ecclesiam sunt, neque intra eam unquam[9] fuisse cognoscimus, Pietatis tuae oculum intendere volueris, infinitam paene in toto Terrarum Orbe dispersam Gentis Iudaeorum multitudinem aspicies. Quamquam enim ad multa milia illi huius gentis accedant, qui per omnes Christianorum Regiones habitare videntur; multo tamen plures ab his, qui Orbem ipsum circuire consueverunt, illi existimantur, qui inter Infideles habitant Nationes.

Praeter Iudaeos autem non parvum esse eorum hominum numerum, qui neque nunc Christum colunt, neque unquam coluisse creduntur, illae testantur Occidentalis Oceani magnae Insulae, (si modo Insulae, et non Continentis partes esse existimantur) quae ad hoc usque saeculum omnibus incognitae, a magnis illis Occidentalibus Regibus repertae fuere, in quibus innumerabilis populorum multitudo habitare dicitur, quibus Christi Nomen nunquam fuisse notum existimatur. Hi omnes, quamquam, eo quod Christianae Fidei veritatem neque nunc quidem suscipiunt, neque unquam suscepisse creduntur, unius conditionis esse dicantur; quoniam tamen diversa illis est Infidelitatis causa, diverso indigere videntur auxilio. Iudaei enim, si recte consideremus, nulla inscitia, aut ignorantia, sed obdurata potius Cordis perfidia Christum non suscipiunt; quem enim illorum Lex, et Prophetae venturum manifestissime praedicant; quem Patres

[621], how would faithful England have come to worship Christ?

If, then, you plan to fulfill your Apostolic office, you will doubtless understand, in your great wisdom and kindness, that you are no less, and perhaps even more obligated to these three classes of men, who are not entirely within the Christian faith, than you are to those who are held in the bosom of the Church. Thus, we do not doubt that you are already carefully and intently pondering how to benefit these classes of men. We trust that Your Holiness will not be offended if we dare to write in some detail about these matters, not because we think that our proposals can possibly have escaped your profound understanding, but rather because, amid the universal rejoicing over your elevation, we simply cannot contain our unlearned voices.

[Part II]

If, then, you care to turn your eyes first of all to the class of men who are outside the Church and have never been within her, you will see the countless multitude of the Jewish race, which is spread over nearly the entire world. For although many thousands of this people belong to the population of Christian areas, those who have traveled around the globe count many more of them among the Infidel nations.

Apart from the Jews, there are many people who do not worship Christ at present and, it is believed, never did so. This is proved by the great islands of the Western Ocean—if indeed they may be considered islands, and not parts of continents. In these islands, which were unknown to all until the present time and which were discovered by the great Kings of Western Europe, a vast multitude of people is reported to dwell, who apparently have never had any knowledge of Christ. These people, since they do not currently accept the truth of the Faith of Christ and have never done so, can be put in the same class [as the Jews]; nevertheless, since the cause of their lack of faith is different, they seem to require a different kind of help. For the Jews, if we look at the matter rightly, fail to accept Christ not through ignorance, but because of the stubborn perfidy of their hearts. Their Law and Prophets clearly foretell his coming, and they dare not deny that their

[622] eorum crucifixisse negare non audent; quem a tot milibus ex
Iudaeis et Gentibus omnibus in unam Fidem congregatis adorari in
universis Orbis partibus non ignorant, hunc suscipere non acquiescunt. Illarum vero extremarum Orbis partium incolae ideo Christum
non colunt, quoniam ipsum Christi nomen ad hanc usque diem
nunquam audivisse recordantur. Quod tamen ita omnino esse non
obstinati contenderimus. Nam licet eam Prophetae vocem, qua at-
testatur, in omnem Terram exiisse Apostolorum sonum, ad futurum
trahere possemus: facile tamen et id evenire potuisse existimamus, ut
vocem Dominum Iesum praedicantium in omnem Terram iam olim
exiisse credamus, temporum autem iniuria factum esse, ut illis in
locis obliteratum ex omni memoria ita sit, ac si nunquam ibi Christus
annuntiatus fuisset. His gentibus eodem morbo, diversa tamen causa
laborantibus, a Te, qui animarum omnium languentium vere medicus
es, diversa sunt excogitanda remedia, quibus, quantum in Te sit, ex
miserabili hac infirmitate, ad Christianae veritatis sanitatem ac vitam
revocentur, priusquam plures eorum in aeternam illam miseriarum
omnium mortem dilabantur.

Iudaeis prodesse fortasse poteris, si ii animi blanditiis, atque omnibus
humanitatis officiis ad Fidem alliciantur; inde vero si allecti converti
noluerint, pro eorum cervicosa perfidia, acerbius, duriusque tractentur: non quod vis aliqua illis inferatur; ad Fidem enim neminem
cogendum esse, sacri Canones definierunt; sed ut videntes illos, qui
ex eis converti voluerunt, foveri, illos vero, qui hoc facere nunquam
acquieverunt, sperni, atque durius haberi, his stimulis, quasi duobus
calcaribus, ad iter Veritatis, et Vitae arripiendum facilius incitentur.
Satis vero a Te blandiri, atque foveri existimabunt, si divitibus conversis, quamquam iniusta arte aquisitas divitias suas habere permiseris. Cum enim, quae illi aliena ex iniqua foeneratione possident,
pro multitudine, ignorationeque personarum, a quibus foenerati sunt,
propriis dominis restitui non possint, plenissime sub Apostolicae
definitionis potestate esse credimus, eas ipsas divitias, cui visum fuerit, et iam ipsis iniuste possidentibus, si convertantur, elargiri. Pauperibus vero, si ad Christi Fidem vere converti voluerint, de Ecclesiae
Bonis, quae victui, vestituique eorum necessaria sunt, provideantur.
Quos enim vi compellere non possumus, non quasi pretio conducere,
sed his vitae subsidiis

[622] fathers crucified him,[5] and they know that he is worshiped by so many thousands of Jews and Gentiles, all gathered into one Faith throughout the world, yet they still refuse to accept him. The inhabitants of those remote parts of the world, on the other hand, do not worship Christ because, they say, they have never heard his name before the present day. That this is true, let us not unreasonably dispute. For although we could apply to the future the words of the Prophet, which testify that the voice of the Apostles has gone forth into all the earth (Ps 19:5), we may also readily suppose that preaching about the Lord Jesus did indeed go into every land long ago, but with the passing of time it was erased from popular memory, just as if he had never been proclaimed there. For these people, who suffer from the same malady for different reasons, it is your task as the true physician of all languishing souls to think up diverse remedies, so that they may be brought back from this pitiful infirmity to the health and life of Christian truth before more of them slip into eternal death, which is the fullness of misery.

You will be able to help the Jews, perhaps, if they are drawn to the Faith by soothing words and every sort of kindness; then, if they refuse to be drawn and converted because of their stiff-necked faithlessness, they may be treated more harshly and severely. Let us not, however, use any force against them, for the Sacred Canons make clear that no one should be compelled to the Faith. Rather, when they see that those who are willing to be converted are enjoying support, and that those who have never consented are spurned and treated more harshly, they will easily be incited by these stimuli, as if by two spurs, to take the road of Truth and Life. Now, they will consider themselves sufficiently flattered and encouraged if you allow wealthy converts to keep their riches, even if they were acquired by unjust means. Since the money that they possess from unjust lending cannot be restored to its owners, owing to the number of people involved and ignorance of their identity, we think that the Apostolic Office has full power to bestow this money, when it seems appropriate, even on those who possess it unjustly, provided that they become converts. Poor Jews, on the other hand, if they are willing to convert to the Faith of Christ, should be provided from the Church's goods with the means to obtain food and clothing. For we believe that those who cannot be compelled by force may legitimately be attracted in this way,

5   The ecumenical council Vatican II, in its Declaration on the Relationship of the Church to non-Christian Religions, *Nostra Aetate*, no. 4, has corrected this ancient error by saying, "What happened in His passion cannot be charged against all Jews, without distinction, then alive, nor against the Jews of today."

[623] allicere, non illicitum esse credimus. Quod si Ecclesiae thesauros in alios usus convertere potius videbitur, quamquam non
facile sit invenire, in quae potiora pietatis opera convertantur, cum
ea misericordia, quae animarum saluti praestatur, verior misericordia sit, quam quae nutriendis corporibus impenditur, poterit tamen
Beatitudo tua, Ecclesiae divitiis nequaquam imminutis, pauperibus,
qui convertantur, misericorditer quaedam elargiri, si divitibus, qui
converti voluerint, aliquam parvam divitiarum particulam in aliquod
fidele aerarium conferre iusseris, in nullos alios usus expendendam,
nisi eiusdem gentis pauperibus, cum conversi ad veritatem fuerint,
per Episcopos elargiendam. Tam vero divitibus, quam pauperibus
commune beneficium existimabitur, si quicumque ad Fidem conversi fuerint, illis donentur Civitatibus, in quibus sacrum suscipere
baptismum elegerint, si pro singulorum virtute, ac industria ad
saecularia, et opportuno quoque tempore, ad Ecclesiastica Beneficia
promoveantur, aliisque huiuscemodi favoribus prosequaris.

Qui vero ex Iudaeis neque veritatis amore, neque his pietatis officiis converti ad Christum voluerint, non iniquum fore putamus, si
durius, asperiusque tractentur; non quod odio illos prosequi ullo
modo Christianis aequum sit, sed ut magna quadam paternae in eos
pietatis norma, quos blanditiis emollire non potuimus, minis, piisque
verberibus ad cor redire quoquo modo cogamus. Acerba autem illis
verbera existimamus futura, si nullatenus inter Christianos foenerari
permittantur, si mercaturae commercia, aliasque artes exercere prohibeantur, si pedagia rerum omnium plus illis aliquantulum augeantur,
quam Christianis hominibus, si non multum temporis in eodem
loco manere, neque ita libere synagogas habere, caeremoniasque suas
exercere permittantur, si nullo modo cum Christianis habitare, aut
ambulare, aut navigare illis concedatur, si manifestissimo signo in
Christianorum regionibus notentur, quo ab omnibus facilius dignosci, ac evitari valeant. Non iniusta esse haec credimus, neque violen-
ta, quae ad conterendam sane cordis eorum duritiam non inutilia
fortasse reperientur.

Si experimentum fieri contingat, non sunt tamen duo illa remedi-
orum genera praetermittenda, in quibus non humanae sapientiae
industriam, sed Divinae pietatis gratiam operari existimamus;[10]
quorum alterum est, ut illis non a quibuscumque, sed ab his, qui a Te
ad hoc opus eligentur, Doctrina,

---

10   non humanae...pietatis gratiam MS; non humanae sapientia industriae, sed
     Divinae pietatis gratia ED

[623] not indeed as if we were hiring them for a price, but by providing them with the necessities of life. But if it seems best to put the treasures of the Church to other uses—although it would be hard to find better works of piety to which they might be applied, since mercy devoted to the salvation of souls is a more genuine kind of mercy than that which is spent on nourishing the body—Your Holiness will be able to give something to poor converts without diminishing the Church's wealth, if you require the rich who opt for conversion to put a small portion of their wealth in a secure treasury, which the Bishops will spend exclusively on alms for poor Jews when they convert to the truth. Moreover, both the rich and the poor will seem to benefit if all who convert to the Faith are granted citizenship in the place where they are baptized, and if they are promoted, in accordance with their individual virtue and industry, to secular and, when it seems appropriate, to ecclesiastical offices, and are granted other favors of this kind.

Those, however, who are unwilling to convert to Christ either for the love of truth or because of these kindly offices can in all fairness, we believe, be treated more harshly and severely. We recommend this not because it is right for Christians to pursue them with hatred, but so that we may follow, as it were, the great rule of a father's concern, and that by using threats and kindly blows on those whom we are unable to soften with flattery, we may somehow compel them to enter into their hearts. We suppose that it will come as a sharp blow to them if they are not permitted to lend money to Christians; if they are prohibited from engaging in trade and other arts; if they must pay in all things slightly higher taxes than Christians do; if they are not permitted to remain for very long in one place and to have their synagogues and perform their ceremonies with as much freedom; if they are completely forbidden to live or walk or sail with Christians; and if they are required in Christian areas to wear a manifest label, so that they can be more easily recognized and avoided. We do not consider these measures unjust or violent, and they will, perhaps, be found useful for softening the hardness of their hearts.

But if this experiment should succeed, two types of remedy should not be overlooked, which we consider to be the work not of human wisdom, but of divine goodness. The first is that the word of life should be untiringly administered to them not by just anyone, but by those you have chosen for this work,

[624] et moribus praeditis verbum vitae incessanter administretur, ut non de Philosophorum rationibus, non de nostrorum Doctorum auctoritatibus, sed de suis propriis Scripturis convincantur, perfidiaque eorum expulsa eis Veritatis lumen, et Sacri Evangelii, Apostolorumque doctrina ostendatur. Fidem etenim nostram, ideo plurimi eorum abhorrere videntur, quoniam, quae nos credimus, minime intellegunt. In quo illud admirabile est, quod nos idolorum cultores existimant, cum nihil ita sit a Christiana veritate alienum, quam ipsum Idololatriae crimen. Hoc enim in universo terrarum Orbe diffusum per solam Christi praedicationem penitus extinctum cognovimus. Alterum vero pii remedii genus est, si pro illis, tamquam pro pereuntibus fratribus ab omni Ecclesia, ac singulis quibusque fidelibus Orationum sine intermissione voces[11] et piarum lacrimarum intercessiones ad Dominum dirigantur: quae devotius fient, si Tu pro illis Orationibus Indulgentiarum munera larga manu contuleris.

His quidem artibus; aut efficacioribus etiam aliis, quae nos pro mentis imbecillitate excogitare non possumus, Domino Iesu auxiliante, multos converti posse non diffidimus; id unum si Tu nobis dederis, Beatissime Pater, ut pietatis tuae oculis ad eorum miseriam conversis, de eorum salute cogitare incipias, si eos Christo lucrifacere cupias. Hoc si praestiteris, non deerunt Tibi salubriora ad hoc opus Sapientium consilia. Non deerunt maxime illius tuae sapientiae profundissimae excogitata argumenta, quibus non dura tantum Iudaeorum corda, sed durissimos etiam lapides valeas emollire. Neque Tu, propterea quod aliquantulum in sua perfidia pertinaciores videntur, de eorum conversione, quasi Tibi nulla spes salutis reliqua sit, minus cogitare debes: quoniam non est ea manus Domini abbreviata, quae de lapidibus filios Abraham suscitare potuit; quin immo potens est Deus excisos in terra ramos inserere. Nam si nos ex oleastro gentilitatis excisi in bonam olivam contra naturam inserti sumus, quanto magis hos secundum naturam suae olivae a Domino inserendos sperare non prohibemur. Non enim ea Divinae Pietatis imminuta est abundantia, per quam ad Petri vocem uno die huius gentis tria milia, alio autem quinque milia ad Dominum Iesum conversi sunt.

Tuum igitur, Beatissime Pater, qui Sanctissimam Petri Sedem tenes, officium est, omnibus modis de Iudaeorum salute sollicitum esse, pro quibus omnibus Apostoli multa

---

11   Orationum sine intermissione voces MS: Orationes sine intermissione, voces ED

[624] and who are endowed with learning and moral character. Let the Jews be convinced, moreover, not by philosophical arguments or the authority of our doctors, but by their own Scriptures; and after their faithlessness has been overcome, let them be shown the light of Truth and the teaching of the Holy Gospel and the Apostles. For most of them appear to shrink from our Faith because they do not understand what we believe. It is particularly remarkable that they consider us idolaters, when nothing is so far from Christian Truth as the sin of idolatry. For we know that when idolatry had spread throughout the entire world, it was only through the preaching of Christ that it was finally eradicated. A second type of kindly remedy is that the whole Church, as well as individual believers, should make unceasing prayers and tearful intercessions to the Lord on behalf of the Jews, as if for perishing brethren. They will do so more devoutly if these prayers receive generous indulgences.

By these or still more efficacious means, which our own weak minds cannot devise, and with the help of the Lord Jesus, many people can no doubt be converted, if you, Holy Father, will grant us this one favor: to turn your kindly eyes toward their misery and to begin to think of their salvation, if indeed you want to gain them for Christ. If you grant this, you will not be without the counsels of wise men, nor will you lack the means devised by your profound wisdom to soften not only the hard hearts of the Jews, but even the hardest rocks. Nor should you, if they seem a little too stubborn in their faithlessness, pay any less attention to their conversion, as if you had no hope left for their salvation. The hand of God, which was able to raise sons of Abraham from the stones, has not been shortened; indeed, God is able to re-graft the branches that have been cut off and have fallen on the ground. If we who had been cut off from the wild olive tree of paganism were grafted, contrary to nature, onto the good olive tree, how much more can we hope that the Lord will graft these naturally onto their own tree (Rom 11:19-24). There has been no diminution of the abundance of God's kindness, through which the preaching of Peter converted three thousand of this race to the Lord Jesus in one day (Acts 2:24) and five thousand in another (Acts 4:4).

Thus it is your duty, Blessed Father, who occupy the Holy See of Peter, to be completely solicitous for the salvation of the Jews, on whose behalf the Apostles did and endured so much

[625] fecerunt, tuleruntque, ut eos ad aemulandum Fidei cultum provocarent, salvos aliquos saltem ex illis facere cupientes. Ubi vero omnia tentaveris, ubi unguenta omnia atque medicamenta adhibueris, insipientiae vero eorum vulnera ita computruisse respexeris, ut curari nullo modo possint, postremum omnium erit, ut illos tamquam morbidas oves a Christianis gregibus ita omnino separari iubeas, ut in nullo Christianae potestatis loco permanere, aut per illum pertransire permittas. Quod statim ante omnia faciendum ausi fuissemus dicere, nisi ad eorum salutem potius respicere, pium, Christianaeque disciplinae opus esse suspicati essemus; et nisi Iudaeorum accessione Infidelium vires augendas fore dubitassemus. Vere enim, si ad Christianae plebis commodum, salutemque pie respexeris, nihil in toto hoc Iudaeorum negotio expediens magis, opportunumque videbitur, quam eos penitus ex omnibus Christianae Dominationis Regionibus, capitis etiam poena constituta, expellere; quoniam praeter illud incommodum, quo Christianam plebem foenerando officiunt, quod sub commodi specie maximum est incommodum, vanissimis superstitionibus gens illa, vanarum superstitionum omnium Magistra, milleque iniquis ac impiis artibus Christianum Populum imbuit. Inde enim inanissimorum somniorum inaniores interpretationes: inde dierum observationes, futurorum praedictiones: inde aliae multae pessimae, humanoque generi perniciosissimae artes, quasi ex omnium impietatum fonte in miserabile Christianum vulgus derivant.

Ut autem longiorem sermonem paucis verbis colligamus, Iudaeorum certe saluti, et Christianorum simul hominum commodo, Fideique puritati optime consulere Te posse credimus, si talem aliquam legem promulgaveris, qua illi intellegant, qui se ad Fidem convertere voluerint, quibus Beneficiis sint sublevandi: qui vero noluerint, quibus sint incommodis afficiendi; Te vero, non in perpetuum, sed ad quemdam usque praefixum annorum numerum conversionem eorum expectaturum denuntiaveris, quo transacto minime permissurum eos inter Christianos ullo modo reperiri declaraveris. Haec vero cum nihil omnino obesse, prodesse autem, Divina auxiliante misericordia, multum possint, nulloque penitus periculo, labore, aut dispendio fiant, non videmus, cur praetermittenda, aut aspernanda omnino videantur.

[625], in order to summon them to the practice of our Faith, since they desired to save some of them at least (Rom 11:4). When you have tried everything, when you have applied every kind of ointment and medicine and have found that their festering wounds cannot be cured, your last resort will be to separate them, like diseased sheep, from the Christian flock, so that they are not permitted to remain in or cross through any Christian country. We would have recommended doing this from the start, but we deemed it a work of Christian charity to look out for their salvation, and we feared that the power of the Infidel would be increased by the addition of the Jews. Indeed, if you consider the advantage and safety of the Christian people, nothing seems more expedient and timely in this whole matter of the Jews than to expel them completely from all the regions of Christendom, even on penalty of death. For apart from the trouble they cause the Christian people with usury—which, although it has the appearance of convenience, is really the greatest inconvenience—that race has imbued Christians with the wildest superstitions, being itself the teacher of all vain superstitions, through a thousand unjust and impious arts. The Jews are the source of those silly dreams and their even sillier interpretations, of superstitions about certain days, of fortune-telling, and many other bad and harmful arts, which flow, as it were, from the font of all impieties into the pitiful Christian people.

To be brief: we believe that you will contribute to the salvation of the Jews, to the good of Christians, and to the purity of the Faith if you promulgate a law making it clear what benefits will be available to those who wish to convert and what disadvantages will be encountered by those who refuse, and if you announce that you will not wait for their conversion forever, but only for a fixed number of years; when this period is over, they will not be allowed to mix at all with Christians. Since these measures can do no harm, but can, with God's help, do a lot of good, and since they can be accomplished without danger, effort, or expense, we do not see why they should be overlooked or rejected out of hand.

SED iam et de illis loqui aggrediamur, qui

[626] neque Iudaicam legem, neque Evangelicam Iesu Christi Doctrinam
suscepisse unquam cognoscuntur, sed misera adhuc idolorum servitute,
vanis, impiisque superstitionibus tenentur, de quorum salute non minus,
immo magis etiam, quam de Iudaeorum conversione Te, Beatissime
Pontifex, cogitare credimus, tum quoniam fratres illos nostros esse
non Te latet (et nos enim aliquando gentes fuimus), tum maxime, quia
miserandi magis sunt, quoniam si quid ipsi fecerunt, id pura ignorantia,
non obstinata perfidia faciunt, et ideo eorum facilior conversio futura
est, quod experientia comprobatum audivimus. Cum enim superioribus
annis Catholici illi occidentales Reges ad transfretandum magnum illud
occidentale Pelagum, variasque ipsius continentis partes perquirendas
naves quamplurimas transmisissent, novit omnibus melius Beatitudo Tua,
quot, qualesque insulae neque antiquioribus Scriptoribus, neque aetatis
nostrae hominibus antea cognitae, ab illis repertae fuerint. Neque Te latet,
quantum habitabilis Terrae, quae sive magna insula, sive continens sit, non
adhuc pro comperto habetur, in hominum cognitionem venerit, in qua
gentes reperiuntur, quae neque Iudaicam sapiunt superstitionem, neque
Christi Veritatem cognoverunt, neque Mahumeti impia haeresi sunt foedatae: sed vano Idolorum Solis, et Lunae, animaliumque diversorum cultui inserviunt. Ad quarum aliquas cum Religiosi illi Principes Deo dicatos
homines, et sacrae Fidei nostrae institutionibus eruditos transmisissent, hi
autem, utcumque lingua, idiomateque illorum percepto, cum illis Christum[12] Crucifixum praedicare coepissent, infinitam paene eorum multitudinem credidisse, Christumque suscepisse audivimus; Te vero, si ita se
res habeat, cognovisse credimus; non falsum autem omnino existimamus,
quod omnes totius Hispaniae populi manifestissime testantur. Dum enim
apud eos Reges ego Petrus pro Venetorum Republica, cui tunc inservie-
bam, Legatus, agerem, hoc ab omnibus aperte praedicari audivi, nullamque prorsus aliam ad eorum gentium conversionem difficultatem esse
accepi, quam eorum linguam addiscere. Ubicumque enim est, qui possit
eis Christum annuntiare, illi in eum verissime credentes, et Fidem, et sacri
Baptismatis lavacrum devotissime suscipiunt; ita ut non Christiani modo,
sed Monachi fieri incipiant. Iam enim in magnos illos Terrae ambitus,
quos occidentalem Indiam vocant, sedecim constructa esse

---

12 Christum: Christianum MS, Christianorum ED

Now, however, we would like to speak about those who

[626] have evidently never received either the Law of the Jews or the Gospel of Jesus Christ, and who are still held fast by the wretched servitude of idolatry and vain superstitions. Their conversion should, we believe, concern you no less—nay, even more—than that of the Jews, Holy Father. For they are obviously our brothers, since we too were pagans once, and, more to the point, they acted from simple ignorance, rather than stubborn faithlessness. Thus, their conversion will be easier, as experience has shown. In recent years the Catholic kings of Western Europe have sent many ships to cross the great western Ocean and to explore the various parts of that continent, and Your Holiness knows better than anyone how many islands they have discovered, and of what kind, which were previously unknown to ancient writers and to men of our own time. Nor are you unaware of the great amount of habitable land that has been discovered— whether it is a continent or a great island remains uncertain— in which peoples are found who know nothing of the Jewish superstition or of Christian Truth, and who have not been soiled with the impious heresy of Muhammad; rather, they are devoted to the empty cult of idols, of the sun and the moon and diverse animals. To some of these peoples those two devout princes sent men who are consecrated to God and well versed in the teachings of our Faith. Having learned somewhat the language of the people, they began to preach Christ Crucified, and at once an almost infinite number, as we have heard, believed and accepted Christ. We trust that if this is true, you already know it; for our part, we do not consider false what all the people of Spain clearly testify to be true. When I, Peter, was acting as an ambassador to those kings for the Venetian Republic, which I was serving at the time, I heard this report openly declared by everyone, and also that they had encountered no difficulty in converting these peoples, beyond that of learning the language. Wherever a man fit to proclaim Christ may find himself, these people put the most genuine faith in him and devoutly receive the Faith and the Sacrament of Baptism. Indeed, they are not only becoming Christians, but even monks. For in those wide stretches of earth that are called the West Indies, sixteen

[627] Monasteria sub B. Francisci Regula, non in illis[13] modo regionibus constanter asseritur, sed ad nos usque haec fama pervenit.

His, Sanctissime Pater, sola ignorantia laborantibus, sic avide, sic libenter audientibus, cumque audierint, Christum suscipientibus non succurrere, magnam ignaviam, maximamque impietatem esse Te existimare credimus. Unde de tantarum animarum salute multo magis, quam Reges illos, Te sollicitum anxiumque futurum speramus, cum id maxime, non Regum negotium, sed Apostolicum potius opus esse non ignores, totumque hoc onus tuis humeris incumbere Te minime lateat; nisi enim pro viribus Tu Christum illis annuntiandum curaveris, Te de animabus eorum in extremo tremendi illius Iudicii examine rationem redditurum fore non ambigimus: nisi Apostolicam Dignitatem ad quietem potius, et otium, quam ad sollicitudines, et ad labores Tibi traditam existimes: nisi Pontificalis apicis honore frui, optimi autem Pastoris onus non subire sine culpa Te posse cogites. Illi enim recto Dei Iudicio minus arguentur: Quomodo enim credent, nisi audierint; quomodo autem audient, nisi illis praedicetur? Ceteri vero omnes Christiani vix aliquam hac in re culpam subibunt: quomodo enim praedicabunt alicui, nisi mittantur? Mitti autem a quo possunt, nisi a Te Christianorum omnium Pontifice Maximo; cum enim summum locum teneas, summamque possideas auctoritatem, sicut magni boni, si ad hoc animum intenderis, sic magni etiam mali, si neglexeris, causa esse poteris. Postquam igitur neque illi credere possunt, nisi audierint, neque audire, nisi illis praedicetur, neque aliquis praedicare, nisi mittatur, neque mitti ullus potest, nisi a Te uno, reliquum est, ut si hi minus, quam fieri potuisset, crediderint, omnis in Te uno culpa reiiciatur. Quare, si saluti tuae consulere in animo est, illarum gentium salutem nullo modo neglegere poteris. Iam enim pastoralis Officii ratione tuam nequaquam quaerere valeas, illorum neglecta salute, neque eorum salutem neglegere, nisi et propriam neglegas. Quod cum factum omnino a Domino sit, Tibi non grave, aut molestum, sed suave, atque gratissimum esse debere existimamus: quoniam non hoc Tibi a Domino opus commissum est, ut laboriosius ad salutem pervenires, sed magis ut ad gloriam virtutibus, sanctissimisque moribus tuis iam praeparatam his meritis facilius accederes, cumulatioremque Beatitudinis aeternae felicitatem susciperes. Quod Tu profundissima, et in

---

13   in illis MS: illis ED

[627] monasteries under the rule of St. Francis have been constructed. This fact has been repeatedly confirmed not only in those regions, but the news of it has also come to us.

Surely Your Holiness knows that it would be the greatest indolence and the greatest impiety not to come to the aid of these people who suffer from ignorance alone, and who so eagerly and gladly hear the Gospel of Christ and accept it when they have heard it. Thus, we hope that you will be much more concerned than those kings for the salvation of such souls, since you know that this is not the responsibility of kings, but the duty of an Apostle, and that the whole task falls upon your shoulders. If you fail to do everything in your power to proclaim Christ to them, you will doubtless render an account for their souls in that last, fearful judgment—unless you suppose that you have been given the Apostolic office to enjoy peace and quiet, rather than care and labor, and that you can innocently enjoy the exalted honor (*honor*) of the Papacy while failing to undertake the burden (*onus*) that falls upon the Supreme Pastor.[6] In the just Judgment of God, those people will suffer less reproach: "For how shall they believe him, of whom they have not heard? And how shall they hear, without a preacher?" (Rom 10:14) Nor will other Christians incur any fault in this matter; for how will they preach to anyone, unless they are sent? By whom can they be sent, except by you, the Supreme Pontiff of all Christians? Since you hold the highest place and possess the greatest authority, you will be the cause of great good if you attend to this matter, and of great evil if you neglect it. And so, since they cannot believe unless they hear, and cannot hear unless someone preaches to them, and since no one can preach to them unless he is sent, and no one can be sent except by you alone, it follows that if these people come to believe less than they might have, the blame will be cast upon you alone. If you are concerned, then, with your own salvation, you will not neglect theirs also; for by reason of your pastoral office you cannot seek your own salvation while neglecting theirs, nor can you neglect their salvation without neglecting yours. Since this has been done by the Lord, we assume that you do not find it burdensome or troublesome, but rather pleasant and most welcome. The Lord has committed this work to you, not that you may come to salvation with greater trouble, but rather that, by these meritorious works, you may attain more easily to the glory that has already been prepared by your virtues and holy way of life, and may receive a more ample share of eternal Blessedness. As you recognize this fact with your profound and

---

6   Giustiniani employs a long-standing word play. "Honor" (honor, honoris), and "burden" (onus, onoris) appears in Jerome's *Letter* 60, and throughout Latin and Italian literature.

[628] Deum tota mentis intentione conversa cognoscens, hanc curam neglegere nequaquam credimus. Sed iam nobis videre videtur, Te intra cubiculum mentis tuae sollicite indagare, si quos idoneos habeas, quos lucri spe ad hoc negotium mittere possis; et quamquam non facile Tibi occurrant, qui possint idonei ministri existimari, non ideo tamen illa animi tui deterretur magnitudo; sed potius, cum idoneos ad haec opera a praedecessoribus Tibi praeparatos non invenias, et Tibimet, et aliis, qui post Te futuri sunt, huiusmodi ministros, magis quam auri, aut argenti thesauros comparare cogitas.

Haec enim duo illa potissimum sunt, in quibus earum gentium saluti consulere poteris: unum, si ad eos electos ex omni Religione peritiores maturioris aetatis viros ad Christum praedicandum miseris, qui utcumque potuerint, vel per interpretes, vel saltem moribus, et vita, si minus sermone potuerint, Christianam illis vivendi rationem ostendant, et iuniores etiam aliqui, qui Fidei sint non ignari,[14] docilesque, si mittantur, non multo tempore, neque magno labore inter illos versantes eorum linguam addiscere poterunt, qua potiti peritia idoneos iam se Tibi ministros praebebunt. Neque dubitare Beatitudinem tuam oportet, an in hac Religiosi fervoris declinatione aliquos reperire valeas, qui ad hoc opus libenter accedant, si a Te mittantur; quoniam, quamquam omnes declinasse a pristino illo Religionis fervore appareat, reliquit tamen sibi adhuc Dominus, quos minus cognoscimus, septem milia virorum, qui non incurvaverunt genua sua coram Baal, et praeter hos nullus adeo ignavus, nullus adeo professionis, servitutisque suae, quam Domino obtulerit, oblitus est, ut Te annuente, non libenter, non avide, non laetanter ad Tibi in Terris, et Christo in Caelis serviendum accedat. Quid enim alii facturi sint, nos ex animorum nostrorum ardore colligimus. Si enim nos, qui heri, aut nudius tertius, relictis saeculi vanitatibus, Christi iugum suscepimus, qui omnium Monachorum postremi, omnium Religiosorum minimi sumus, omnibusque minus idonei, ut ad hoc opus vel postremi a Te eligamur, id tamen non desiderare non possumus, et si a Te nobis mitti contigerit, id magni muneris loco habituri sumus. Nihil enim in hac vita nobis optatius contingere posset, quam inter Gentes, quae Christum minime cognoscunt, religiosum Christi nomen, non temere a nobis hoc praesumentes, sed a Te missi praedicare. Quod etiam quamplurimos alios,

---

14 ignari MS: ignorari ED

[628] God-centered vision, you cannot, we trust, neglect this undertaking. Rather, we imagine that in the recesses of your mind you are pondering whether you have suitable men that you may profitably send to this work. If fitting ministers do not easily come to mind, you are not thereby discouraged; rather, if you find that your predecessors have not left you suitable men for this task, you suppose that you are acquiring such ministers for yourself and your successors rather than treasures of gold or silver.

Now, these are the two most important means of attending to the salvation of these peoples. The first is to send learned and mature men from every religious order to preach Christ to them; and even if these men have not mastered the language, they will be able through interpreters or simply by virtue of their character and manner of living to show them the Christian way of life. If you also send younger men who are sufficiently versed in the Faith and teachable, they will be able in a short time and without much trouble to learn the language, and with this knowledge they will provide you with suitable ministers. Nor should Your Holiness doubt that in this time of declining fervor in religious life you will find men who will gladly undertake this work if they are sent. For even if it seems that all have fallen away from the original fervor of religious observance, the Lord has left himself seven thousand, whom we hardly know, who have not bent their knees before Baal (1 Kgs 19:18). Beyond these, there is no one so lazy or forgetful of his profession and the service that he has offered to God, that, with a nod from you, he would not willingly, gladly and joyfully come to serve you on earth, and Christ in heaven. What others will do, we gather from the ardor of our own soul. For we, who only yesterday or the day before left the vanities of the world and took upon us the yoke of Christ, who are the last of monks and the least of all religious, and less suited than all others to be the last ones chosen for this work—even we cannot fail to desire it, and if we happened to be sent by you, we would consider it a great boon. Nothing, indeed, is more desirable in this life than to preach the sacred name of Christ among the nations that do not know him, and to preach him not presumptuously and on our own authority, but as men whom you have sent. That there are many others

[629] quanto idonei magis sunt, tanto etiam ardentius desiderare non dubitamus.

Alterum vero, quod non tantum his gentibus, sed aliis etiam omnibus prodesse posse non ambigimus, illud est, quod nunc tamquam novum a nobis minime excogitatur, sed a Sanctissimis antiquioribus Fidei nostrae Patribus inventum cognovimus, qui animadvertentes, quod Linguarum gratiam, quam super Apostolos Dominus in die Pentecostes effudit, (idque peccatis nostris sic exigentibus) accipere non meremur, sine Linguarum autem cognitione infidelibus, barbarisque nationibus, quibus omnino debitores sumus, Christum praedicare non possumus; ad sacrosanctas illas universales synodos congregati, et Spiritus Sancti lumine afflati constantissimis definitionibus statuerunt, in omni Christianorum loco, ubi studia vigerent Litterarum, illud proximum summa diligentia curandum, ut omnium Gentium Linguae, quarum principales Hebraica, Graeca, Latina, et Araba fore censentur, quantum fieri posset, addiscerentur, edocerenturque non quod aliqua curiositate in his Linguis iuniora ingenia occupari vellent, sed quod sic fieri debere censerent, ut ad praedicandum Christum in omnibus gentibus et nationibus plurimi idonei evaderent. Quod et illi non tacuerunt, qui post illos fuere Sancti Pontifices, sed eadem confirmantes apertissime declaraverunt. Has oblivionis caligine obrutas Sanctissimas Patrum Sanctiones si Tu non edicto modo, sed opere ipso in lucem revocabis, non dubitamus, Te non multo post tempore plurimos habiturum idoneos, quos ad omnes Gentes ad Christum Iesum Crucifixum nuntiandum, et praedicandum mittere possis. Proderit huic operi, si ex illis Occidentalibus insulis, et ex omnibus simili ratione regionibus iuniores aliquos ad Te adduci curaveris, qui non ut servi Tibi ministrent, sed ut per Monasteria, quae sanctiora sunt, distributi et linguam pariter nostram, et Fidei Christianae veritatem addiscant, et linguam quoque propriam aliquos doceant. Si enim ad eos aliquos[15] miseris, et ex illis quosdam ad Te adduci curabis, facillime fiet, ut hac mutua consuetudine nos linguam eorum, illi vero nostrae Fidei veritatem addiscant. Unde ad Fidei cultum in illis regionibus disseminandum duplex Tibi praeparabitur instrumentum, dum hac arte nobis extraneae linguae peritiam, illis vero ignotae veritatis agnitionem parabis.

Sed haec, Sanctissime Pater, pacis sunt opera. Qui enimvero Dei armis nullo

---

15   aliquos MS: alienos ED

[629] who, just as they are more suitable, will desire it more ardently, we have no doubt.

The second thing that will doubtless benefit not only these nations, but all others as well, is not something that we ourselves have just invented, but which was discovered by the ancient and Holy Fathers of our faith. They observed that although we are unworthy to receive the gift of tongues, which the Lord poured out on the Apostles on the day of Pentecost—for our sins prevent this—we are unable, without the knowledge of languages, to preach Christ to unbelieving and barbarian nations, to which we are altogether debtors. And so, when the fathers assembled at the ecumenical councils and were inspired by the light of the Holy Spirit, they firmly decreed that in every Christian land where the study of letters flourished, special care should be taken to learn and teach the languages of all the nations (principally Hebrew, Greek, Latin, and Arabic).[7] They did so not because they hoped that the study of these languages would occupy the curiosity of young minds, but because they deemed it necessary, so that many suitable persons would come forth to preach Christ among all nations and peoples. Nor did the holy Popes who followed them remain silent on this matter, but they confirmed their predecessors' acts by open declarations. We have no doubt that if you bring to light the forgotten edicts of the Holy Fathers, not only in word but in deed, you will soon have many persons fit to be sent to all nations to preach and proclaim the Crucified Christ. It will also help to have certain young men sent to you from these western islands and indeed from all nations, not to serve you as slaves, but to be distributed throughout the more observant monasteries, that they may learn the true Christian faith and teach others their own language. If you send men to those people and have some of them brought to you, this mutual exchange will make it possible for us to learn their language and for them to learn the truth of our Faith. Thus you will prepare for yourself a double instrument for sowing the Faith in those regions, when you gain for us knowledge of a foreign tongue and for them knowledge of an unknown truth.

Now these, Holy Father, are the works of peace. Those who do not resist

7   The council of Vienne (1311-1312) decreed that that teaching posts in Hebrew, Greek, Aramaic and Arabic be established at Paris, Oxford, Bologna and Salamanca.

[630] pacto resistunt, armis impugnandi, atque ad Fidem trahendi
nequaquam sunt: sed cum his potius, qui duritia cordis Fidei nostrae
veritatem non recipiunt, partim humanitatis officiis, partim minis,
ac piis verberibus, ut diximus, ita agendum est, ut eorum pertinax
propositum emolliatur, frangaturque. Cum his vero qui sola ignorantia a Christianae veritatis semita aberrant, praedicatione et doctrina,
sic omnia tractanda fore existimamus, quibus ad rectum Fidei callem
ipsi revocentur. Haec eorum omnium, qui nec impraesentiarum
Christum suscipiunt, neque unquam suscepisse videntur, pastoralis
Officii cura, quamquam magna, tua tamen animi Sapientia, atque
generositate est minor.

[Part III]

NEGOTIUM vero, quod Tibi cum his superest, qui nunc extra Ecclesiam omnino sunt, neque Christianam veritatem recipiunt, aliquando tamen intra Ecclesiae gremium fuisse, et Christi Fidem suscepisse
cognoscuntur, maius quidem est, non autem magnitudini tuae impar
esse poterit. Nam qui non cordis duritia, non veritatis ignorantia, sed
armorum saevitia verbo Dei resistunt, piis Ecclesiae armis impugnandi, subiiciendique sunt. Quemadmodum enim, qui nunquam veritatis
Fidem susceperunt, ut ad Fidem accedant,[16] cogendi nequaquam sunt,
sed aliis artibus alliciendi, sic illi, qui, suscepta Fidei veritate, ab ea
impie discesserunt, et non rationibus, sed gladiis illi resistunt, armorum violentia, ut ad cor redeant, et veritatem suscipiant, sunt urgendi.
Quod si id minus facere voluerint, non crudele, non impium, sed max-
imae pietatis opus est, eos piis armis opprimere, atque iusta Ecclesiae
dextera trucidare. Sacrorum enim Canonum auctoritas, quae non nisi
Spiritus Sancti virtute emanavit, Haereticos homines, illos scilicet
omnes, qui semel suscepta veritate impie ab ea recesserunt, non solum
aliis omnibus violentiae generibus cogendos esse, ut ad Fidei redeant
pietatem; sed nisi redierint, opprimendos statuit.

Quod Tu, Sanctissime Pater, cui omnia sunt Ecclesiastica Decreta
optime cognita, non ignoras, quam autem illis periculosum sit, quibus a Sacris Ecclesiae legibus, a Sancto scilicet Spiritu haec provincia
demandatur, vel minima aliqua ex parte huiusmodi Dei praecepta

---

16   accedant: accendant MS, accendantur ED

[630] the weapons of God should certainly not be opposed with arms and compelled to the Faith. With those, indeed, who in the hardness of their hearts do not receive the truth of our faith, we may use humane methods in part, and also threats and kindly blows, as we have said, so that their stubborn resolve may be softened and broken. But those who have wandered from the path of Christian truth merely out of ignorance should, we think, always be approached in preaching and doctrine in such a way that they will be recalled to the straight path of the Faith. The burden of pastoral care for all those who neither accept Christ at present nor seem ever to have accepted him in the past is great indeed, but less than the wisdom and generosity of your soul.

[Part III]

Still greater is the work that remains for you regarding people who are now outside the Church and reject Christian truth, but who, we know, were formerly within the Church's bosom and accepted the Faith of Christ. Nevertheless, the magnitude of this work will not exceed your own greatness. Those who resist the word of God not from hardness of heart or ignorance of the truth, but with the violence of arms, must be opposed and subdued with the devout weapons of the Church. Just as people who have never received the Faith should not be compelled to come to it, but should be attracted by other means, so those who once accepted the truth of the Faith and have impiously deserted it, and who resist it not with reasoning but with swords, must be urged by force of arms to enter into their hearts and to accept the truth.[8] If they are unwilling to do this, it is not a cruel or impious act, but rather one of the greatest piety, to attack them with devout weapons and to crush them with the just right arm of the Church. For the authority of the Sacred Canons, which emanates from the power of the Holy Spirit, states that heretics—those who have accepted the Faith and then impiously abandoned it—should not only be compelled by every kind of force to return to the practice of the Faith, but should be crushed if they refuse to do so.

This fact is known to you, Holy Father, since you are well acquainted with all the statutes of the Church. The peril to those whom the laws of the Church—that is, the Holy Spirit—require to exercise this authority, if they spurn these divine precepts even in the least

---

8 The view that Islam is a Christian heresy is already present in the writings of John of Damascus (c.655-c.750). Vatican II did not endorse this view. Muslims throughout the ages have not previously been Christians. Vatican II did state that Christians and Muslims worship the same God.

spernere, (sanctae enim Leges, nonnisi Divina praecepta sunt) exemplo nobis Saul et Achab esse possunt. De eorum namque altero,
quoniam contra praeceptum Domini, quod per Samuelem audierat,
Regi Amalech pepercerat,

[631] dixit Dominus: Poenitet me, quod constituerim eum Regem,
quia verba mea opere non implevit, et vere secundum quod illi idem
Propheta dixerat, abiecit eum Dominus, ne esset Rex. Alteri autem,
quoniam Regem Syriae, quem dederat Dominus in manibus eius, vi-
vum abire permisit, dictum est: Quia dimisisti virum dignum morte
de manu tua, erit anima tua pro anima eius, et populus tuus pro
populo eius. Sed et inter magna populi Israel crimina per Psalmistam
recensetur, quod non disperdiderunt gentes, quas dixit Dominus illis,
unde iratus est eis, et tradidit eos in manus gentium.

Haec autem, ne Tibi, populisque tuae Fidei commissis contingant,
Te, quoniam primum Apostolicae Dignitatis apicem ascendisti, ante
cetera omnia cogitare coepisse credimus, quomodo impium hoc
hominum genus, aut ad pietatem Fidei revocare, aut delere omnino
possis a facie Terrae. Hoc enim Amplitudinis, Dignitatisque Romani
Pontificis munus esse non dubitas. Hoc magnanimitate, Sapientiaque tua nogotium usque ad haec tempora reservatum a Domino
credimus. Hoc illud est unicum, quod non inani aliqua, sed solida,
stabili, sempiternaque gloria in universum Orbem Terrarum Te
merito supra omnes, qui ante Te fuere, Romanos Pontifices extollere
potest, et ad illam simul immortalitatis beatam gloriam sublevare.
Hoc a Te omnes, qui Christum colunt, totis votis expostulant, omni
fiducia expectant. Hoc illud unum est, quod Beatissimi illi Apostolorum Principes Petrus et Paulus a Te, qui nunc eorum locum tenes,
exigunt. Si enim illi homines pauperes sine imperio, omni Idolorum
cultura penitus destructa, universum Terrarum Orbem Christianae
Fidei subiecerunt, Te, qui et Dignitate maximus es, et divitiarum
thesauris abundas, supremumque Imperium possides, nisi ab hoc
impiorum hominum genere Orbem ipsum liberaveris, nequaquam
dignum Successorem eorum arbitrabuntur. Hoc unum illud est, in
quo Sancti omnes Pontifices, qui ante Te fuere, Beataeque omnes
illae Caelestis Gloriae mentes postremum virtutis tuae experimentum sumere expectant. Hoc illud denique est, ad quod peragendum
Dominus noster Iesus Christus Tibi eius in Terris vices praeter tuam,
omniumque expectationem, commisit. Hoc nisi praestiteris, certissime nihil praestiteris, nihil omnino Christianis hominibus, nihil
Caelestis Gloriae Civibus, nihil Terrarum Caelorumque Domino
praestiteris. Hoc[17] vero

---

17   Hoc MS: haec ED

degree—for the holy laws are none other than the precepts of God—can be demonstrated by the examples of Saul and Ahab. To the former, who spared King Amalek despite the command he had received through Samuel

[631], the Lord said: "I repent that I have made Saul king, for he has forsaken me, and has not executed my commandments"; and, as the same prophet had warned, "God rejected him from being king" (1 Sam 15:11, 23). To the latter, because he had allowed the King of Syria, whom God had delivered into his hands, to depart with his life, God said, "Because you have let go out of your hand a man worthy of death, your life shall be for his life, and your people for his people" (1 Kgs 20:42). Moreover, referring to the great crimes of the people of Israel, the Psalmist says: "They did not destroy the nations of which the Lord spoke unto them," and so he was angry with them and "he delivered them into the hands of the nations" (Ps 106:34, 40-41).

Lest the same things happen to you and to the peoples committed to your trust, you, who have ascended to the highest position of Apostolic dignity, doubtless have begun to ponder before every other matter how this impious race of men can either be recalled to the practice of the Faith or wiped from the face of the earth. Indeed, you have no doubt that this is the burden of the greatness and dignity of the Roman Pontiff. For our part, we believe that this task has been reserved by the Lord for your wisdom and greatness of soul. For this is the one thing that can raise you above all previous Pontiffs of Rome with a glory that is not empty, but solid, enduring, and eternal throughout the world; and indeed it can raise you to the blessed glory of immortality. This is what all who worship Christ beg of you and await with full confidence. This is the one thing that the princes of the Apostles, Peter and Paul, whose place you now hold, require of you. For if those men, being without power, managed to destroy the cult of idols and to subject the entire world to the Christian faith, they will hardly deem you, who enjoy the highest dignity, who abound in wealth, and who possess supreme power, to be their worthy successor unless you deliver the world from this race of impious men. This is the one thing that the holy Pontiffs who preceded you and all the blessed spirits in heavenly glory await as the final proof of your virtue. This is the one thing, finally, for the completion of which our Lord Jesus Christ entrusted his place on earth to you, contrary to your own expectation and that of everyone else. If you do not accomplish this, you will surely not accomplish anything, either for Christians everywhere, or for the citizens of heavenly glory, or for the Lord of heaven and earth. If you do accomplish this

[632] si praestiteris, omnia certe Te praestitisse censebimus; quoniam, nisi hoc confeceris negotium, nihil omnino est, quod recte succedere Christianis possit. Hoc autem confecto, omnia ad vota sponte sua consequentur. Quae quidem Tu omnium melius intellegens, totam mentis tuae vim ad hoc unum iam convertisse credimus. Non enim ullo modo existimamus, Te videre posse tot milia commissarum Tibi ovium a veritatis semita aberrare, atque in adversarii illius Leonis fauces incidere, et magno Pietatis zelo non succendi, alioquin non Pastorem, sed Mercenarium potius Te esse ostenderes. De his enim, qui aliquando Fidei veritatem excoluisse cognoscuntur, quamquam ab ea longissime recesserunt, nemini dubium esse potest, quod inter commissas Tibi a Domino oves connumerandi sunt.

Tua igitur si ad hoc hominum genus cura prospiciat, statim videre poterit, omnes, qui Mahumetis saevissimae, foedissimaeque Bestiae[18] Haeresim sequuntur, huiusmodi esse. Nihil enim aliud est Mahumetanorum hominum nefanda religio, quam impia quaedam haeresis, armorum violentia, temporum longitudine confirmata. Mille enim prope elapsi anni iam sunt, quod antiquissimus humani generis hostis saevissimum nequitiae suae ministrum Mahumetum excitavit, qui partim occasione Schismatum, et Haeresiarum, quibus ea tempestate vexabatur quam maxime Christi Ecclesia:[19] partim armorum vi ac fraude, illam coepit nefandissimam legem, vivendique spurcissimum ritum tradere, quo nunc Christiani nominis[20] inimici Mahumetani omnes utuntur: qui ex septem principalioribus Orbis Ecclesiis, quae Patriarchali Dignitate fulgebant, unicam tantum Romanam Christianis reliquerunt, ceterisque omnibus occupatis, atque in impiissimum, non Dei, sed Diaboli cultum conversis, Christianam magna ex parte Religionem destruxerunt, Christianumque omnino nomen delere avidissime concupiscunt. Cum enim post Domini nostri Iesu Christi Ascensionem, omnibus Idolorum superstitionibus destructis, universus Terrarum Orbis apostolica praedicatione Christum suscepisset, hi surrexerunt impii Mahumetis sectatores, qui inter nos, qui hanc sub Christi nomine Europam habitamus, et illos, qui Christum etiam adorantes Africae, Asiaeque illas maximas Regiones incolunt, interpositi, quasi murus ita nos ab eis, et illos a nobis separant, quod quamquam multo plures illi sint Christiani, quam nos sumus, eorum tamen cognitionem aliquam habere vix possumus.

---

18   Bestiae: Destiae MS, Daciae ED, audaciae *Barletta*
19   vexabatur...Ecclesia: vexabat quam maxime Christi Ecclesia MS, vexabat quam maxime Christi Ecclesiam ED
20   nominis MS: hominis ED

[632], however, we will conclude that you have accomplished everything. For if you do not complete this task, there is nothing that can properly succeed for Christians; but when it is completed, every kind of success will follow of its own accord. Since you understand this better than we do, we are certain that this matter has already received your full and undivided attention. Indeed, we cannot imagine that you are able to tolerate the sight of so many thousands of the sheep committed to your care wandering from the path of truth and falling into the jaws of that Lion, our adversary (1 Pet 5:8), without being inflamed with a great and pious zeal. If it were otherwise, you would be showing yourself to be not a shepherd, but a hired hand (John 10:11-12). No one doubts that those who formerly observed the truth of the Faith, though they have fallen far from it, are to be numbered among the sheep committed to your care.

And so, if you should cast a glance of concern toward this class of men, it will become obvious that all who follow the heresy of Muhammad, that savage and foul Beast, are such as I have said. Indeed, the accursed religion of the Muslims is nothing other than an impious heresy, which has been strengthened by the violence of arms and the passage of time. Nearly a thousand years have passed since the ancient enemy of the human race roused Muhammad, the minister of his wickedness, and he, in part with the help of schisms and heresies, with which the Church of Christ was greatly troubled at the time, and in part by using armed force and deception, began to teach that unspeakable law and foul manner of living that all Muslims, the enemies of Christianity, currently observe. Of the seven principal churches that once enjoyed patriarchal dignity, they have left to Christians only the Church of Rome; the rest have been occupied and turned to the impious service not of God, but of the devil. Thus they have destroyed the better part of Christendom and eagerly seek its complete annihilation. It was after the whole world, following the Ascension of our Lord Jesus Christ and the destruction of all idolatrous superstition, had accepted Christ by the preaching of the Apostles, that these impious followers of Muhammad arose; now, placed like a wall between us who inhabit Christian Europe and the Christians who dwell in the great regions of Africa and Asia, they separate us from them, and them from us. These other Christians are far more numerous than we, and yet we have scarcely any contact with them.

[633] Ipsi vero tamquam membra a suo capite divisa varias patiuntur
infirmitates, neque ab eis resurgere, nisi capiti suo iterum coniungantur,
ullo modo possunt. Coniungi autem minime valent, nisi interpositus
hic impietatis murus destruatur.

Ut igitur illis consulas, qui tot millia numero in ea haeresi cotidie nas-
cuntur, educanturque, qui omnino in aeternum pereunt; ut Christianis
Orientalibus, qui innumerabiles sunt, a Romana Ecclesia, non aliqua
nequitia, aut discordia, sed huius generis interpositione divisi, subve-
nias; a capite enim divisa membra salutis sanitatem consequi non possunt; ut nobis etiam, qui hanc Europae partem incolimus, providas;
illi enim, nisi deleantur, eorum quae possident, nunquam contenti,
etiam quod reliquum Christiani nominis est, occupare aggredientur,
cum pacis huius gentis saevitia[21] impatiens semper extiterit; ut universis orbis partibus hoc impietatis veneno, aut misere infectis, aut quae
miserius occupari timent, pius succurras, oportet Te, Beatissime Pater,
cui universi orbis, totiusque humani generis cura, non ab hominibus
modo, sed a Domino ipso demandata est, hanc orbis subversionem,
Fidei Christianae destructionem, tot milia animarum aeternam perditionem, neque neglegentia spernere, neque desidia[22] neglegere, neque
proprii commodi amore parvifacere, neque timore derelinquere, neque
aliis minoribus occupationibus differre, neque conficiendi negotii
desperatione deserere, sed potius maxima animi alacritate, magnani-
mitateque congruam virtutibus tuis provinciam intrepide suscipere, et
omni alia cura seposita, nullis laboribus, nullis dispendiis, nullis vigiliis
aut incommodis parcentem,[23] cum Domini Nostri Iesu Christi auxilio
perficere:[24] In ea enim perficienda unum a Te solum Dominus ipse
quaerit, ut quemadmodum ille Te in Ministrum suum eligere dignatus
est, ita Tu ad praebendum temetipsum illi Ministrum accommodes,
non ut tuam, sed Tu Domini tui causam suscipias, neque ullo modo ita
modicae sis Fidei, ut de operis perfectione dubitare incipias. Si enim
Domini causa haec est, quod nemo unquam negabit, non deerunt
Divinae Sapientiae recta, opportunaque ad rem ipsam perficiendam
consilia, non deerit Omnipotentis fortitudo, quae adversariorum vires
confringat. Ab eo aderunt Tibi omnia, quae ad rem pro votis confi-
ciendam optari possunt. Tu modo hanc ipsam provinciam intrepide
aggredere. Cum enim per semetipsum possit Deus has impias gentes

---

21   huius gentis saevitia MS: huiusmodi gens ED
22   desidia *Barletta*: dessidia MS, dissidia ED
23   parcentem: parcens MS, parcendo ED
24   perficere *Barletta*: proficere MS, ED

[633] They, for their part, like members separated from their head, suffer various infirmities, from which they cannot begin to recover unless they are joined again with their head. They can in no way be joined, however, unless the wall of impiety that has been placed between us is destroyed.

And so, that you may attend to the many thousands who are born every day into that heresy and are brought up in it, and who are perishing for all eternity; that you may help the countless Eastern Christians, who are divided from the Roman Church not by any wickedness or discord, but rather by this interposition; for members divided from their head cannot enjoy health; that you may provide for us, who inhabit this part of Europe; for unless these people, who are never content with what they have, are completely destroyed, they will attempt to occupy the rest of Christendom, since this savage race has never been satisfied with peace;[9] and that you may come to the rescue of the entire world, which is miserably infected with this impious poison or fears to be more miserably overwhelmed: it behooves you, Holy Father, to whom the care of the whole world and of the entire human race has been entrusted not only by men but by the Lord himself, not to overlook the overthrow of the world, the destruction of the Christian faith, and the eternal perdition of so many thousands of souls. It behooves you, indeed, not to reject this task through negligence, or to neglect it through laziness, or to despise it through love of your own comfort, or to abandon it through fear, or to postpone it for other lesser occupations, or to give it up through despair of ever finishing the task; but rather with the greatest alacrity, magnanimity and fearlessness to undertake a commission that is congruent with your virtues, and putting every other concern aside, and sparing no labor, expense, vigilance, or inconvenience, to make progress with the help of our Lord, Jesus Christ. In undertaking this charge the Lord himself requires one thing from you: just as he has deigned to choose you as his minister, you must try to show yourself as such, not to take up your own cause, but rather that of your Lord, and never to be of such little faith that you begin to doubt the success of the work. If this is the cause of the Lord— which no one will ever deny—you will not lack the right and timely counsels of Divine Wisdom for completing the task, nor will you lack the strength of the Almighty, which breaks the power of his adversaries. From him you will have everything that can be desired for successfully finishing this work. For your part, take this charge in hand without fear! God could wipe these impious nations

---

9   This is a misunderstanding of Islam. The Qur'an could be described as a program toward peace. One of God's names is Peace, and God calls to the home of peace (Qur'an 10:25). In the history of Muslim spokesmen of peace one could name Badshah Khan (1890-1988).

[634] solo voluntatis eius nutu delere a facie universae terrae, ut
tamen Tibi, et his, qui tecum in hac expeditione futuri sunt, aeternae
vitae praemia, caelestisque felicitatis gloriam cumulatius tribuat, hanc
Tibi, tuisque promerendae illius Beatitudinis viam aperuit, labo-
resque proponit, ut mercedem omni labore imparem suscipias. Meminit enim sublimitas tua, Sanctissime Pater, quoniam cum ad delen-
das Cananaeorum, et reliquorum Imperiorum gentes Moysem, atque
Iosue post eum elegisset Dominus, omnes demum in eorum manibus
tradidit. Nec Te latet, quae, et quanta mirabilia supra omne id, quod
ab humano ingenio excogitari, humanisque viribus perfici potuisset, praestitit illis Deus, cui non erat difficile in magno, aut in parvo
numero vincere, cum unus ex illis mille hostium viros persequeretur,
cum ad clamorem populi, clangoremque tubarum firmissima moenia
dilaberentur, cum lapides de Caelo ad instar grandinis illos interfi-
cerent, qui manus militum Domini effugissent. An Tu maiora etiam
his, occultioraque affutura Tibi Domini auxilia diffidis? Sed minime
diffidendum est, quoniam si vero Dei zelo pia Tibi voluntas aderit,
facultas Tibi a Domino deesse non poterit, quo auxiliante, etiamsi
solus cum fratribus tuis inermis contra has impias gentes procederes,
de victoria minime diffidendum esset. Non enim oblitus es, quomodo
saevissimum Christiani, Romanique nominis hostem, qui tam ingenti
exercitu, furoris plenus, victoriis exultans ad desolandam Urbem pro-
cedebat, ille Sanctus Pontifex, cuius Tu Tibi nomen delegisti, inermis
obvius procedens paucis verbis terruerit, fregerit, superaverit, Urbem,
Italiamque servaverit, captivos redemerit. Sed quoniam Deus, qui
semper omnia in omnibus operatur; universas enim creaturas eius
instrumentum fore non ambigimus; non semper infinitam suae Maiestatis potentiam his mirabilibus ostendit; omnia, quae ipse in hac
tam sancta expeditione mirabiliter facere posset, hominum potius
industria ac labore, dum occulte consilia, viresque tribuet, et maxima
semper, licet non semper aperta, auxilia conferet, confici permittet,
ob idque tantam Tibi potestatem tuam ad Dignitatis auctoritatem
praestitit, ut si ad humanas etiam solum vires respicias, Te posse hoc
negotium conficere non diffidas.

Quae enim sint Pontificis vires; quae Christianorum Principum
omnium, quibus potentia praeis, Te latere non potest. Nam quamvis
pia Domini dispensatione factum

[634] from the face of the earth by his own power and will alone; nevertheless, that he might shower on you and those who will join this expedition the rewards of eternal life and the glory of heavenly joy, he has opened for you and yours this way of earning that blessedness, and has assigned you labors, that you may gain wages that no labor can equal. You remember, Holy Father, that when the Lord chose Moses and then Joshua to destroy the Canaanites and the other kingdoms, he finally delivered all these into their hands. Nor are you unaware of the great miracles, beyond everything that the human mind can imagine or human strength accomplish, that God performed for them. It was not difficult for God to conquer with great numbers or with small, since a single man pursued a thousand enemies (Deut 32:30), and the strongest walls collapsed at the shout of the people and the blast of trumpets (Josh 6:11-20), and stones from heaven like hail killed those who fled from the hands of God's soldiers (Josh 10:11). Do you doubt that God will give you greater and more miraculous help than this? You should not doubt it in the least. For if your pious will is joined with the zeal of God, God will not fail to grant the ability; and with his help, even if you should go forth alone and unarmed with your brethren against these impious nations, you cannot have the least doubt that you will conquer. Surely you have not forgotten how that ferocious enemy of Christianity and Rome, full of madness and exulting in victory, who was proceeding with a great army to despoil the City, was terrified, broken, and defeated by that holy Pontiff whose name you have chosen, who went forth unarmed, and with a few words saved Italy and ransomed her prisoners?[10] But since God, who always does all things in all—for we do not doubt that all creatures will be his instruments—has not always shown the infinite power of his majesty by such miracles, he will surely grant that everything he could have performed miraculously in this holy expedition will be accomplished through the industry and labor of men, while he secretly supplies the wisdom and strength, and he will always bestow the greatest, if sometimes concealed, assistance. This is why he has given such power and authority to you, so that even if you consider human strength alone, you will not doubt that you can complete this task.

You cannot be unaware of the strength of the Pontiff and of all Christian princes, over whom you excel in power. It is true that by the kindly dispensation of the Lord

10   Pope Leo I (440-461), according to a tradition, met Attila before Rome (452), and the advance of the Huns stopped.

[635] sit, ut multi ante Te Pontifices propriam non cognoverint
potestatem, ne quasi saeviores belluae in proprios greges grassaren-
tur immanius, si suarum maiorum virium cognitores fuissent: Tibi
tamen ad pietatis opera iam converso, Tibi, inquam, qui ad Christi
Iesu imitationem animam tuam pro ovibus tuis tradere paratus es,
qui per ostium ingressus, tamquam verus Pastor, pascere Dominicum
gregem, nequaquam autem mactare venisti, incognitam esse Christianorum virtutem, tuaeque Sedis auctoritatem, ac potestatem nullo
modo credimus. Dum enim superioribus annis Pontifex Maximus
omnes Christianos Principes et Reges concordia iungit, proque arbitrio suo discordia dividit, dum Principes ipsi in Christiani nominis
perniciem, bella, et impie quidem, exercent, viresque suas in semetipsos experiuntur, quae sit Christianorum hominum virtus, quae
sit Pontificis in omnes Christianos auctoritas atque potestas, non
Tibi modo, sed et multis etiam aliis pie considerantibus innotescere
potuit. Si enim, qui ante Te Beatissimi Petri Sedem tenuerunt, solum
ad Christianorum Principum animos inter se conciliandos, ac contra
ipsos Christiani nominis hostes incitandos Apostolica auctoritate usi
essent; si tantum Christiani sanguinis, atque etiam auri pro Christiana pietate contra perfidas has nationes dimicando effusum, profu-
sumque fuisset, quantum pro minimae huius Italiae partis Imperio
his proximis annis effusum audivimus, non esset, Beatissime Pater,
non inquam esset Iesu Christi Domini, et Dei nostri sepulcrum in infidelium potestate; non tot milia in Dei honorem constructa Templa
Daemoniorum cultui deservirent; non infinita Christianorum multitudo infidelibus subiecta esset nationibus; non denique Christiana
Religio in derisum ac multorum hominum subsannationem reperi-
retur; sed haec Tibi Sanctissime Pontifex a Domino reservabantur,
ut virtutibus tuis meritam, pietatique tuae quoquo modo debitam
mercedem condonaret.

Tu igitur, Piissime Pater, qui in ea temporum opportunitate, ad
Pontificalis potestatis apicem ascendisti, in qua et Christi Principes
omnes armatos habent exercitus, ac inter se dissidentes, in qua Principes ipsi ad concordiam, et pacem nequaquam redire poterunt, si ad
expugnandos communes hostes unanimiter non convenerint, in qua
etiam infideles civilia inter se bella exercent, divisique facilius superari
poterunt. Utere modo, utere Sapientia animi tui, utere a Domino
Tibi concessa Auctoritate,

[635] many Pontiffs before you have not known their own power, lest, like savage beasts, they should attack their own flocks more viciously when they realized their superior strength. To you, however, who have already turned to the works of piety, who are prepared, in imitation of Christ, to give your own life for your sheep, and who have entered through the gate like a true shepherd and have come to feed the Lord's flock and not to kill it, to you, I say, the strength of Christians and the power and authority of your See is not, we firmly believe, unknown. For in previous years the Supreme Pontiff has united all Christian princes and kings in concord or, according to his whim, divided them by discord, and the princes themselves have impiously brought disaster and war upon Christianity and tried their own strength against each other. Consequently, not only you, but many others who carefully consider the matter, can see how much strength there is among the Christian people, and how much authority and power the Pontiff has over all Christians. If those who held the See of Blessed Peter before you had used their apostolic authority only to reconcile Christian princes and to incite them against the enemies of Christianity, and if as much Christian blood, and money as well, had been spent on fighting for the Christian religion against those faithless nations, as was spent, we hear, in recent years for control of this tiny part of Italy,[11] the Sepulcher of our Lord and God Jesus Christ would not, Holy Father—indeed, would not be in the hands of the Infidel,[12] and so many thousands of churches constructed in honor of God would not be serving the cult of demons; a countless multitude of Christians would not be subject to infidel nations, and the Christian Religion would not be the object of derision and murmuring among so many. These accomplishments, Holy Father, were reserved for you, that God may give you a reward equal to your virtues and worthy of your piety.

And so, most kindly Father, since you have ascended to the summit of pontifical power at this opportune moment, when all Christian princes have armed troops engaged in mutual conflict, and when these princes cannot return to peace and concord unless they come together to defeat a common foe, and when even the infidels are fighting civil wars among themselves, and being thus divided can now more easily be conquered—only use the wisdom of your mind, use the authority that the Lord has granted you! Turn those Christian arms,

---

11   Pope Julius II allied himself with Louis XII of France, Holy Roman Emperor Maximilian I and Ferdinand II of Aragon in 1508 against the Republic of Venice. This League of Combrai defeated the Venetian forces in the Battle of Agnadello, 1509.

12   When the Muslim forces besieged Jerusalem in 637, Patriarch Sophronius agreed to surrender only to the Caliph. Umar came to Jerusalem to accept. Sophronius invited him to worship in the Holy Sepulcher, but Umar declined lest Muslims desire to make it into a Mosque. Umar did entrust the keys of the Sepulcher to the Nusseibeh family to end the disputes among Christians over control of the church. The family still has custody of the keys.

[636] Christiana arma, quae huc usque in proprio sunt foedata sanguine, in propriis grassata visceribus, converte in impiorum Fidei, Religionisque, ac Libertatis Christianae hostium caput; nulla enim alia ratione ad pacis conditiones suscipiendas commoti Christianorum Principum animi facilius inter se convenire poterunt, quam si, Te auctore, Te Duce contra infideles has pessimas nationes eorum rabies convertatur. Vidimus saepe male inter se dissidentes Fratres, seque invicem armis petentes, quibus si communis hostis occurrerit, statim unanimes, quae in semetipsos exercebant, contra extraneum arma converterunt. Sic quidem hac tempestate fiet Pater Optime. Si enim Tu Christianis Principibus communem Fidei Christianae Libertatis hostem impugnandum obtuleris, sane depositis odiis, paceque inter se firmata, concordibus animis ad communem hostem delendum convenient. Pacem namque Christianis reddere nequaquam poteris, si Christiana arma contra Infideles convertere non tentaveris, si armorum exercitum, maleque convenientium animorum furores in communes hostes non immiseris: et nisi sese offerret impraesentiarum haec tam sancta, tam laudabilis, tam bonis omnibus optabilis contra infideles expeditio, inquirenda, desiderandaque vel ea ratione maxime fuisset, ut vesana Christianorum odia, inimicitiae, bella hac sola occasione extinguerentur.

Non enim, ut insanum vulgus existimat, componenda sunt prius Italiae negotia, ad pacemque Christiani Principes compellendi, ut ad Infidelium postremam expugnationem unanimiter Christiani omnes accendantur; sed ante omnia potius illis commune bellum est proponendum contra communes Religionis inimicos. Tunc enim facilius quascumque volueris pacis conditiones propriarum simultatum obliti suscipient, cum Te docente communem hostem, quem impugnare magis oporteat, adesse intellegent. Facilius namque est, armatos, instructosque exercitus ex impiis ad pia, sanctaque proelia convertere, quam ad quietem, armorumque depositionem persuadere, ubi maxima, et in bello spes victoriae non desit, et in victoria divitiarum omnium, maximorumque Imperiorum acquisitio proponatur. Si enim, Te admonente, quae sint Infidelium divitiae, Christiani milites, qui praedae cupiditate in nostrae Religionis populos saepissime grassantur: si quam ingentia sint eorum Imperia Christiani Principes, qui sola dilatandi Imperii ambitione Italiam alter alteri quam avide rapere gestiunt, Te docente, cognoverint: ea

[636] which until now have been fouled by Christian blood and raised against Christian breasts, against the head of the impious enemies of Christian faith, practice, and liberty. In no other way will the minds of Christian princes be moved to undertake terms of peace and more easily come to mutual agreement, than if you initiate and lead the way by which they can turn their rage upon these wicked, faithless nations. We have often seen brothers, who were in fierce disagreement and seeking weapons against each other, suddenly share the same mind, when some common enemy arrived on the scene, and turn the arms that they were raising against each other upon the stranger. So it will be at this time, Holy Father. If you urge Christian princes to oppose the common enemies of Christian liberty, they will surely put down their arms, make peace among themselves, and with wills united come together to destroy the common foe. Indeed, you will surely not succeed in bringing peace to Christians unless you endeavor to turn Christian weapons and armies against the Infidel and to divert the rage of contentious spirits against a common enemy. If this holy, praiseworthy, and universally desired expedition against the Infidel did not currently present itself, it would have been worthwhile and desirable merely as an occasion for extinguishing the poisonous hatred, enmity, and wars that exist among Christians.

Thus one should not, as common people foolishly believe, first settle affairs in Italy and compel Christian princes to make peace, so that they may then be motivated to make a united, final assault on the Infidel. Rather, one must begin by proposing a common war against the common enemies of religion. Then, forgetful of their quarrels, they will easily accept whatever terms of peace you wish, when you make it clear to them that the common enemy, who must be opposed, is already threatening. It is easier to redirect armed men and armies from impious to pious conflicts, than to induce them to make peace and lay down their arms—especially when you set before them the hope of victory in war and the acquisition of wealth and great kingdoms. If you show them the wealth of the Infidels, Christian soldiers, who from a desire for plunder so often attack people of our own religion, will launch wars against the Muslims with the same eagerness of mind. Likewise, Christian princes, whose only wish is to increase their power and who now so eagerly try to seize Italy from each other, will follow suit, once you show them the greatness of the Infidels' territory. Both soldiers and princes will proceed against them with the same

[637] animi alacritate haec contra impios Mahumetas bella aggredientur: ea strenuitate in illis exercebuntur, ut facilis, et cita innocuaque Christianis omnibus victoria sit futura. Congrega Tu modo Sapientia, auctoritateque tua Christianos Principes, et quae in propriis visceribus convertenda iam paraverunt arma, illa eadem in saevas et Christiani Sanguinis sitibundas Belluas converte. Nunc enim quando inter se dissident Infideles, et non modo gentes contra gentem, Rex contra Regem; sed et Frater contra Fratrem maximis odiis saevissima bella exercent, facilius Tibi victoria promittitur. Regnum enim in seipsum divisum, extraneo superveniente hoste, diutius stare non potest, sed facillime desolatur.

Vides, Beatissime Pontifex, nisi dissimulare omnino volueris, quot et qualia sint, quae Te ad suscipiendum negotium urgent compelluntque. Ut autem, quae diffusius diximus, brevibus colligamus, commissae Tibi a Domino hae sunt oves, quae intra Dominicum gregem aliquando fuere, nunc autem extra Ecclesiae pietatem egressae in saevissimi Leonis fauces inciderunt, atque in aeternum pereunt. Armis huiusmodi homines impugnandos piae, sanctaeque Leges statuunt. Et Tu tot continue pereuntium animarum interitus otiosus spectator esse sustinebis? Innumerabiles sunt Christianorum hominum multitudines, quae, hoc pariete interposito, a Romana Ecclesia, ab eorum scilicet Capite, divisa sunt membra. Neque coniungi illi possunt, nisi medius ille paries destruatur: et Tu tantarum sub Christi vexillo degentium animarum salutem neglegere poteris? Saevissimi Fidei nostrae hostes, regnandi aviditate, destruendi Christiani nominis inextinguibili siti, eorum quotannis augentes Imperium, a Christianis Imperia, Libertatemque auferre conantur, nostrisque paene cervicibus miserrimae servitutis iugum iamiam imponere videntur; et Tu, qui Christianorum Pontifex Maximus a Domino electus es, tantum Christianae Reipublicae periculum videre dissimulabis? Christianorum odia, inimicitiaeque, quibus miserae Christiani nominis reliquiae rapinis, incendiis, ac caedibus consumuntur, non alia ratione facilius sedari possunt, neque Christianis omnibus vera pacis tranquillitas reddi, quam si communis hostis Christianorum omnium armis pereat: et Tu, qui Regum et Principum, pro eorum in Pontificem Maximum reverentia ac observantia, voluntates moderaris ac regis, et merito quidem, quoniam eius Domini vices geris, in cuius manu sunt corda Regum,

[637] strenuous effort, with the result that all Christians will obtain an easy, quick, and painless victory. Only use your wisdom and authority to assemble the Christian princes, and turn the weapons that they have prepared for their own breasts against the savage beasts that thirst for Christian blood. Now, when the Infidels are divided amongst themselves, and when not only nation wars against nation and king against king, but even brother fights against brother with the most savage hatred, an easier victory is assured. A kingdom divided against itself when a foreign enemy arrives can stand no longer, and is easily destroyed.

You see, Holy Father, unless you wish to conceal the truth altogether, how many weighty considerations urge and compel you to undertake this task. To summarize briefly what we have said at some length: to you have been entrusted these sheep who once were in the Lord's flock, but who, after wandering away from the Church's observance, have now fallen into the jaws of the savage lion and are perishing for all eternity. The good and holy laws state that such men must be opposed with arms. And will you be able to remain idle when so many souls continually perish? There are countless multitudes of Christians who, because of this wall placed between us, are dismembered from their head, the Roman Church, and they cannot be joined to her unless this wall is destroyed. Can you neglect the salvation of so many souls living under the banner of Christ? The savage enemies of our faith, with their desire for power and their inextinguishable thirst for the destruction of Christianity, increase their power every year and try to wrest from Christians their realms and liberty, and they virtually impose on our necks the yoke of wretched servitude. Will you, who have been chosen Supreme Pontiff by the Lord, pretend that you do not see the danger to the Christian Commonwealth? The mutual hatred and enmity of Christians, on account of which the miserable remnant of Christianity is consumed by rapine, fire, and slaughter, cannot easily be calmed, nor can true peace be restored to all Christians in any other way but that the common enemy of all Christians should perish by arms. And can you, who moderate and rule the will of kings and princes in accord with their reverence and obedience to the Supreme Pontiff—and rightly, since you are the Vicar of the Lord, in whose hand are the hearts of kings—

[638] quidquam aliud cogitare, curareve poteris, quam communem
Christianorum omnium exercitum contra infideles Nationes instruere,
atque coactis in unum Christianorum viribus, communem eorum hostem
oppugnare, cum maxime, si ad humanas tantum vires respicias, contrari-
am Tibi victoriam polliceri possis, sed et[25] in Domini Iesu Christi auxilio
confisus de huius impiae haeresis destructione, horumque impiorum
hominum abolitione nequaquam valeas dubitare. Tempus enim Divinae
ultionis iam advenisse, neque ulterius posse Dominum nefandissimam
gentis huius superstitionem, immanissimosque eorum mores sustinere
credimus: praesertim cum Te pium, religiosum, Christiani Nominis
studiosum, liberalem, magnificum, magnanimum, in consiliis sapientem,
in promissionibus fidelissimum, in arduissimis rebus strenuum, ad Ponti-
ficalem Beatorum Apostolorum Sedem sublevatum conspicimus. Neque
enim alium in universo hominum genere Te uno magis ad haec conficienda negotia idoneum[26] eligere potuisse credimus, neque mortalium
quempiam esse, qui haec ipsa Te ardentius optaverit unquam; quoniam
non modo, postquam Romanorum Cardinalium ordini tenera adhuc aetate annumeratus accessisti, sed ab ipsa infantia tua hoc tam sanctum, tam
pium desiderium in pectore tuo versatum audivimus. Neque in universo
Terrarum orbe[27] quempiam esse iudicamus, qui sapientius possit[28] opportuna, salubriaque consilia excogitare; et quae maturo consilio excogitata
fuerint, opere ipso perficere; ob idque tanta iam mentis intentione Te hanc
provinciam suscepisse non dubitamus, versarique in hac ipsa quam plurimas cogitationum tuarum credimus. Et quamquam temeritatis notam sapere videatur, haec ad Te scribere, quae Tu ipse multo profundius cogitas,
multo melius intellegis, quam nos, qui ea Tibi recensere audemus, dabis
tamen in tanta exaltatione tua, Christianaeque Reipublicae exultatione
temeritati nostrae veniam Beatissime Pater, et nos, quae semel coepimus,
pro tuae benignitatis abundantia prosequi permittes.

Mahumetani omnes saevissimi Christiani nominis hostes, contra quos
optamus quam maxime, speramusque Christiana omnia arma, Te auctore, Te Duce, quam citissime conversa videre, quamquam eandem, relicta
Christiana pietate, nefandissimam Mahumeti haeresim superstitione
nimia sequantur; non omnibus tamen eadem fuit ad hanc impietatem via,
non eadem est vivendi ratio, non eadem regnandi

---

25   sed et: et MS, sed ED
26   idoneum MS: *om.* ED
27   orbe MS: orbem ED
28   possit MS: posset ED

[638] contemplate or care for anything other than to lead a common army of all Christians against the infidel nations, and having combined the power of Christians into one force, attack their common enemy—particularly when, taking only human power into account, you can assure yourself of victory? But since you trust in the help of the Lord Jesus Christ, you can have no doubt that you will destroy this impious heresy and wipe out these impious men. We believe that the time of divine vengeance has arrived, and that the Lord can no longer tolerate the unspeakable superstition of this race and its monstrous ways, especially when we see that you, a pious and religious man, who are zealous for Christianity, liberally educated, distinguished and magnanimous, wise in counsel and faithful in your promises, and strenuous in the performance of difficult tasks, have been raised to the Pontifical See of the Blessed Apostles. Indeed, we believe that God could not have chosen any human being more suitable than you for accomplishing these tasks, nor has any mortal man desired them more. For we have heard that you cherished this holy and pious desire in your heart not merely from the time that you entered, while still a young man, into the order of Roman Cardinals, but even from your childhood.[13] Moreover, we believe that there is no one in the world who has greater wisdom to devise fit and serviceable plans, and, when timely strategies have been formed, to bring them to execution. Hence we are certain that you have already focused your attention on this undertaking, and that you are giving as much thought to these matters as you can. Although it may smack of presumption, Holy Father, that we should write to you on matters that you yourself are considering with greater profundity, and which you understand better than we who are recounting them to you, you will surely pardon our temerity at this time of your exaltation and of the exultation of the Christian Commonwealth, and in the abundance of your kindness you will permit us to finish what we have begun.

All Muslims, those savage enemies of Christianity, against whom we hope and pray to see all Christian arms turned, as soon as possible, under your leadership and guidance, have abandoned Christian practice and superstitiously follow the same unspeakable heresy of Muhammad; but the road by which they came to this impiety was not the same for all, nor do they all have the same manner of life, the same style of governing,

13   Giovanni de' Medici became cardinal in 1488 at the age of thirteen, and became Leo X in 1513 at the age of thirty-seven.

[639] conditio, non unum idemque Imperium, non unus Princeps;
sed quantum nos ipsi cognoscere potuimus, huius haeresis alii sunt,
qui passim ab omnibus Turcae, alii, (vulgaribus utemur vocibus) qui
Mauri appellantur, non nominibus tantum, sed rebus etiam ipsis ab
invicem diversi, quibus, praeter impiissimae superstitionis observantiam, nulla paene est communicatio, cum et diversas Orbis partes
occupent, diversa Imperia habeant, diversamque penitus regnandi
rationem, et praeter haec ita moribus, animisque male conveniant,
ut ingentia inter utramque gentem bella quam saepissime exerceant,
utriusque tamen gentis illud commune est, quod in earum utraque
alii sunt in ea haeresi nati, et illorum locorum, quae habitant, vere
indigenae, qui ex impiis parentibus orti nullum Christianae Fidei
Sacramentum susceperunt, Turcae, ac Mauri propriis eorum ap-
pellationibus nominati. Alii vero, qui Christianis parentibus geniti,
sacrosanctaeque Christianae Religionis lavacro suscepto a teneris
annis, ab ipsis parentibus aut vi, aut fraude sublati deservire, et haeresim illam sequi instruuntur, quamquam et multi sint, qui nefanda
quadam impietate agitati, ex Christi Fide, quam nec intellegere pro
cordis eorum duritia, neque operibus servare pro eorum immunditia
poterant, maturioris aetatis sponte prope iam sese in hoc infidelitatis barathrum proiiciunt, hos omnes apud Turcas Ianizeros, apud
Mauros Mamaluccos vulgari sermone vocari audivimus. Commune
autem est utrisque Dominis inservire, et arma tractare. Ianizeri enim
apud Turcas peritissimi sunt milites; Mamaluchi vero apud Mauros
non solum militiam omnem exercent, ita ut arma tractare illis, qui
vere Mauri sunt, non permittant, verum etiam ex eorum numero is
semper eligitur, qui supremam totius gentis illius potestatem habeat.
Nam sicut omnibus his, quos Turcas vocamus, unicus est Imperator,
qui neque electione, neque sorte aliqua deligitur, sed per legitimam
successionem ad Imperium accedit, neque ex alia, quam ex Ottoma-
norum Familia esse permittitur, ita opposita fere ratione, qui Maurorum Sultanus (sic enim Imperatorem appellant) futurus est, hic ex
eorum numero, qui Christianis sint ex parentibus orti, et baptismum
susceperunt, esse oportet, et nisi saepius etiam venundatus pluribus
Dominis inservierit, ad eam dignitatem minime idoneus est promo-
veri, neque aliqua apud eos Regni successio reperitur,

[639] and the same government or prince. As far as we can determine, there are some of this heresy who are popularly called Turks, and others—we will use the vernacular terms—called Moors, who differ from each other not only in name but also in fact. Apart from their common impious superstition, there is practically no common ground among them, since they occupy different parts of the earth and have diverse realms and thoroughly different forms of government. Moreover, they differ in customs and attitudes to such an extent that they often wage great wars against each other. Nevertheless, they have this in common, that in both nations there are some who were truly born into that heresy and who are native to the countries they inhabit, and, having been born of impious parents, never received the sacrament of the Christian faith; these are the Turks and Moors, properly so called. Others, however, were born of Christian parents and received the water of the holy Christian Religion in their tender years, but were snatched from their parents by fraud or force and compelled as slaves to follow that religion. Then there are also many who, driven by some unspeakable impiety from the Christian Faith, which they could neither understand because of the hardness of the hearts nor follow because of the foulness of their character, freely cast themselves as adults into this pit of infidelity. We hear that among the Turks all these are called "Janissaries," and among the Moors, "Mamelukes." Their common duty is to serve their masters and to bear arms. Among the Turks, the Janissaries are the most skilled soldiers, and among the Moors the Mamelukes not only comprise the whole army—in fact, they do not allow real Moors to bear arms—but one of their number is always chosen to hold supreme power over the whole nation. Indeed, all those whom we call Turks have one ruler who is not chosen by any election or lottery but comes to the throne by legitimate succession, and who may not come from any family but that of the Ottomans. By contrast, the Sultan of the Moors—for so they call him— must be chosen from among those who have Christian parents and have been baptized, and unless one has also been sold more than once and has served several masters, one fails to qualify for this dignity. No form of succession is found among them,

[640] sed uno mortuo alius, qui propria potestate, aliorumque
consortium favoribus sit potentior, ad huius gentis imperium, non
votorum suffragiis, sed armorum potius vi deligitur. Turcarum autem
gens maior, potentiorque Maurorum gente existimatur; quippe quoniam ampliora potentioraque Imperia sub Turcarum sunt potestate,
apud quos non solum, qui Christianis sunt ex parentibus orti, sed
omnes pariter, qualescumque fuerint, armis exercentur, ad bellaque
sunt idonei; apud Mauros vero illi solummodo, qui post Baptismum ad eam impietatis haeresim accesserunt, quos et servos esse, et
Mamaluccos vocari diximus, arma et bella sic tractare consueverunt,
ut indigenis, et qui ex ea sunt haeresi orti, neque arma contingere,
neque domi habere, neque equos ascendere permittant; sed miserabili quadam servitute oppressis, aut otio, deliciisque, aut mercatura
illis vacare proprium est; unde fit, ut Turcarum Imperatori facile sit,
cum voluerit, innumerabilem paene virorum multitudinem ad bella
armare; Maurorum autem Sultano, sic ab eis appellato, exercitum
quindecim virorum milia vix habere liceat. Praeter enim hos, qui
Mamaluchi dicuntur, alios nequaquam milites habent. Hi vero ad
eum, quem diximus numerum, aut raro perveniunt, aut nunquam.

Vides, Pater Beatissime, quantum gens distet a gente, quam diversa
regnandi ratio, et quam dispar sit in utraque hominum conditio. Valde autem ab utraque eorum diversa tertia quaedam huius vanissimae,
impiissimaeque superstitionis gens est, eorum scilicet, qui Reccabitarum more, neque Civitates incolunt, neque domos habent, sed in
tentoriis, in tabernaculis cum uxoribus, filiis, gregibus, et armentis
inhabitant. Haec ferocissima gens est, quae neque serere, neque
arare, neque putare[29] unquam didicit, sed nihil aliud omnino, quam
arma tractare, furari, ac rapere novit. Hi Arabes propterea fortasse
appellantur, quoniam eorum maxima pars Arabiae montes occupat.
Non unus illis Imperator, non unus est Princeps, sed ut quisque aut
ingenii virtute, aut alia est ratione potentior, sic aliquorum Principem
seipsum facit, qui tamen potentioribus etiam Principibus subesse
et obtemperare novit. Hi si quando in unum cogantur, ad multa
virorum milia accedunt, ita ut legitimum Maurorum Sultano bellum
inferre non dubitent, neque ipse Maurorum Imperator hanc gentem
unquam delere potuit, quamquam id saepius efficere

---

29   putare MS, *Barletta*: potare ED

[640] but when one Sultan dies, another man, who is more powerful both in his own right and through the favor of others allied with him, is chosen to govern this nation—not by a popular vote, but by force of arms. The nation of the Turks is considered greater and more powerful than that of the Moors, because the Turks control larger and more powerful realms, and not only those born of Christian parents, but all alike, of whatever sort they are, bear arms and train for battle. Among the Moors, on the other hand, only those who have come to that heresy after Christian Baptism, and who, as we said, are slaves and are called Mamelukes are accustomed to handle arms and engage in warfare, while natives who are born into that heresy are not permitted to handle weapons or to have them at home, or even to ride a horse; but being oppressed by a pitiful kind of servitude, they devote themselves to idleness and pleasure or to commerce. Thus it happens that the ruler of the Turks is able, whenever he wishes, to arm a virtually incalculable multitude of men, while the so-called Sultan of the Moors can possess an army of scarcely fifteen thousand; for apart from the so-called Mamelukes, they have no soldiers at all. Even these rarely, if ever, amount to the number we have just given.

And so you see, Holy Father, how much these races differ from each other, how different is their manner of government, and how unequal their condition. There is a third group of persons belonging to this vain and impious religion, altogether different from the first two, who, like the Rechabites,[14] have neither cities nor homes, but dwell in tents with their wives, children, flocks, and herds. This is a most ferocious race, which has not learned to sow, or plough, or think; indeed, they know nothing other than the use of arms, theft, and plunder. These are called Arabs, perhaps because most of them dwell in the mountains of Arabia. They do not have a single ruler or prince, but as each of them excels in character or in some other respect, he makes himself leader of a group, although he also acknowledges and obeys more powerful princes. If these should ever be unified, they would amount to many thousands of men, and they would not hesitate to wage war on the Sultan of the Moors, nor has the Moorish leader ever been able to destroy them, although he has tried

---

14   The Rechabites appear in the Bible only in Jer 35:1-19 as the followers of Jonadab, the son of Rechab. They are described as living without houses, wine, sowing or planting. Jonadab (also Jehonadab) occurs with his group in 2 Kgs 10:15-28, as Jehu becomes king of Ancient Israel, ninth century B.C.E. The house of Rechab is mentioned in 1 Chron 2:22. They appear nowhere else in history.

[641] omnibus viribus, et extraneis etiam accitis auxiliis ipse tenta-
verit; quod iis, qui Romanorum volverunt historias, nequaquam mirum
esse deberet; quoniam nec ipse Pompeius, qui primus hanc gentem
est persecutus, neque alii Romani Imperatores, vel quando eas Regiones cum pace regebant, vel quando cum Iudaeis bella gerebant, hanc
latrunculorum gentem delere potuerunt. Quamquam autem ipsi ea
tempestate Mahumetis cultores esse non possent, quoniam non adhuc
illa bellua exorta fuerat: hanc tamen latronum multitudinem absque
civitate, absque firma sede Arabiae montes illi incultiores semper
habuere, ita ut ex ea Reccabitarum antiquissima progenie omnes illos,
quos nunc Arabes vocamus, facile descendisse credamus.

His tribus adeo inter se diversis eiusdem superstitionis gentibus,
quartum postremo genus adiicitur, non minus et in his, quae ad
Religionem, et in his, quae ad morum concordiam spectant, ab illis
diversum. Huius autem generis homines, cum plurima Christianae
Fidei suscipiant Sacramenta, Christum potius, quam Mahumetum
colere videntur; quamquam ipsi nec veram Christianae Pietatis Fidem
recipiant, neque Mahumetis nefandam deserant superstitionem.
Hi sunt, qui sub nominatissimo, potentissimoque Persarum, atque
Medorum Principe Sophi ab omnibus nuncupato[30] militantes, maxima
contra Turcas, et alias gentes bella his praeteritis annis exercuisse,
Persiam, Mediamque, et alias regiones subegisse dicuntur, quorum inclitum ducem Sophi communi vocabulo nuncupatum, sapientissimum,
victoriosissimumque esse Iuvenem, et qui se Christianis hominibus
amicissimum profiteatur, ab omnibus passim audivimus.

Haec autem omnia, quae ad aures usque nostras pertingunt, quaeque
Tibi notissima apertissimaque fore non dubitamus, Sanctitati Tuae
commemorare voluimus, non quod aliquid eorum, quae diximus, Te
nescire existimemus, (absit enim haec a nobis insana cogitatio) sed
potius consulto haec ad Te scribere decrevimus, ut mirari nemo possit, qui haec ipsa audierit, si in tanta huius iniquae gentis divisione,
atque diversitate facilem Tibi Victoriam futuram speramus. Nam
si quattuor, quae numeravimus infidelium genera, Turcae, Mauri,
Arabes, et qui magnum Persiae Regem sequuntur, in unum convenire
possent, omnesque simul a Christianis Principibus essent impugnandi, minime Tibi de victoria diffidendum esset, quoniam praeter
Divinum Omnipotentissimi

---

30   nuncupato MS: nuncupati ED

[641] with all his resources and even with the help of foreign troops. This will come as no surprise to those who have read the Roman historians; for neither Pompey, who was the first to attack this race, nor the other Roman commanders, even when they ruled the entire area in peace or when they were waging war against the Jews, were able to destroy this nation of robbers.[15] In those days, of course, they could not have been followers of Muhammad, because that Beast had not yet arisen; but the wilder mountainous regions of Arabia have always been home to this multitude of robbers, who have no city or fixed dwelling place. From this it is easy to conclude that the people we now call Arabs descended from the Rechabites, the most ancient people of the region.

To these three races, which differ from each other despite their common superstition, a fourth and final class may be added, no less different from the first three in matters of religion than of customs. People of this class, who accept for the most part the mysteries of the Christian faith, seem to follow Christ rather than Muhammad, although in fact they neither accept the true Christian faith nor reject Muhammad's foul superstition. These fight for the famous king of the Medes and Persians, whom everyone calls Sufi,[16] and have reportedly waged great wars in recent years against the Turks and other nations and have subdued Persia, Media, and other regions. We have heard from every source that their leader, who is called by the common title Sufi, is a wise and victorious young man who professes to be friendly to all Christians.[17]

All these things, which have come to our ears and which are doubtless well known and obvious to you, we did not wish to communicate to Your Holiness because we thought that you were ignorant of them—God forbid that we should have such a foolish idea! Rather, we decided to write you so that no one who hears these things will be surprised that we hope for an easy victory, given the great division and diversity of this wicked people. If the four classes of Infidels that we have named, the Turks, Moors, Arabs, and those who follow the King of Persia, could unite, and if Christian princes had to fight them all at the same time, you would still have no cause to lose hope of victory; for apart from the divine help of our almighty

15 The future emperor Pompey invaded Judea in 63 B.C.E. and made it a Roman territory. The first Jewish Revolt against Rome was 69-74 C.E., and the second revolt was 132-135.

16 Sufism began by the ninth century C.E. in Muslim lands. It is characterized by ascetic and mystical practices. Sufis arose among the Sunni and later included some Shi'i. They trace their spiritual lineage to Muhammad and base their piety on the Qur'an. Sufis, as do other Muslims, hold both Christ and Mary in very high regard.

17 This refers to Ismail 1 (1487-1524), the founder of the Safavid dynasty in Persia. He had some political contacts with a few European leaders.

[642] Salvatoris Iesu Christi auxilium, humanae adhuc Tibi, si modo
Christiani Principes invicem convenire voluerint, ad gentem hanc
abolendam, penitusque destruendam satis abunde suppetunt vires.
Cum vero haec una infidelium multitudo in multas iam divisa gentes
sit, quibus nulla est inter se communicatio, nulla concordia, sed
odia, inimicitiae, ac bella potius intercedunt, mirari quis poterit, si
certissimam Tibi, Christianisque omnibus nos victoriam promittere
audemus?[31]

Et quamquam hi omnes pro communi eorum impietate armis merito
essent oppugnandi, non omnes tamen simul Te iudicare credimus,
nunc armis aggrediendos fore; sed pro eorum diversitate, diversa a
Te aut conversionis, aut subversionis illorum, si id minime poterit[32],
opportuna remedia excogitari.[33] Quorumdam namque non sic omnino
desperanda conversio est, ut penitus intentata relinquatur. Cum enim
omnes Christum, tamquam Dei halitum ita honorare, ita laudare, ac
praedicare soleant, ut etiam Christi nomen blasphemantibus atro-
cissimae mortis poena sit constituta, facile certe esse poterit, hos, aut
horum quamplurimos ad Christi veritatem convertere, si modo ipsi
audire paterentur, et nos illis Christi Fidem praedicare parati essemus.
Sed impurissimus ille Mahumetus, qui nulla ratione illam, quam
tradebat, superstitionem constare, facileque rationibus subverti posse
intellegebat, illud praecipuum sectatoribus suis mandavit, quod falsae
superstitionis eius dogmata, non rationibus, sed potius armis defen-
derent; et si qui contra eam loqui auderent, tamquam maximum nefas
attentati fuissent, nequaquam vivere permitterentur. Hoc si lex non
obstaret, de omnium conversione, aut certe de maiori eorum parte
non esset omnino desperandum. Sed cum palam omnibus praedicare
Christum, Christianam Veritatem proponere, superstitionis illius
vanitatem aperire non liceat, quis prohibet, Beatissime Pater, illum
Persarum Regem (ut ab eo, quem postremum numeravimus, nunc in-
cipiamus) qui se Christum potius, quam Mahumetum colere gloriatur,
qui Christianum nomen non solum non abhorrere, sed et quam maxime honorare solet, per sapientissimos, dignissimosque viros, quorum
Tibi tanta copia est, suasionibus, pollicitationibusque sollicitare, qui de
Christiana etiam veritate illum instruant, Fideique pietatem persuadere
conentur? Audire enim ipse non recusabit. Et si Christianorum

---

31   nos victoriam promittere audemus: non volueris victoriam permittere audemus
      MS, non voluerit victoriam permittere ED

32   minime poterit MS: minime non poteris ED

33   excogitari MS: excogitare ED

[642] Savior, Jesus Christ, you have sufficient human strength to eliminate and utterly destroy this race, if Christian princes are willing to come together. Since, however, these many Infidels are divided and have no common project or agreement, but in fact hatred, enmity, and war stand between them, who can be surprised that we dare to promise you and all Christians a certain victory?

And although it would be right for you to attack all these nations on account of their common impiety, we do not believe that you must attack them all at once. Rather, in keeping with their diverse circumstances, you may ponder timely remedies for their conversion or, if this proves impossible, for their destruction. For the conversion of some of them is not so much beyond hope that it may not be tried. Since they all honor, praise, and preach Christ as the "Breath of God,"[18] so that even to blaspheme the name of Christ is punishable by a cruel death, it will certainly be possible to convert them, or a great number of them, to the truth of Christ, provided that they are willing to hear, and we are ready to preach, the Faith of Christ. But that foul character, Muhammad, who understood that the superstition he was teaching could not possibly endure and could easily be overcome by reason, expressly commanded his followers to defend the teachings of his false superstition not by reason, but by arms, and that if any should dare to speak against it, they should be accused of the greatest crime and not be permitted to live.[19] If this law did not stand in the way, there would be no reason to despair of their conversion, or at least of the majority of them. Since, however, it is not possible to preach Christ openly and to propose to all the truth of Christianity and to disclose the emptiness of their superstition, who prevents you from approaching the King of the Persians—I will start with the last-mentioned case—through prudent and worthy men, of whom you have such a great supply, who will instruct him in Christian truth and encourage him toward the practice of the Faith—since he professes to honor Christ more than Muhammad, and who not only does not abhor Christianity, but gives it the greatest respect? He will certainly not refuse to listen. If, moreover, in the name of all Christian princes

---

18 Qur'an 4:171. "The Messiah, Jesus son of Mary, was no more than God's apostle and His Word which He cast to Mary: a spirit from Him" (Translation N. J. Dawood, 1997 edition). Or "Christ Jesus the son of Mary was (no more than) a messenger of Allah, and His Word, which He bestowed on Mary, and a Spirit proceeding from Him" (Translation 'Abdullah Yusuf 'Ali, 1991).

19 Only in the defense of God and his messenger, the Qur'an allows decapitation, crucifixion, maiming or exile if the attackers do not repent. Qur'an 5:33.

[643] Principum omnium nomine, auxilia ad expugnandos Turcas sibi inimicissimos hostes peterent, si rationibus, suasionibus, ac apertissimis documentis sibi arcana Religionis nostrae panderentur, surdas fortasse non averteret aures. An quoniam longe a nobis abest, neglegendus omnino est? An quoniam minus haec forsan profutura timemus, idcirco nullo sunt modo attentanda? Siccine Apostoli Sancti impios Tyrannos, idolorum cultores, aut neglegentia, aut timoris causa minus adoriebantur? Haec aliis fortasse, quasi insanientium hominum deliramenta videri poterunt, dicentque, qui haec a nobis audierint: vestri illi recessus, vasta illa eremi solitudo vos ad insaniam redegerunt. At Tu, Beatissime Pontifex, qui de Domini auxilio nunquam diffidere didicisti, quique Pontificis praecipuum munus esse, semen Divini Verbi spargere, plantare, atque irrigare, deque eius incrementum curam Deo relinquere nunquam dubitasti: iam quos ad hunc Principem summos auctoritate, sapientia, atque doctrina viros possis mittere, cogitare coepisti, qui et ad Fidem Christi illum adhortari, et contra impios Turcas, hostes non suos minus, quam nostros incitare valeant. Neutra enim parvifacienda causa est. Nam si uni huic homini vel veritatis ratione, vel latius et regnandi ambitione Christianam Fidem suscipere persuaderi omnino potuerit (quod facilius tanto fieri posse sperandum est, quantum ipse Christianum nomen habere, et Christiana plurima Dogmata suscipere gloriatur) considera tu Pater, quot animarum milia Christo lucratus eris. Principe enim Fidei nostrae veritatem suscipiente, omnes, quae sub eo sunt, innumerabiles populorum multitudines eundem ritum, fidemque eandem suscipient; quoniam inclitum hunc Persarum Regem populi sub eo degentes adeo colunt, ac venerantur, ut maximum nefas putarent, si eum, quem summopere diligunt, in omnibus non sequerentur. Si vero id illi minus persuaderi poterit, quid Tibi unquam obesse potest contra Turcas, quos ante omnia Te oppugnare velle existimamus, eius auxilio uti? Et quamquam ipse in infidelium adhuc numero censeatur, non videmus, cur Christiano exercitui, quem Te iam contra Turcarum gentem parare credimus, non maximo auxilio sit futurus. Dum enim Christiani ex una parte Turcas aggredientur, et hic potentissimus Rex ex altera eos oppugnare coeperit, vindicaberis Tu quidem Beatissime Pater de inimicis tuis. Ad eum vero contra Turcarum

[643] these emissaries should ask for help to expel the Turks, their bitterest enemies, and if by reasoning, persuasion, and the clearest proofs they should disclose the mysteries of our religion, he would not, perhaps, turn a deaf ear to them. Should this king be ignored, simply because he is far from us? Because we fear that we shall have little success, should we not attempt it? Did the Holy Apostles fail to meet impious tyrants, who were idolaters, out of negligence and fear? To others, perhaps, these remarks of ours will seem like the ravings of madmen, and they will say, "Your withdrawal and the great silence of the hermitage have driven you insane." But you, Blessed Pontiff, who have learned never to lose faith in the help of the Lord, and that your principal task as Pontiff is to sow, plant, and cultivate the word of God, and who have never hesitated to entrust to him its increase, have surely begun to consider which of the men who excel in authority, wisdom, and learning you may send to this prince, to urge him to embrace the Christian Faith and to incite him against the impious Turks, his enemies no less than ours. For neither cause should be disdained. If this one man can be persuaded, either by reason of the truth or by ambition to rule more widely, to accept the Christian faith (which can more easily happen, we may hope, because he boasts himself a Christian and accepts many Christian dogmas), just think, Holy Father, how many thousands of souls you will have gained for Christ. For when a prince accepts the truth of our Faith, all the innumerable multitudes of people who are under him will accept the same worship and the same faith. Indeed, the subjects of this king esteem and venerate him so much that they would think it unlawful not to follow him, whom they love so much, in all things. If, however, he cannot be persuaded, what prevents you from using his help against the Turks, whom, we believe, you are most eager to attack? Although he is one of the Infidels, we do not see why he cannot be of great assistance to the army that we believe you are already preparing to fight the Turkish nation. When the Christians assault the Turks from one side and this powerful king begins to attack them from the other, you, Blessed Father, will be avenged upon your foes. No effort will be required to arouse him against the power of the Turks

[644] potestatem incitandum nullus omnino labor est futurus, cum ille huius infidissimae gentis inimicissimus sit, et iam multa inter utrosque bella peracta ad nullam eos concordiam venire permittant. Et qui ex semetipso ad oppugnandas has gentes avidissimus est, qualem futurum speramus, si et rationibus incitetur, et Christianos omnes illi auxilio futuros maximis viribus polliceatur?

Quare non irridenda sunt a Te haec ipsa, quae scribimus, quippe qui multo etiam ante cogitaveris Principis huius conditionem maximam Tibi occasionem praebere, vel ad suae gentis conversionem, vel ad Turcarum omnium subversionem, si modo non desint Tibi, qui deesse non possunt, sapientissimi, prudentissimique viri, qui a Te missi haec prudenter apud eum tractare valeant. Hoc autem consilium, qui pro eorum pusillanimitate approbare non poterunt, quid dicturos existimamus, cum Te maiora, magisque ardua attentantem, non ad hunc Principem modo, de quo spem bonam concipere possimus, sed ad magnum illum Maurorum Imperatorem, quem Sultanum vocitant, de cuius conversione nulla forte hominibus nostri temporis spes est reliqua, viderint Legatos, Oratoresque, atque cum iis viros peritissimos destinare, ut ad rectam Christianae Fidei veritatem eum redire rationibus, manifestisque suasionibus persuadere possint. Neque certe mirari decet, si et hoc dignum quidem Sapientia, ac Dignitate tua consilium minus probaturi aliqui sint, cum Sapientes Mundi huius, qui se sapientes cum dixerint, stulti omnino facti sunt, divina etiam consilia in rerum creatione, aut dispensatione saepe minus approbare consueverint. Multi enim sunt, qui quae ipsi non viderint, aut non intellexerint, qua fiant ratione, ea a nemine videri, et frustra fieri arbitrantur. Tu vero Beatissime Pontifex pro Sapientia tua huiuscemodi hominum iudicia, ut semper consuevisti, parvifaciens, altiori mentis consideratione, hunc, quem diximus Maurorum Imperatorem respiciens, deque eius conversione non desperandum existimans, ad eum idoneos pro hoc munere obeundo Legatos mittes. Quid enim magis desperandum videbatur, quam Romanos olim Imperatores, aliosque Reges Terrae idolorum cultui servientes ad Christi Fidem evocare, et hoc nihilominus Domino auxiliante factum vidimus. Nam qui impugnare, destruereque Christianam Religionem modis omnibus conabantur, ipsi hanc eandem postmodum Fidem susceperunt. Nunc autem, cum idem Dominus

[644], since he is a bitter enemy of that faithless race, and the many wars that have already been fought between them will not permit them to come to an agreement. Since he is eager on his own account to fight these races, what attitude do we expect him to have when he is encouraged by reason and the promise that all Christians will help him with their utmost strength?

And so, you should not laugh at the things we have written, since you have already noted that the position of this prince offers you an excellent opportunity to convert his nation or to overthrow the Turks, provided that you do not have a shortage—and this is impossible—of wise and prudent men whom you can send to handle this matter properly. We can well imagine what cowards who disapprove of this plan will say when they see that you attempt still greater and more difficult things, and that you send ambassadors and orators not only to this prince, concerning whom we have reason to hope for success, but also to the great leader of the Moors, whom they call the Sultan, for whose conversion our contemporaries no longer, perhaps, have any hope, and that you send learned men to persuade him with reason and clear arguments to return to the truth of the Christian Faith. Nor should it be any wonder that some will not approve of this plan, which is worthy of your wisdom and dignity, since the wise men of this world—who, when they call themselves wise, become altogether foolish—are accustomed even to disapprove of the plans of God in his creation and ordering of things. Indeed, there are many who believe that things they do not see, or whose reason for being they do not understand, are seen by no one or come into being for no purpose. But you, Holy Father, in keeping with your wisdom, will reject, as you always have, the judgment of such men, and as you give more careful thought to the leader of the Moors and the real possibility of his conversion, you will send to him appropriate representatives. What indeed, ever seemed more hopeless than to bring the rulers of Rome and other idolatrous kings of the world to the Faith of Christ, and yet we have seen this accomplished with the help of the Lord; for those who were determined to attack and destroy the Christian Religion accepted, in a short time, this very Faith. Now, since this is the same Lord

[645] sit, qui omnes homines vult salvos fieri, numquid et Tibi, si
modo pia intentione, rectoque Fidei nostrae[34] zelo res huiuscemodi
attentaveris, ea negaturus est auxilia, quae Principibus aliis, qui et
homines ipsi fuere, largissime tribuit? Numquid latere sapientiam
tuam potest, magnam, ad huius Principis conversionem attentandam,
sperandamque, occasionem Tibi praebere, quod non ille, qui penitus
Christi nomen nunquam cognoverit, Christianam Religionem suscipere persuadendus sit; sed ille potius, qui Christianis ex parentibus
ortus, Christianaeque Fidei maximum illud sacrae ablutionis Sacramentum suscepit, et plurimos fortasse annos Christianam secutus est
Religionem, ad Christum, quem impie dereliquit, pie est revocandus?
Non possumus enim existimare illum, aliosque omnes, qui a Christo
post baptismum recesserunt, non saepius pia Domini dispensatione
inter arcana pectoris de conversione sua aliqualiter stimulari. Adde,
quod hunc Christianam Fidem reliquisse, Mahumetis impietatem
rationis examine suscepisse, quod scilicet plus veritatis, et pietatis in
ea esse superstitione, quam in vera Christi Religione ratione aliqua,
aut iudicio approbaverit, nequaquam est suspicandum; sed certe a
Christo ad Mahumetis superstitionem vel ignorantiae caecitate, vel
dominandi aviditate conversum esse credimus. Quod si ignorantia
veritatis hoc factum esse censebimus, quid magis pium, quid magis
Apostolicae curae congruum, quam ignorantia aberrantem in viam
veritatis, admonendo, docendo, observandoque reducere? Si vero
regnandi ambitione ad eam impietatem accesserit, facilior etiam
futura Tibi eius conversio est. Cum enim nullus sit, qui proprios filios
divitiarum, honoris, Regnique successores relinquere non maiori
desiderio ambiat, quam ea ipsa possidere; hic autem, si in ea, quam
suscepit, perversitatis haeresi, permaneat, nullam filiis suis Regni successionem sperare omnino possit: quid facturum eum credimus, si Tu
Summus Christianorum Pontifex, cuius maxima est apud externas
etiam Nationes existimatio, maxima illi auxilia polliceri coeperis, ad
Regni eius in filios successionem, et nepotes statuendam? An ille, qui
ut regnaret, Christum pro Mahumeto deserere non timuit, ut filiis, et
nepotibus idem Regnum firma successione relinquat, Mahumetum
deserere, et ad Christum redire formidabit, si modo illi Christianorum auxilia ad successionem huiuscemodi Imperii eius firmandam,

---

34 nostrae MS: nostro ED

[645] who desires that all men be saved (1 Tim 2:4), do you suppose that if you attempt such things with a pious intention and proper zeal for our Faith, he will deny you the help that he generously granted to other princes who were no more than men themselves? Surely you are aware that we have good reason to attempt and to hope for the conversion of this prince, because the one whom we must persuade to accept the Christian Faith is not altogether ignorant of Christianity, but was born of Christian parents and received the great Christian sacrament of Holy Baptism, and may have practiced the Christian Religion for many years. Cannot such a one, who impiously deserted Christ, be generously recalled to him? We cannot imagine that he, and all others who have wandered from Christ after Baptism, are not somehow moved, in the secret places of their hearts, to think about conversion. Moreover, it cannot be supposed that this man left the Christian Faith and accepted the impiety of Muhammad by a rational examination, or that he somehow reasoned or came to a judgment that there was more truth and piety in that superstition than in the true religion of Christ. We must believe instead that he was converted from Christ to Muhammad's superstition through blind ignorance or ambition to rule. But if we suppose that he did this out of ignorance of the truth, what could be more kindly or congruent with apostolic charity than to lead one who is straying in ignorance back to the road to truth by teaching, admonishment, and personal concern? If, on the other hand, he has come to this impiety through ambition to rule, his conversion will be still easier. For there is no one who does not more strongly desire to leave his sons as successors to his wealth, honor, and power than to possess them himself. This man, however, if he persists in the heresy he has embraced, cannot hope that his sons will succeed to his throne. What, then, do we think he will do if you, the Supreme Pontiff of the Christians, whose reputation is great even among foreign peoples, begin to promise him the greatest assistance in establishing a succession for his sons and grandsons? Surely one who did not hesitate to desert Christ for Muhammad in order to rule will not shrink from deserting Muhammad and returning to Christ in order to leave the same royal power to his sons and grandsons by a firm right of succession, provided that Christians promise the help needed to guarantee

[646] ampliandumque Regnum polliceatur? Quae quidem auxilia, si ad Christum convertatur, Te illi promissurum fore minime dubitamus. Converti vero ad eum perfacile poterit, quem fortasse intrinsecus colere, adorare, et Deum verum confiteri non cessat, quamvis exterius perversam Mahumetis perfidiam sequatur. Multos enim ex ea gente homines esse audivimus, aliquos etiam cognovimus, qui Christianam pietatem ita intra pectoris sui secreta custodiunt, ut saepius Christum Iesum deprecari soleant, ut ab illa impia, quam sequuntur, haeresi eos liberare dignetur. Fit enim in illis, quod et in nobis fieri sentimus, ut cum in aliquem vitiorum laqueum incidimus, liberari cupimus, oramusque, et cum nos ipsos liberare possimus, id facere nolumus. Hoc multis eorum evenit, ut cum infidelitatis, impietatisque laqueum, quo tenentur, non ignorent, ad Christum redire cupiant. Redire tamen aut timore, aut propriae dignitatis amore, aut misera consuetudine alligati non audent, ita ut, quod maxime cupiunt, idem omnino nolle videantur. Quod si talem Principis huius animum invenies, quid difficultatis futurum est, ut, Te rationibus suadente, pollicitationibusque maximis alliciente, ad Christum palam convertatur, si tuo, Christianorumque omnium auxilio conversus cum fuerit, regnum suum confirmare, ampliareque, et filiis suis, nepotibusque legitima successione relinquere speraverit.

Quae vero de gentis huius Principe diximus, eadem omnia de principalibus apud eum viris affirmare possumus. Quoniam et ipsi, et omnes, qui in eo Regno alicuius sunt existimationis, Christiani fuere, sacrique fontis baptismatis participes; et dummodo eundem apud Principem locum sint habituri, quem nunc habent, facile illis erit ad Fidei Christianae conversionem eorum Principem sequi, illis fortasse ex eis dumtaxat exceptis, qui ad summam Imperii dignitatem ambiunt. Hi enim de Regni successione minus cum Principe convenire posse existimabuntur. At vero si eis dominia Civitatum, quae illis a summo eorum Principe cum nulla spe, nedum successionis, sed neque firmitatis traduntur, firma, et quae filiis suis per successionem sint duratura promittantur, nonne et ipsi libentissime conditionem suscipient? Qui vero, si etiam expugnata Turcarum gente aliqua eius Imperii pars his, si conversi fuerint, polliceatur, nonne sponte ad Christum convertentur? Principe vero, principalibusque eius viris conversis, nonne

[646] this succession and to increase his power. Indeed, we do
not doubt that you will promise this assistance, if he converts to
Christ. Nor will he find it difficult to convert to the One whom he
inwardly, perhaps, does not cease to worship, adore, and confess as
the true God, although he outwardly follows the twisted perfidy of
Muhammad. For we have heard that there are many men of that
race—and we have also known some of them—who observe the
Christian religion in the recesses of their hearts, so that they often
pray to Jesus Christ to free them from the impious heresy that
they follow. These men experience what we sometimes discover in
ourselves, namely that when we fall into some trap of vice, we desire
and pray to be freed, and although we can free ourselves, we are not
willing to do so. So it is with many of these people; since they are
not ignorant of the noose of infidelity and impiety by which they are
held, they wish to return to Christ; yet, bound by fear or by love of
their own prestige or by wretched custom, they do not dare to do so.
Thus, they seem to be unwilling to do what they most desire. If you
find the mind of this prince to be such, what difficulty will there be in
his openly converting to Christ, if you persuade him with reason and
win him over with great promises, and if he hopes that, with your
help and that of all Christians after his conversion, he will strengthen
and increase his realm and leave it by legitimate succession to his
sons and grandsons?

Moreover, all that we have said about the leader of this nation can be
affirmed about the principal men who attend him. For they too, and
indeed all persons of distinction in this realm, were once Christians
and partakers of the holy font of Baptism, and if they can retain
the position with respect to the prince that they now enjoy, their
conversion will easily follow his—with the exception only of those
who aim at the supreme power; for these will be less likely to agree
with the prince concerning the succession. But if they are promised
the control of cities, which they currently receive from the prince
without the hope, not only of succession, but even of security, as a
firm possession and one that will endure through succession, will
they not also gladly undertake this new condition? Moreover, if
some part of the defeated Turkish Empire is promised to them upon
conversion, will they not willingly be converted to Christ? And when
the prince and his principal attendants have been converted, will not

[647] universa Maurorum gens Christum suscipiet? Nam omnes ex
hac gente, qui Mamaluchi nuncupantur, Imperatoris, et reliquorum,
qui sub eo Principum servi sunt, Christiani et ipsi cum fuerint, cumque
etiam multi eorum intra occulta pectoris Christianam quoquo modo
pietatem servent, nonne statim Dominos insequentes, ad Christum
revertentur? Qui vero ex ea haeresi orti sunt, impiisque progenitoribus
nati, infidelium locorum, et veri indignae illius superstitionis alumni,
quos proprie Mauros appellari diximus, difficilius fortasse converti
posse existimabuntur. At vero, si quae sit in omnibus illis hominibus
illius, cum qua nascimur omnes, naturalis iustitiae observantia: signa-
tum est enim super homines lumen vultus Domini, quo iudicia eius
in semetipsa[35] iustificata conspiciuntur, quam illi miro quodam modo
conservare videntur, iustitiamque Dei appellant, contra quam aliquid
nec facere audent, neque promittere possunt: si quae sit etiam in ea
haeresi de Christo opinio, quae maxima sane est, considerare voluerimus, non adeo difficilem eius gentis conversionem existimabimus; quae
quidem, si audire Christianam veritatem pateretur, nullo labore, nulla
difficultate ad illam converti potuisset. Christum enim maximum non
solum Prophetam, sed Dei halitum, natumque ex Virgine profitentur:
nullam legem Christi Evangelio nedum praeferendam asserunt: verum
Christi nomen honore maximo prosequuntur; ita ut iis, qui illum blas-
phemaverint, saevissima mortis sit poena constituta. Ipsum vero tanto
minus mortuum credunt, quanto magis Dei halitum esse[36] existimant;
maximeque Christianam veritatem in hoc aberrare suspicantur, quod
Christum Dei Filium, verumque proinde Deum, et mortuum fuisse
credimus. Non enim intellegere valent, quomodo et Deum esse, et mori
potuisse dicamus. Quae si illis, ut facile posset, declarabuntur, pedibus,
manibusque, ut dici solet, in Christianam venient veritatem. Imperatore vero earum gentium, et iis, qui dominantur conversis, quibus
prohibere ulterius Christi praedicationem, veritatisque declarationem
poterunt? Sed et illud etiam eveniret, ut, nemine praedicante, si illi, qui
dominantur, qui scilicet post baptismum ad eam impietatem accesserunt, converterentur, tota gens reliqua Fidem susciperet.

Verum enim vero quid pergimus pias Sanctitatis tuae aures his
sermonibus ulterius obtundere, cum potissimum haec, quae diximus,
omnia paucis verbis perstringi possint? Nihil

35   semetipsa *Barletta*: semetipso MS, ED
36   esse MS: *om.* ED

[647] the entire race of the Moors accept Christ? For all those who are called Mamelukes serve the ruler and his princes; and since they were once Christians themselves, and since many somehow maintain Christian piety deep in their hearts, will they not immediately follow their leaders and return to Christ? Those, however, who are native to this heresy, who were born of impious parents and are the true offspring of infidel regions and this unworthy superstition, and who, as we have said, are properly called Moors, will perhaps be more difficult to convert. Nevertheless, if they have any regard for that natural justice with which we are all born—for the light of the Lord's countenance is signed upon men (Ps 4:6) and by it his judgments are seen as justified unto themselves (Ps 18:10, Vulgate; righteous altogether, Ps 19:9, RSV)—which these people seem wondrously to preserve, calling it the justice of God, and they dare not do anything or make any promises against it—and if this heresy has any idea of Christ—which, in fact, is very exalted—we should not suppose that the conversion of this race will be so difficult. If they are at all willing to listen to the truth of Christianity, they will be converted to it with no trouble or difficulty. For they not only profess that Christ was a great prophet, but also that he is the Breath of God and was born of a virgin. They say that no law is superior to the Gospel of Christ,[20] and they pay to Christ's name the greatest honor, so that those who blaspheme his name are punished with a cruel death. They believe that he cannot be dead, inasmuch as he is the Breath of God. Indeed, they suppose that Christianity is most mistaken in the belief that Christ, the Son of God and therefore God himself, also died; for they cannot understand how we can say both that he is God and that he could die. If these things are explained to them—and this can easily be done—they will come "on hands and feet," as they say, to Christianity. When the ruler and the leaders of these peoples have been converted, from whom will they be able to prohibit the wider proclamation of Christ and of the truth? It may even happen that, following the conversion of the leaders who came to this impiety after Baptism, the whole race will accept the Faith without a preacher.[21]

But why do we continue to assault Your Holiness' ears, when our argument can be summarized in a very few words? We simply

---

20   When the Qur'an says that the *Injil* was revealed, the reference is not to the message of the New Testament or to the texts themselves, but to what Muslim belief holds was an undistorted form of that which was fully revealed later. The Qur'an is held to be the final revelation of God.

21   The idea that Islam is a Christian heresy and that, thus, Muslims had been baptized remained popular among some until the Second Vatican Council.

[648] enim aliud his suasionibus dicere voluimus, quam nos existimare
Te, priusquam contra Turcas Christianorum Principum exercitum
ducas, iam excogitasse, duos hos maximos Mahumetanae gentis Principes, quorum alter Christi nomine gloriari solet, quamquam Christi
fidem non sequatur: alter vero Christianus cum iam fuerit, maximum-
que Christianae Fidei Sacramentum susceperit, Mahumetanae superstitionis caput se esse asserit: per Oratores, Legatos, Nuntios, viros scilicet Dignitate, Sapientia, Virtute, Sanctitateque praeditos adire, ut per
illos, si his Principibus persuaderi Christiana veritas possit, in omnes
ipsis subiectos populos Christi Nomen diffundatur; aut si id minus facere poterunt, eos Principes incitare, et contra Turcarum Imperatorem
commovere, aut secum saltem convenire, ne illi auxilio sint futuri, cum
a Christianis impugnari coeperit. Haec omnium summa. Neque enim
existimare possumus Te contra perfidam saevissimamque Turcarum
rabiem arma ante capere velle, quam horum duorum potentissimorum
Imperatorum animos attentaveris, si vel ad Christum converti acqui-
escant, vel Turcis bellum una Tecum inferre velint, vel Te inferente,
arma contra Te non sumere polliceantur. Magni enim momenti haec
habenda esse iudicamus, in utram partem vertantur, ad eam, quam Te
omnino contra Turcarum gentem parare expeditionem credimus. Vere
enim eorum, quae Te pro pastorali Tibi iam demandata cura facturum
iudicamus, illud maximum, praecipuumque omnium existimamus, non
contra omnes simul Infidelitatis Mahumetanae sectatores, sed contra
Turcarum gentem, contra scilicet potentissimos eorum, et in perfidia
pertinaciores, quos nulla alia ratione, quam armorum vi adire facile
potes, et quos etiam nostrae non Fidei modo, sed et libertatis inimicos
nunc maxime sentimus, nostrisque cervicibus imminere cernimus,
maximum et potentissimum Terra, Marique Christianorum omnium
exercitum, quanto citius pro rerum magnitudine fieri possit, instruere.

Neque Te differre hoc velle arbitramur, cum nunc et armatos, ad
bellaque paratos Christianos omnes habeas, et illi insperata[37] fraternae cladis novitate inter se quam maxime dissentiant. Haec enim ad
expeditionem accelerandam Te invitant. Nam dum fratres de Regno
maximis odiis pugnant, aut dum fraternae discordiae quaedam adhuc
reliquiae supersunt, si Tibi partem eorum imbecilliorem coniungere
curaveris, facile

---

37 insperata MS: in speratae ED

[648] mean to say that, as we see it, you have already decided to approach those great leaders of the Muslim race—one of whom glories in the name of Christ, although he does not follow the Christian faith, and the other of whom was once a Christian and received the great sacrament of Christianity, but now asserts that he is the head of the Muslim superstition—before you lead an army of Christian princes against the Turks; and that you will employ ambassadors, messengers, and orators—that is, men endowed with prestige, wisdom, virtue, and holiness—to the end that these leaders may be persuaded of the truth of Christianity and the name of Christ may be spread through all their subject peoples. If this is impossible, you will incite and rally them against the Emperor of the Turks, or at least obtain their agreement not to come to his aid when Christians attack him. This is the sum total of the matter. Nor can we imagine that you will want to take up arms against the perfidy and savage madness of the Turks before you have tested the minds of these two powerful commanders, to see whether they will convert to Christ, or wage war with you against the Turks, or promise not to oppose you with arms. We consider the outcome of these undertakings very important for the expedition that we believe you are preparing against the Turkish nation.[22] Indeed, of all the things we think you shall do in accordance with the pastoral care required of you, we consider this the first and greatest: to raise as quickly as possible, in view of the size of the undertaking, a great and powerful army and navy of Christians, not to attack all the followers of the Muslim infidelity at once, but rather the Turks, who are the most powerful and stubborn in their perfidy, whom you can influence only by arms, and whom we now find to be the greatest enemies of our faith and liberty and an imminent threat to our lives.

Nor do we suppose that you will put this off, since you now have all Christians armed and ready for war, while our enemies are fighting among themselves in the novelty of fraternal slaughter. These circumstances invite you to hasten the expedition; for when brothers fight desperately over some kingdom or when traces of fraternal discord remain, if you take care to win over the weaker party, you will easily defeat the stronger.

---

22 There had been calls for Christian leaders to join against "the enemies of the faith" or "the infidels" for some time by Julius II and by Lateran Council V.

[649] potentiorem expugnabis. His vero expugnatis, nisi converti ad Fidem et illi acquieverint, imbecillioris facilior erit expugnatio. Neque hoc fraudis nomine refugiendum est contra Fidei hostes, qui iisdem artibus totam Graeciam (male inter se convenientibus, qui imperare debuerant) Christianis abstulerunt. Unica Tibi haec Turcarum gens, hoc tantum huius gentis imperium abolendum est; quoniam hoc, quod potentissimum infidelium genus est, destructo, nullus Tibi labor futurus est, reliquos omnes huius perfidiae sectatores, aut ad Fidem revocare, quod maxime optandum est, aut pro Christianae pietatis zelo a facie universae Terrae abolere. Numquid superato maximo, potentissimoque divitiis et numero virorum, bellandique peritia Turcarum Imperatore, poterit Tibi Maurorum Princeps cum parvo servorum eius exercitu resistere? Numquid audebunt illi Latrunculorum Principes contra exercitum tuum Turcarum victoria gloriosum stare? Numquid Princeps ille Sophi, qui Turcarum impietatem detestando, magnam sibi auctoritatem acquisivit, maximamque hominum multitudinem adiunxit, contra exercitum Christianum ipse, qui Fidem Christianam extollit, pugnare vellet, aut si pugnaret, resistere ullo modo poterit? Numquid nam illi Reguli, qui Africae littorales Regiones occupant, resistere Christianis viribus poterunt, quibus unus tantum ex Christianis Principibus Regna solet auferre, quos et sic parvifaciendos diximus, ut in ea, quam superius prosecuti sumus, Mahumetanae gentis divisione, eos connumerare noluerimus; tum quoniam et parva eorum potentia est, et ab aliis hominibus paene toto orbe divisi sunt; tum maxime quoniam in eorum expugnatione, non Christianorum modo omnium, sed Sanctae Ecclesiae solummodo exercitum, si Hispaniae Regibus coniungatur, sufficere posse existimamus? Unum igitur solum Mahumetanae gentis est imperium, quod totis Christianorum viribus, nunc maxime civili bello labefactatum, ad desolationem paratum sese praebeat, aggrediendum esse credimus. Hoc ipsum Turcarum Imperium si superaveris, de tota infidelium gente actum esse dicere possumus. Nullus enim erit, qui aut audeat deinceps, aut possit Tibi resistere. Ad hoc vero Turcarum Imperium expugnandum, gentemque impiissimam delendam, maximo Tibi auxilio futurum est, si aliquem, aut plures eiusdem infidelitatis Reges, ac Principes vel ad Fidem convertere poteris, vel ad inferendum tecum

[649] When these have been defeated, the conquest of the weaker will be easier, unless of course they are willing to be converted. Nor should we recoil from this "fraudulent" strategy against the enemies of the Faith, who used the same arts to wrest all of Greece from Christians, who should have ruled but could not get along with each other. Only the Turkish nation and its power must be destroyed; for when this, the most powerful race of Infidels, has been eliminated, it will be no trouble for you to bring the remaining adherents of this perfidy back to the Christian Faith, as we hope, or with Christian zeal to wipe them off the face of the earth. When the Emperor of the Turks, our greatest and most powerful enemy in terms of wealth, number of men, and skill in battle, has been defeated, will the leader of the Moors be able to resist you with his small army of slaves? Will those princes of petty thieves dare to stand against your army, glorious in victory over the Turks? Will the "Sufi," who has acquired great authority and assembled a vast number of men by detesting the impiety of the Turks, be willing to fight against a Christian army, and if he does fight, will he be able to withstand it? Surely those princelings who hold the regions of coastal Africa will not be able to resist Christian power, when even one Christian prince is able to wrest their kingdoms from them, and since they are so insignificant that in our summary of the Muslim nation we did not even bother to mention them. For their power is slight and they are divided from other men by practically the entire globe, and we believe that to defeat them one does not require an army made up of all Christians, but only the forces of the Holy Church, if they are joined by the Kings of Spain. Therefore we believe that there is one Muslim realm that must be opposed with all our strength, and which is ready for destruction because it is now much weakened by civil war. If you overcome the Empire of the Turks, we can say that the entire race of Infidels is doomed; for there will be no one who will dare or be able to withstand you. But if you intend to attack the Turkish Empire and destroy this impious race, you will find it very helpful to convert one or more kings from among the Infidels, or to persuade them to join you

[650] Turco Imperatori bellum, vel saltem ad nullum praestandum
illi auxilium persuaseris. Persuadere autem si poteris, nemo scit, nisi
opportuno congruoque ordine per idoneos viros attentaveris.

Haec omnia, quae diximus, antequam exercitum contra hos ducas,
attentanda censemus, ut maiori spe, et alacritate Christiani milites ad
bellum accedant; in quo tanto firmius victoriam se consecuturos credent, quanto Tibi plura et infidelium auxilia coniunxeris; quamquam
sine externo auxilio satis superque virium Christianis Principibus
inesse certissimum est, si modo singuli Christianorum Principes tantum Tibi ad expugnandos infideles exercitum praebeant, quantum,
cum inter se pugnaturi sunt, parare consueverunt. Si enim ex multis
Christianorum Principum exercitibus in unum convenientibus,
exercitum unum constituas, non Turcarum Imperatores, non omnes
infidelium Principes, non orbis universus illi resistere ullo modo poterit; et Sanctae Ecclesiae exercitui si Italiae solum vires coniunxeris,
tantum contra Turcas Terra, ac Mari exercitum, Classemque tradu-
cere poteris, ut nequaquam ea gens, quamquam ferocissima sit, Tibi
resistere audebit. Quid futurum non sit, si Italiae viribus, Gallorum,
Germanorum, Hispanorum, Britannorum, Pannonum, Helvetio-
rumque potentias pro tua maxima Sapientia coniunxeris, nemo est
qui non videat. Si enim has Nationes, quarum singulae, si omnibus
viribus suis utantur, ad profligandos Turcas sufficere possunt, omnes
simul, aut aliquam saltem cum reliquis Italiae, Sanctaeque Ecclesiae
viribus coniunxeris, nonne die soleque clarius victoriam in manibus
tuis videre etiam hebetes possunt?

Sed praeter Regum, Principum, et aliarum potentiarum publicos
exercitus, cum semel Te contra infideles pugnaturum esse publicis
indiciis declaraveris, et his, qui Tibi auxilio futuri sunt, sanctamque
hanc expeditionem aut armis, aut divitiis adiuverint, Indulgentiarum,
ut fieri solet, larga munera contuleris: videbis profecto privatorum
hominum ex omni Provincia, ex omni Christianorum Provincia,
et Regione tantam ad Te accedere propriis stipendiis militaturam
multitudinem, ut eo solo exercitu pro numero, virtuteque militum su-
peraturum Te impiam illam gentem, sperare merito possis. Ut enim
reliquos, qui pietatis zelo ad haec se paratos offerent, taceamus, ex his
solum, qui sacram Religionem professi sunt, ex omni scilicet Religiosorum hominum conditione,

[650] in waging war against the Turkish Emperor, or at least not to give him any assistance. Whether you can persuade them to do so, no one knows, unless you make the attempt in proper order through suitable intermediaries.

We believe you should try all the things we have mentioned before you lead an army against the Turks, so that your Christian soldiers will go to battle with greater hope and enthusiasm; for they will have greater confidence in gaining the victory if you have obtained help even from the infidels. Nevertheless, even without external aid there is clearly more than enough strength among Christian princes, if each of them presents you with an army for conquering the infidels as great as that which he is accustomed to raise for battle against his fellows. If you create a single army from the many assembled forces of Christian princes, neither the Turkish Emperor nor the princes of the Infidels nor the entire world will be able to withstand it. And even if you can join the army of the Holy Church with the strength of Italy alone, you will be able to lead so great an army and navy on land and sea that the Turkish race, ferocious though it may be, will not dare to stand against you. What, then, will happen if you apply your wisdom to combine the strength of Italy with the power of the French, the Germans, the Spaniards, the Britons, the Hungarians, and the Swiss, no one can fail to see. Each of these nations, if it used all of its strength, would suffice by itself to rout the Turks; if you join all of them together, or at least one of them with the forces of Italy and the Holy Church, is it not as clear as daylight, even to the dim-witted, that the victory is in your hands?

Once you have publicly declared that you intend to fight the Infidels and have supplied generous indulgences, as is the custom, to those who come to your aid and assist this holy expedition with arms and money, you will see, in addition to the public armies of kings, princes, and other potentates, such a multitude of private individuals coming at their own expense from every Christian province and territory that you can reasonably hope to overcome that impious race with this army alone, given its size and the virtue of its soldiers. In addition to all the others who, in their pious zeal, will show themselves ready for this task, you will have many thousands of brave men from the ranks of professed religious of every sort,

[651] si id modo tu consenseris, aut imperaveris, multa milia fortissimorum hominum habebis, qui, quod minus exercitatione posse existimabunt, fervore Spiritus, Fideique ardore strenuissime proficient.
Cernes praeterea eos, qui minus ad pugnam idonei sunt, imbecilles
scilicet viros et mulieres, et ceteros, quibus aut longior aetas, aut
familiarium rerum cura, aut alia causa ad capessendum arma impedimento est, tantas in tuo aerario pecunias conferre, tot Thesauros
Sanctissimae Ecclesiae elargiri, ut illis solum innumerabilem possis
virorum armare, alereque multitudinem. Cum vero exercitus partem
aliquam movere iam coeperis, nulla est futura Christianorum natio,
nulla civitas, nullum oppidum, nulla denique domus, quae pro viribus
Tibi auxilia non libenter, atque magna cum laetitia subministret. Et
qui pro paupertatis eorum exiguitate, quod afferant, non habebunt,
Orationibus Te, piisque vocibus prosequentur. Accurrent ad Te ex
omnibus Regionibus, per quas exercitum, aut classem ducere decreveris multa undique auxilia, et ut reliqua omnia taceamus, ea solum
Graeciae pars, quae Christianis adhuc reservatur, maxima certe Tibi
et terra, et mari auxilia subministrare poterit, et pro Religionis zelo,
et pro gentis illius odio, id minime dissimulabit. Reliquas praeterire
insulas possumus; Rhodum vero praetermittere non possumus, quae,
quamquam minime, aut numero virorum, aut divitiis contra eam
gentem sufficere possit: animorum tamen virtute, bellique exercitatione tantum valet, ut ceteris omnibus Christianis aut otio languescentibus, aut impiis odiis sese invicem lacescentibus, atque dilacerantibus, ipsa sola adversus totum Turcarum Imperium continuis bellis
pugnare audeat, et nunquam sine victoria pugnare consuevit. Si enim
ceteri omnes Christiani Principes, singuli pro viribus suis, sic Turcis
indefessi hostes sese praebuissent, ut ea una insula semper praebuit,
nequaquam tantum impia illa gens crevisset, sed et omnis huiuscemodi pestis multo iam tempore de medio ablata esset; quae non satis
ampla, neque multum hominibus, aut divitiis abundat, una Insula
contra Turcas bellandi provinciam sustinere audet: et Tu Sanctissime
Pater, cum omnium Christianorum multitudine, et innumerabilibus
divitiis eandem provinciam suscipere dubitabis?

Postremo vero loco, ut quod omnium maximum, praecipuumque
est, recenseamus, cum semel pugnare Christianus exercitus coeperit,
minimumque

[651] if you consent to it or command it; what they feel they are lacking in military capability, they will diligently supply in spiritual fervor and the ardor of faith. Moreover, you will see that those who are less suited for battle, such as invalids, women, and the rest whom advanced age or domestic responsibilities or some other cause prevent from taking up arms, will contribute so much wealth to your treasury and so much money to the Holy Church that with these alone you will be able to arm and feed a countless multitude of men. And when you have begun to move some part of the army, there will be no Christian nation, no city or town, and finally no house that will not gladly and joyfully supply what assistance it can. Those who in their poverty will not have anything to offer will support you with prayers and pious words. From all the regions through which you decide to lead your army or fleet, much support will come your way. To give just one example, that part of Greece which is still the preserve of Christians will be able to supply the greatest assistance on both land and sea, and from zeal for their religion and hatred of the Turkish race they will scarcely try to conceal it. We may pass over the other islands, but we cannot fail to mention Rhodes, which, though she hardly suffices in numbers of men or wealth to oppose the Turkish nation, is so mighty in terms of courage and skill in war that while all other Christians languish in idleness or attack and lacerate each other with impious quarrels, she alone dares to fight against the entire Turkish empire in continual wars, and has never fought without victory. If all the other Christian princes had shown themselves to be such indefatigable enemies of the Turks as that island has always done, that impious race would never have grown so great, but the whole plague would long ago have been removed from our midst. This one island, which is neither great nor populous nor wealthy, dares to assume the task of fighting against the Turks; will you, Holy Father, hesitate to assume the same task with a multitude of Christians and countless riches to support you?

The last and greatest point is this: once the Christian army has begun to fight, and some small sign

[652] aliquid Christianae victoriae signum apparuerit, centena milia millium Christianorum, qui in illis Turcarum Imperio subditis Regionibus vivunt, excitabuntur, armaque, quibus minime egent, assument. Et dum tuus pugnare adversus illam gentem parabit exercitus, iam ab illis citius, quam credi potuisset, totum confectum negotium aspicies. Illi enim tum Religionis et Libertatis amore, tum propriarum animarum neglectu, si semel exercitum tuum intuentes insurgere contra Tyrannum illum pessimum audebunt, ita pugnaturi sunt, ut nullus omnino ex tota illa gente reliquus futurus sit. Adeo enim illis miserum est inter impios Religionis hostes in extrema, miserabilique servitute vivere: ita gentis illius occulto, sed tamen magno odio fervent, ut pro Religione, pro libertate, pro multarum iniuriarum vindicta, pro ingentium odiorum siti exsaturanda, minima quaeque victoriae spes excitare eos ad pugnandum possit. Satis excitati vero eo impetu, eo fervore, ea audacia pugnaturi sunt, ut unusquisque eorum pro plurimis futurus sit. Intestino autem, familiarique inimico excitato, neminem certe illius gentis evasurum speramus, illis namque maxime, qui a tam miserabilis servitutis asperrimo iugo ab eo Tyranno Mahumeticae impietatis potentissimo propugnatore tot iam annis premuntur, vindictam reservari a Domino credimus, cuius semper ex alto auxilium Tibi affuturum, non vaticinandi ratione, sed Fidei veritate polliceri possumus; quamquam haec omnia, quae connumeravimus, nihil aliud, quam magna, quae Tibi praestantur auxilia, esse credamus; a quo etiam unum aliud Beatitudini tuae conceditur, quod Te multum super omnia haec existimare censemus. Quid enim tot habere exercitus, tot pecunias, tanta externarum gentium, tanta fidelium auxilia prodesse possent, si qui haec moderaretur, regeretque, deesset? Cum enim Te pastoralis officii sollicitudo, Ecclesiaeque Romanae[38] non parva, neque parvifacienda negotia, Lateranense iam celebrari coeptum Concilium, quod Te prosequi velle non dubitamus, fidelium omnium cura a Romana Urbe, ab Apostolica Sede longius discedere non facile permittant, ille, qui nihil Tibi omnino ad haec magna, aliaque maiora conficienda deesse voluit, alterum Teipsum Tibi tribuit Iulianum, Maximum, magnanimum, vereque magnificum Fratrem tuum, quem nonnisi ad maxima huiuscemodi natum credimus. Hic enim cum et consilio, et

---

38   Ecclesiaeque Romanae *Barletta*: Eccl\u1d43q: Ro. MS, Ecclesiaque Romana ED

[652] of a Christian victory has appeared, millions of Christians who live in areas subject to the empire of the Turks will rise and take up arms, in which they are hardly lacking. And while your army prepares to fight against that nation, you will see the whole business accomplished faster than one could imagine. These people, for love of their religion and liberty and with small regard for their own lives, as soon as they see your army and dare to rise against that wicked tyrant, will fight so fiercely that not a single Turk will be left alive. Indeed, it is so miserable for them to live in extreme and wretched servitude among the impious enemies of their religion, and they burn with such great, though concealed, hatred for that race that the least hope of victory will rouse them to fight for their religion, for liberty, to avenge many insults, and to satisfy their immense hatred. Once they have been roused, they will fight with such force, such ardor, and such daring that each of them will count for many soldiers. When this internal and familiar enemy has been aroused, we are hopeful that not one of the Turks will escape; for we believe that God has reserved vengeance especially for those whom the tyrant, the most powerful champion of the Muslim impiety, has oppressed for so many years under the harsh yoke of such wretched slavery. That the Lord's help will always be available to you we can promise not by way of a prophecy, but with the truth of the Faith (Ps 121:1-2; Ps 124:8). And yet, all the things that we have enumerated must be considered nothing other than the great helps given to you by God, who has also granted one other thing to Your Holiness, which, we believe, you must esteem above all these. For what profit would there be in having so many armies, so much money, and the help of so many foreign nations and Christian faithful, if there were not someone to direct and guide them all? Since the responsibilities of your pastoral office, the great Roman Church and its affairs—which are not to be underestimated—the recently begun Lateran Council, which we are certain you will wish to continue, and the care of all the faithful will not easily permit you to be absent for long from the city of Rome and the Apostolic See, the Lord, who has willed that you should lack nothing necessary for this and other greater accomplishments, has granted you another self: Julian,[23] your great, magnanimous, and magnificent brother, who, we believe, was born for such great endeavors. For since he is distinguished in wisdom and prudence, and

---

23   Giuliano de' Medici was already mentioned in the first section of the Libellus. Giustiniani and Querini had recently gone to Florence to confer with Leo X. Giuliano, the younger brother of Leo X, was then ruling Florence and had invited them to the city to finish matters of the Camaldolese order. Giuliano was named Duke of Nemours in 1515. He was killed in 1516 at the age of 37.

[653] rerum prudentia polleat, et animi fortitudine, atque incredibili virtute praestet, Fideique pietate ferveat, et nullos pro Religionis zelo labores suscipere, ulla pericula subire formidet; et ut virtutum eius, quae numerari per singula non possunt, summam paucis verbis concludamus, cum Tibi in omnibus persimilis sit, nihil aliud in hac vita optare videtur, quam Christiana arma contra impios Christi hostes primus omnium movere. Hic Tibi a Domino, qui cuncta Divina Sapientia moderatur, praeparatus est, ut Tu a Beata illa Apostolorum Sede non discedens, neque pastoralem Fidelium sollicitudinem relinquens, alterum Te habere possis, cui[39] intrepide omnia, quae contra infideles illas nationes agenda decreveris, committere valeas, ut sic et Fideles Leonem Summum Pontificem in Apostolica Sede residentem habeant, et Infideles Leonem alterum Summi Pontificis Fratrem Iulianum, contra se exercitum ducentem, pugnantemque sentiant. Quae vero sit Viri illius praestantia, Tu Beatissime Pater, optime intellegis, scisque nihil omnino tam magnum, tam arduum committi Iuliano posse, quo ipse multo maior animi virtute, sapientia, et fortitudine non inveniatur. Tacemus Iulium religiosissimum, prudentissimumque virum consobrinum tuum, aliosque plurimos, quos Tibi paratos a Domino ad haec negotia perficienda Te cognoscere non dubitamus.

Cum igitur ea omnia praeparata Tibi sint a Domino, quae ad hanc expeditionem optare Tibi potuisses, non est, cur minoribus Te occupari permittas, aut differre hoc maximum a Domino Tibi oblatum negotium patiaris. Et quamquam dici soleat minime auferri, quod differtur; veritatem tamen illam Poetae sententiam credimus: semper scilicet nocuisse differre paratis. Nam cum saepe saepius opportuna se nobis offerat occasio, si in aliud tempus differatur, eam a nobis aufferri videmus. Quando enim Tibi, ut cetera omnino taceamus, continget, armatos iamiam instructosque Christianorum omnium Principum exercitus habere, et hostes de Imperio inter se dissidentes invenire? Quoniam autem et Christianis pacem, quam citius fieri potest, Te reddere velle credimus, et has paratas Tibi a Domino occasiones nequaqam amittere: utcumque rebus Italiae compositis (nulla enim iniqua conditio est, qua nobis ad maiora, melioraque perficienda occasio praestatur) absque dilatione exercitus, Classesque Christianorum Principum contra impios hos Christianae Fidei, Christianaeque Libertatis hostes Te missurum iudicamus.

---

39   cui MS: qui ED

[653] is endowed with outstanding courage, incredible virtue, and fervent piety, and in his zeal for our religion is not afraid to undertake any work or face any danger, and—to summarize his virtues, which cannot be counted—since he is in all respects like you, he evidently desires nothing else in this life than to be the first to lead Christian forces against the impious enemies of Christ. This man has been prepared for you by the Lord, who rules all things with divine wisdom, so that you, without departing from the Apostolic See and abandoning your pastoral concern for the faithful, may have another self to whom you may confidently entrust everything that you decide must be done against those infidel nations, and that while the faithful have a "Leo" sitting upon the Apostolic Throne, the Infidels may find that another "Lion," Julian, the brother of the Supreme Pontiff, is leading an army to attack them. The excellence of this man is best known to you, Holy Father, and you know that nothing too great or arduous can be committed to him without his proving superior in virtue, wisdom, and courage. We pass over your cousin Julius,[24] a pious and prudent man, and many others, who you no doubt realize have been provided to you by the Lord for completing this task.

Since the Lord has prepared for you everything you could want for this expedition, there is no reason to allow yourself to be occupied by lesser things or to defer the great task which the Lord has given you. And although people often say that "what has been deferred is not taken away,"[25] we think that the truth is in the saying of the poet: "For those who are ready, there is always harm in delay."[26] For we observe that when an opportunity presents itself again and again and the work is postponed to another time, the opportunity is eventually taken away. When will you have the occasion—to omit, for a moment, all other considerations—to possess the armed and battle-ready armies of all Christian princes, and to find your enemies disaffected with their empire and with each other? But since we perceive that you want to bring peace to Christians as soon as possible and not to lose the opportunities which the Lord has granted, we believe that, no matter how matters are settled in Italy—for no condition is unjust, if it provides an opportunity to accomplish better and greater things—you will send without delay the armies and fleets of the Christian princes against those impious enemies of the Christian faith and Christian liberty.

---

24   Giulio de' Medici, a cousin of Leo X, became an adviser to that pope, was made a cardinal, and became Pope Clement VII (1479-1534, pope 1523-1534).

25   The saying is from Arnobius Junior's *Commentaries on the Psalms* from the fifth century. Augustine also has this idea in his Tractate on the Gospel of John, also fifth century.

26   This is from *Pharsalia* by Lucan, first century C.E.

[654]

[Part IV]

Post huius vero gentis expugnationem, post Mahumetanae penitus
perfidiae destructionem maiora multo, non tamen difficiliora Tibi
superesse negotia conspicimus. Destructo enim, dissipatoque hoc
infidelium Nationum pariete, qui inter Te, et eos Christianos, qui minus nobis cogniti, extremas Asiae, Africaeque regiones incolunt, medius interpositus viam Tibi ad eorum salutem curandam intercludere
videbatur, maior cura, novusque rerum ordo suboritur. Cum enim,
ut superius commissum Tibi, tuaeque subditum Potestati hominum
genus in quattuor hominum conditiones dividentes dicebamus,
praeter eos, qui nunquam Christianae Fidei pietatem susceperunt, et
eos, qui ab ea iam suscepta impie discesserunt, de quibus hucusque
sermonem fecimus, multo valde plures sint homines, qui Christianum quidem nomen cum habeant, Christianae tamen veritatis ita
quaedam suscipere, quaedam autem non suscipere videntur, ut si intra Ecclesiam sint an extra, nostrum nullo pacto sit definire: relinquitur Tibi, Beatissime Pater, post infidelium gentium excidium (quod
nisi Tibi defueris, cito futurum speramus) horum Christianorum
omnium cura, quae ob magnam Nationum, Linguarumque diversitatem, et hominum in qualibet earum innumerabilem multitudinem,
locorumque distantiam, sicut maximos labores, sollicitudinesque, ita
uberrimos certe, ac dulcissimos Tibi fructus est paritura. Neque enim
existimare possumus, aut invincibilem illam animi tui fortitudinem,
laborum multitudine terreri, aut magnam illam mentis tuae pietatem
optatissimos Christianae pietatis fructus, animarum scilicet salutem,
spernere.[40] Scis enim Apostolicae Dignitatis proprium esse omnium
Ecclesiarum sollicitudinem gerere. Nam si neque Iudaeorum perfidia,
neque Mahumetarum impietas, atque saevitia Te ab eorum, quantum
per Te fieri potest, cura non liberat: quomodo sine salutis propriae
discrimine poteris tantarum Christianarum Nationum, quae ignorantia potius, quam ulla malignitatis nequitia aberrant, curam
neglegere, non videmus.

Si qui vero sunt, qui aut non alios esse in universo Terrarum orbe
Christianos, quam istos, quos omnes novimus, qui Europam incolunt, aut maiorem esse infidelium, quam Christianorum numerum
existiment: hi nimirum magna rerum ignorantia,

---

40   spernere MS: sperare ED, desperare *Barletta*

[654]

[Part IV]

After the defeat of this nation and the complete destruction of the Muslim perfidy, many greater, but scarcely more difficult tasks remain for you, as we see it. For when this wall of infidel nations, which was placed between you and those virtually unknown Christians who inhabit the furthest reaches of Asia and Africa, and which seemed to preclude your caring for their souls, has been destroyed and cleared away, a greater concern and a new order of business arises. As we were saying, the human race, which has been entrusted to your care, is divided into four classes of men, and apart from those who never received the Christian faith and those who received it and have impiously deserted it—about whom we have spoken thus far—a far larger number of men can be called Christians, but seem to accept some parts of the Christian faith and not to accept others, so that we are not qualified to say whether they are in the Church or out of it. Thus, it is left to you, Holy Father, after the extermination of the Infidels—which, unless you disappoint yourself, we hope shall come soon—to care for all these Christians. Because of the great diversity of nations and languages and the incalculable multitude of people and the great distances involved, this task will surely bring you much labor and care, but also the greatest and sweetest rewards. Nor can we imagine that your invincible fortitude will be daunted by the amount of work involved, or that your kindly intention will spurn the most desirable fruit of Christian piety, the salvation of souls; for you know that it belongs to the apostolic office to care for all Christian churches. If neither the perfidy of the Jews nor the impiety and savagery of the Muslims frees you from the obligation of caring for them to the extent of your ability, we cannot see how you will be able, without danger to your soul, to neglect the care of such great Christian nations, who err through ignorance rather than any wicked malice.

If there are some people, however, who think that there are no other Christians in the world than the ones we know, who live in Europe, or that the number of Infidels is greater than that of Christians, such persons are suffering from a colossal ignorance of the facts.[27]

---

27 Although population estimates before the modern age are not based on any data from that time, in 1500 more territory seems to have been controlled by Muslim

[655] inscitiaque laborant. Habet namque Africa plurimas, habet et Asia multo etiam plures Christianas Nationes, innumerabiliumque fidelium populorum multitudines, quae multo maiora Terrarum spatia, latioresque regiones, quam tota ipsa sit Europa, occupant. Et nisi Tibi haec notiora, quam nobis esse crederemus,[41] ex ipsa Orbis descriptione ostendere possemus; minimam eam esse Orbis partem, quae ab infidelibus, sive Turcis, sive Mauris possidetur: maximas, ingentissimasque relinqui Africae, ac Asiae regiones, quas Christiani certissime inhabitant, quorum pro regionum capacitate, habitantiumque frequentia tantus est numerus, ut multo sine ulla proportione plures illos esse, quam omnes simul Europae Christianos, ac reliquarum orbis partium infideles absque aliqua temeritate et iudicari possit, et certis rationibus, ipsaque rerum experientia comprobari.

Hi vero omnes, quoniam si in omnibus Fidei nostrae articulis, ac in universis sanctae Romanae Ecclesiae definitionibus, quae ad salutis attinent necessitatem, recte, an minus recte sentiant, nescimus; neque hoc esse adhuc definitum ab ipsa, quae Fidei mater est, Apostolica Sede, cognovimus; ideo an intra Ecclesiam, an extra illam sint, non nostrum, neque cuiusquam alterius, quam Beatitudinis tuae esse id definire, diximus; quamquam has omnes nationes, et populos, quasi praecisa corporis membra esse non ignoramus. Quippe, quoniam minus, quam opus esset, Capiti suo, Romano scilicet Pontifici adhaerent; quoniam tamen, si dissentiendi voluntate, aut excusabili aliqua ignorantia hoc illis accidat, nescimus: ideo nisi a Te uno, et ab Ecclesia ipsa, quid de illis credendum sit, definiatur, neque damnare illos, neque approbare ullo modo audemus. Scimus eos, qui voluntarie a sancta Romana Ecclesia vel minima in re dissentiunt, qui non omnia Apostolica decreta suscipiunt, ab ipsis sacris Canonum definitionibus damnatos esse. Si vero isti voluntaria nequitia, an satis excusabili ignorantia minus Romanae Ecclesiae, Romanique Pontificis decretis tribuant, quam par sit, nescimus, neque aperte hoc adhuc definitum censemus. Neque mirum fortasse videri potest, si maxima locorum distantia (magna enim inter nos, et illos maris aequora, magnaque Terrarum spatia interiacent, mediusque interponitur Infidelium Nationum paries) si Linguarum diversitate factum sit, ut quemadmodum plurimis eorum, qui Europam incolunt, ita illi incogniti omnino sint,[42]

---

41   crederemus *Barletta*: credimus MS, ED
42   sint MS: sunt ED

[655] Africa has many Christian peoples, and Asia many more, and these places contain a great multitude of faithful who occupy a much larger space of the earth than all of Europe itself. Did we not suppose that you know these things better than we do, we would be able to prove from a map that the part of the earth possessed by the Turks and Moors is very small, while the remaining regions of Africa and Asia, where Christians undoubtedly live, are vast indeed.[28] In view of the capacity of these regions and the density of the population, the number of people is so great that we can presume, without any fear of error and by sure reasoning and experience itself, that those Christians are disproportionately more numerous than all those of Europe put together and more numerous than the Infidels of the remaining areas.

Since we do not know whether all these correctly hold to all the articles of our faith and to all the definitions of the Holy Roman Church that pertain to our salvation, and since we understand that this question has not been definitively answered by the Apostolic See, which is the mother of our Faith, we have affirmed that it is not up to us or to anyone else but Your Holiness to define whether they are in the Church or outside her. Of course, we know that all these nations and peoples are like the severed limbs of a body, since they are not joined as they should be to their head, the Roman Pontiff; but whether this has come about because of willful dissent or some excusable ignorance, we do not know. Therefore, what we must believe about them should be defined by you alone and by the Church herself, and we do not presume either to condemn or approve them in any way. We know that those who voluntarily dissent from the Roman Church in even the smallest matter or who do not accept all the Apostolic decrees are condemned by the sacred definitions of the Canons. But whether it is because of voluntary wickedness or from an excusable ignorance that these people pay less heed than they should to the decrees of the Roman Church and the Roman Pontiff, we do not know, nor do we think the question has been clearly settled to this point. Nor will it seem surprising, in view of the great distances involved—for between us and them lie great oceans and great expanses of land, and a wall of infidel nations is placed in the middle—and the diversity of their languages, not only that most Europeans are unaware that these Christians

---

rulers than by Christian rulers. *Atlas of the World's Religions* (2nd ed; eds. Ninian Smart and Frederick Denny; Oxford University Press, 2007).

28   Magellan began his circumnavigation of the world in 1519, six years after the *Libellus* was written.

[656] ut[43] neque ullos esse existiment: sic illis vel omnibus, vel aliquibus nationibus, et populis aut incognitum omnino, aut parum notum sit, Romanum Pontificem esse, qui caput omnium Ecclesiarum, et Christianorum Princeps sit, cui non adhaerere, cui non oboedire, cuius non omnia Decreta suscipere, a Christo discedere, et Christianae pietatis veritatem non custodire censeant. Quis enim Romanorum Pontificum hoc populis illis, praeter Graecos fortasse, aut per nuntios, aut per litteras declaraverit, quando sunt ad oboediendum Ecclesiae Romanae vocati, et ipsi oboedientiae debitam promissionem praestare renuerunt? Si enim pro hoc, aliove in his, quae ad Fidem attinent, errore unquam ab Ecclesia damnati sint, nescimus: ideo eos si intra, an extra Ecclesiam sint, definire ausi non sumus, ne forte, quos Ecclesia damnat, nos incaute probaremus, aut quos probat, temere damnaremus.

Sive tamen iam ab Ecclesia damnati, sive non adhuc damnati dicantur, hoc affirmare audemus, in maximo apertoque satis salutis propriae discrimine eos versari, qui Romanae Ecclesiae praesunt, si has Pontificali Officio commissas Christianorum omnium Nationes aut omnino neglegere statuunt, aut parum curare decernunt, aut maiorem curam, et sollicitudinem terreno Sanctae Ecclesiae Patrimonio, quam tantorum Christianorum saluti impendunt. Castra enim, Civitates, Regna, et Imperia, quae Sanctae olim Ecclesiae donata, nunc patrimonium eius vocari consuevit, tueri, aut ex Tyrannorum eripere potestate, nemo est qui damnare audeat. Hoc tamen uno negotio ita Summi Pontificis mentem occupari, ut pretiosiorem in conspectu Domini tantorum Christianorum populorum salutem aut neglegat penitus, aut immortalibus animis lucrandis minorem, quam terrenis acquirendis divitiis sollicitudinem impendat, damnabile qui non existimant, illi, quale proprium praecipuumque sit Pastoralis Dignitatis officium, ignorare videntur. Tanto enim curae, sollicitudinique Pastoris immortalium animarum salus magis, quam terrenarum Civitatum, aut Regnorum vindicatio commissa est, ut pro unius etiam solius animae salute, omnes Ecclesiae thesauri, omnia Regna et Imperia exponenda sint. Si enim boni Pastoris munus esse non ignoramus, pro ovibus suis animam suam ponere, pro anima autem commutationem nullam dari posse non ambigimus: relinquitur certe, ut qui minorem ovibus suis, quam terrenis divitiis curam impendit, non boni

---

43 ut MS: tu ED

[656] exist, but also that the latter—perhaps all of them, or at least some nations—have little or no knowledge of the existence of the Roman Pontiff, who is the head of all churches and the Prince of all Christians, such that failure to adhere to him, obey him, and accept all his decrees is considered the same as deserting Christ and abandoning the truth of the Christian Faith. When has a Roman Pontiff declared this either through letters or messengers sent to these people—with the possible exception of the Greeks—summoning them to obey the Roman Church, and they have refused to give the required pledge of obedience? We do not know whether they have ever been condemned for this or for some other error in matters of faith, and so we have not ventured to say whether they are in the Church or outside her, lest through lack of caution we approve those whom the Church has condemned or rashly condemn those whom the Church has approved.

But whether they are said to be condemned by the Church or not, we venture to say this: those who preside over the Roman Church are in the greatest peril for their souls if they decide to neglect or to show too little concern for these Christian nations, which have been entrusted to the Pontifical office, and to have more care and concern for the Church's earthly patrimony than for the salvation of so many Christians. No one would condemn the act of protecting and rescuing from the hand of tyrants the castles, cities, kingdoms, and empires that have been donated to our Holy Church and that we are accustomed to call her patrimony. But that the mind of the Supreme Pontiff should be wholly absorbed in this task, so that he either neglects the salvation of vast Christian populations—which are dearer in the sight of God—or is less concerned with gaining immortal souls than with acquiring earthly riches, surely deserves condemnation, and those who think otherwise are clearly ignorant of the first and proper task of the pastoral office. A Pastor is so much more accountable for the salvation of immortal souls than for his claims to earthly states and kingdoms, that all the treasures and all the realms and empires of the Church should be expended for the salvation of even one soul. We know that the duty of the good Shepherd is to lay down his life for his sheep, and that nothing can be exchanged for the soul. It is certain, then, that one who is less concerned with his sheep than with earthly riches is not playing the role of a good

[657] Pastoris, sed iniqui potius mercenarii locum teneat, et Patris familias praeceptis minus obtemperans, rationem villicationis suae redditurus, in magno animae propriae discrimine versetur. Tu vero, Sanctissime Pater, cui haec omnia, quantum unicuique sunt maxima, immo magis, quam alicui alteri notissima, apertissimaque sunt, et qui concessa Tibi a Domino Pastoralis officii dignitate, non ad propriae salutis detrimentum, sed ad pleniorem sempiternae felicitatis acquisitionem uti decrevisiti: ita curarum tuarum sollicitudines rebus pro meritis impertiri curabis, ut memor esse videaris, quod non Petro solum, sed in Petro Tibi etiam, qui nunc eius locum tenes, a Domino dictum sit: non iura Ecclesiastica tuere, non vindica civitates, non divitias cumula, sed pasce oves, pasce agnos meos, quamquam verae Ecclesiae iura tueri, est animarum salutem omnibus modis curare. Quae enim Ecclesia est, nisi animarum congregatio? Quae autem iura, aut bona Ecclesiae huius sunt, nisi recta Fides, boni mores, salusque ipsa animabus[44]promissa sempiterna? Tu, inquam, Beatissime Pater, cui nulla rerum ignorantia officere potest, ut aureis vasis neglectis, fictilibus solum curam adhibeas tuam: cui nulla divitiarum immoderata cupido, nulla intemperans regnandi ambitio mentis aciem, Fideique adimere poterit: cui demum nulla hominum gratia, nullum odium, nulla vindictae libido dominari poterit, aut Te transverso ducere calle, secundum Domini praeceptum, et maiora facere, et minora non omittere curabis, et pro harum nationum et populorum salute nullos labores, nullas sollicitudines, atque curas subire dissimulabis. Vere enim verecundiae, et pudori Tibi futurum existimares, si aliquis eorum, qui hanc ante Te Beati Petri Sedem tenuerunt, plus laboris subiisse, et plures Ecclesiae thesauros exposuisse pro terrenis Civitatibus a Tyrannorum Dominatione vindicandis inveniatur, quam[45] Tu pro tot populis, nationibusque, tot scilicet mille milibus animabus a Diaboli servitute liberandis, et ad Ecclesiae unitatem, ac proinde ad aeternae salutis infinitam iucunditatem perducendis, facere paratus sis.

Sunt autem, Beatissime Pater, quantum nos non solum studio legendi, sed peregrinandi labore cognoscere potuimus, praeter omnes Christianos, qui Europam occupant, septem Christianorum nationes minus fortasse plurimis cognitae, quae diversas orbis partes incolunt, et sub aliis, et aliis Regibus vivunt, et Principibus.

---

44   animabus: anibus MS, omnibus ED
45   quam MS, *Barletta*: cum ED

[657] shepherd, but rather that of a wicked hireling, and that when he disobeys the precepts of the Master of the house and must give an account of his stewardship, he will be in great danger for his soul. But you, Holy Father, who clearly understand all these things better than anyone else—although they are important to everyone—and who have decided to use the pastoral office which the Lord has granted you not to the detriment of your salvation, but for the fuller acquisition of eternal happiness, will apportion your concerns in such a way as to show that not only Peter, but you also, who now hold his place, have been commanded by the Lord: "Do not protect the rights of the Church or press your claim to states or accumulate wealth, but tend my sheep and feed my lambs" (John 21:15-17). Of course, to defend the rights of the true Church is to care in every way for the salvation of souls. For what is the Church, except a gathering of souls? What are the rights or the goods of this Church, except right faith, good morals, and the eternal salvation that is promised to souls? But you, holy Father, whom ignorance cannot persuade to neglect vessels of gold and to care only for those of clay, whose faith and concentration cannot be shaken by an immoderate desire for wealth or ambition for power, and who cannot be ruled or led astray by men's favor, hatred, or vindictiveness, will do greater things and not neglect the little things, according to the Lord's precept, and will not hesitate to undertake every labor, care, and concern for the salvation of these nations and peoples. Indeed, you would consider it an occasion of shame and disgrace if one who held the See of Peter before you should be found to have undertaken greater labor and expended more of the Church's resources for claiming earthly cities from the domination of tyrants than you are prepared to do for the liberation of so many peoples, nations, and so many thousands of souls from the slavery of the devil, and to lead them to the unity of the Church and ultimately to the infinite joy of eternal salvation.

Now, Holy Father, to the best of our knowledge gained by travel as well as reading, there are seven Christian nations in addition to the inhabitants of Europe. These are, perhaps, largely unknown because they inhabit diverse regions of the earth and live under various kings and princes.

[658] Diversas autem has diximus septem nationes, quae distant ab invicem, non sicut Campania ab Apulia, aut Emilia ab Etruria, sed multo, verbi gratia, magis quam Gallia ab Hispania, aut Pannonia differunt a Germania; quippe quae singulae earum latissimis diffusae regionibus, magno locorum spatio a ceteris separentur, quibus nec imperium, neque vivendi leges, aut habitus, neque religionis ritus, neque Linguarum idioma commune sit. Utuntur enim singulae, ut ex uno hoc in ceteris omnibus, quantum ab invicem diversificentur,[46] facile perpendere possis, non modo tanta sermonis diversitate, ut neque salutandi officio invicem communicari possint, sed tanta in scribendo disparitate, ut forma, modo, ordine, numeroque litterarum, multo magis, quam Graeci a Latino, aut ab Hebraeo Arabes, hae singulae inter se differant a singulis nationibus. Sunt, qui paucioribus, quam nos utuntur, elementis: sunt, qui plusquam centum, et quinquaginta litteras habent, qui non syllabas ex litteris conficiunt, sed singularum syllabarum vim singulis diversis characteribus scribunt, aliqui Latino, Graecoque more de sinistro, alii Hebraeo, Araboque instituto ex dextro in sinistrum scribendo procedunt. Forma vero, sonus, ac nomina ipsarum litterarum in singulis nationibus ita diversa sunt, ut nulla penitus, aut in scribendi forma, aut sono proferendi sit communicatio, nisi in quantum harum nationum una est, quae licet non simili omnino charactere, simili tamen voce Graecis utitur litteris novem, quas Graeci non habent: nihilominus additis quibusdam novem litteris, ita a Graeco idiomate separantur, ut Graecus neque eorum scripta legere, neque sermonem intellegere valeat.

Ceterum, si de his solum nationibus nobis nunc apud Te sermo habendus esset, et quas earum, quaeque incolant regiones, quos Reges, et Principes habeant, et quibus in his, quae ad Fidem attinent, diversis utantur caeremoniarum viribus, quantum nos cognoscere potuimus, scribere non pigeret; ex quibus, quam magnae ipsae fuerint, quamque[47] a ceteris aliis et locorum distantia, et omnibus vitae officiis diversae, palam fieret. Sed ne multa scribentes, dum singula diffusius explicare voluerimus, sermo nimium protrahatur: quantum ratione locorum ab invicem distent, hoc solo argumento dignosci facile potest, quod eorum aliae nigros, aliae fuscos, aliae candidos homines habeant. Et quemadmodum ex eo, quod de Linguarum,

---

46   diversificentur: diversificent MS, ED
47   quamque: quamquam MS, ED

[658] We have used the term "diverse" in the sense that they are distant from each other, not as Campania is distant from Apulia or Emilia from Tuscany, but rather more than France is distant from Spain or Hungary from Germany. For they are scattered over the widest spaces, and separated from each other by such a great distance that they do not have the same government, laws, way of living, religious rites, or language. Indeed, their languages are so different from each other—we cite this one instance, that you may estimate their diversity in other respects—that not only are they unable to greet each other in speech, but even their systems of writing differ in the form, the order, and the number of the letters more than the Latin alphabet differs from the Greek or the Arabic from the Hebrew. Some of them use fewer letters than we do; others use more than one hundred and fifty, since they do not create syllables from letters, but express syllables with distinct signs.[29] Some write, in the manner of Latin and Greek, from left to right, while others, in the manner of Hebrew and Arabic, write from right to left. The forms, the sounds, and the names of the letters themselves in different nations are so different that there is absolutely no common writing or pronunciation among them, except insofar as there is one system which, having characters that are somewhat dissimilar in form from the Greek but similar in value, uses nine letters that the Greeks do not have.[30] Nevertheless, with the addition of the nine letters, their alphabet is so far removed from the Greek language that a Greek can neither read their script nor understand their language.

Now, if we had to speak about these nations alone, we would not be averse to writing down, in so far as we are able, what regions they inhabit, who their kings and princes are, and what religious ceremonies they use; from these things it would be clear how great they are and how vast is the distance between them both in space and in all the usages of life. But lest, in our desire to explain things in detail, we write too much and overextend our discourse, this alone is sufficient to show their distance from each other: the inhabitants of some of these regions are black, some are brown-skinned, and some are white. Just as anyone can judge their diversity from what we have said about their differences in language and letters,

29 This may refer to the Ethiopic script which included various vowels with different consonants, making it seem to be syllabic. Other Semitic languages have fewer letters than Latin and Greek, and are often written only in consonants with no vowels.

30 Giustiniani probably refers to the Coptic and Cyrillic scripts which derived from Greek, adding additional sounds.

[659] Litterarumque diversitate diximus, qualiter sit harum nationum ab invicem diversitas, facile arguere quisque potest, ita ex hoc
uno, quod dicturi sumus, non difficile erit, singularum nationum
magnitudinem cognoscere. Praeter enim illius Principis Presbyteri
Ioannis, qui Abissinis, Iacobinisque imperat, satis certam potentiam,
quae maior omnino existimatur, quam Turcarum simul, ac Maurorum vires, aliae, una sola earum est nationum, quae quinque Reges,
totidemque Regna habet, quorum singuli et regionum latitudine, et
virorum multitudine, et divitiarum copia Maurorum Sultano nihilo
inferiores existimantur. Et quamquam huic reliquae minime sunt
aequales, maximos tamen, potentissimosque fore non ignoramus.

Haec autem, et alia quaedam de his septem Christianorum nationibus tum legendo, tum maxime videndo cognovimus; non quod ad
has omnes nationes peregrinati simus, sed quod ibi fuimus, ubi ex
singulis nationibus multi homines, multaeque familiae continue degunt. Dum enim ego Paulus visendi, venerandique[48] Sepulcri Domini
Nostri Iesu Christi causa in Syriam navigassem, inter cetera, quae
cognoscendi studio per tres continuos menses, quibus in Ierusalem
circumiacentibus locis sum immoratus, inquirere volui, hoc unum
fuit. Cum enim primis illis diebus, quibus Ierusalem applicueram,
Sancti Sepulcri Ecclesiam, quae ab infidelibus lucri gratia clausa
custoditur, ingressus essem, inveni ex harum nationum singulis
viros aliquos in eo voluntario carcere se mancipantes, et in hymnis,
et psalmis, aliisque Religionis obsequiis Domino servientes. Magna
enim, amplaque cum ea sit Ecclesia, pro singulis nationibus seorsum sunt loca separata, in quibus cellulis angustissimis constructis
ex omni natione duo, aut tres, aut quattuor separatim inhabitant.
Praeter enim nonnullos ex Beati Francisci Ordine, qui in ea continue
degunt, quique soli sunt ex universa Europa, septem adhuc ibidem
aliae Christianorum, ut diximus, nationes reperiuntur, lingua, moribus, habitu, caeremoniarumque ritu valde ab invicem dissidentes,
neque ex illis nationibus illi tantum pauci, qui in ea vivunt Ecclesia
Ierosolymorum sunt, sed ex earum singulis multi religiosi viri, famili-
aeque multae inveniuntur; ita ut ex omni populo illius Civitatis, quae
satis est habitata, plusquam tertia pars ex his Christianorum gentibus
esse censeatur, praeter multos alios, qui extra civitatem, ecclesias, et
domos,

---

48   venerandique MS: visitandique ED

[659] so too it will be easy to appreciate the size of particular nations from what we are about to say. For in addition to the well-known realm of Prester John,[31] who rules the Abyssinians and Jacobites, and whose kingdom is believed to be larger than those of the Turks and Moors combined, one of these nations has five kingdoms and five kings, each of which is believed to be not inferior to the Sultan of the Moors in territory, population, and wealth. While the remaining nations are not equal to this one, we know that they will be both very great and very powerful.

These facts and others have become known to us through reading and especially by sight—not because we have traveled to all these countries, but because we have spent time in a place where many persons and communities from all of them dwell together. For when I (Paul) sailed to Syria to see and venerate the Tomb of our Lord Jesus Christ, and I spent three months in the area around Jerusalem, among the various things that I wished to learn, I made this the particular object of my inquiry. During the first days of my stay in Jerusalem, when I entered the Church of the Holy Sepulcher— which the Infidels keep closed in order to make money[32]—I found men from these nations undergoing voluntary imprisonment and serving the Lord in hymns, psalms, and other religious observances. Although it is a large and spacious church, there are separate places for the various nations, in which two, three, or four of them inhabit the tiny cells that they have constructed. Apart from some friars of the Order of St. Francis, who live there permanently and who are the only Europeans present, seven other Christian nations are represented, who are very different from each other in language, customs, dress, and ritual. In addition to the few who actually live in this church, many other religious persons and houses from these nations reside in Jerusalem, so that more than a third of the entire population of the city, with is rather large, is believed to come from these Christian nations, in addition to many others who have churches and homes,

---

31   There were many legends of a Prester John which circulated broadly in Europe from the twelfth century through the seventeenth century. He was sometimes thought of as a priestly king who ruled over a kingdom surrounded by Muslim peoples or other lands. His geographical reign was imagined to be in many different directions beyond the known world.

32   As mentioned above (sec 635), the Caliph entrusted the keys to the Nusseibeh family to enable peace among the quarreling varieties of Christians who maintain different part of the large church.

[660] quasi Monasteria quaedam habent. Fuit enim mihi inter cetera illis diebus cura, non solum eos, qui Ierusalem habitant, saepius convenire, sed extra civitatis moenia, loca singularum nationum adire, ut usu interpretum, quantum potui interrogando, aliquid de illis cognoscere, a quibus et ea, quae diximus, et alia nonnulla didicimus.

Sunt autem istae nationes, ut earum tandem nomina exprimamus: Abissini, qui nigri sunt, immo subfusci, et ab ortu Nili usque ad Aegyptum infra Nili, ac Oceani terminos sub eo satis noto Principe Ioanne Presbytero ab omnibus nuncupato, habitare dicuntur. His caeremoniarum ritu satis similes, sed colore multum diversi sunt Iacobitae; albi etenim sunt. Armenii vero alii nuncupantur, qui ex nomine ipso, quam Orbis incolunt partem, cognoscuntur; formosi siquidem homines, ac valde Religiosi. Alii autem sunt Georgii, reliquis ditiores, quibus in Sepulcri Ecclesia locus, ubi Dominus fuit crucifixus, deputatus est. Cum enim amplitudine sua Calvarii Montis partem illam, in qua crucifixus est Iesus, et Horti locum, ubi Sepulcrum in saxo erat excisum, comprehendat, his nobilissimis Georgiis, et aliis ditioribus nobilissimus locus datus est, et multa in Ierusalem, atque etiam circumcirca Ierosolymam loca, ecclesias, domos, ac praedia possident. Et illi hi certe sunt, de quibus a fide dignis, senio, Sacerdotioque venerandis hominibus didicimus: quinque huius gentis Reges Sultano, ut diximus, esse non inferiores. Praeter hos sunt et Suriani, et Maronitae, ex quibus non multi tunc temporis Ierosolymis erant. Maronitae enim illi sunt, qui Libanum montem et circa eum adiacentia loca occupant. Gabrielem namque virum ex eodem S. Francisci Ordine, linguarum peritia insignem in Episcopum receperunt, qui eos in Ecclesiae Romanae oboedientia custodit, conservavitque. Hae sunt sex, quas narravimus nationes, quibus si Graecos aliis[49] notiores addamus, septem, sicut praediximus, Orientalium, Meridionaliumque Christianorum nationes habebimus. Hi vero, qui Graeci censentur, et qui Constantinopolitanae Ecclesiae ritus servant, plusquam centum familiae sunt apud Ierosolymam, Romanaeque Ecclesiae mores non suscipiunt. Sunt et alii huius nationis paene innumerabiles, qui per totam Graeciam, et in omni tam Turcarum, quam Maurorum regione degunt.

Commune autem his omnibus nationibus est Romanae Ecclesiae minus adhaerere; Romanum Pontificem aut non

---

49   aliis MS: alios ED

[660] similar to monasteries, outside the city. Among other things, I took pains to visit not only the Christians who live in Jerusalem, but also the places they had founded outside the walls, and with the help of interpreters I questioned them as much as I could and learned these and other facts about them.

The names of these nations are as follows. First are the Abyssinians, who are black—or rather, dark brown—and who inhabit the area stretching from the source of the Nile to Egypt between the river and the ocean. They are said to be ruled by the famous prince known as Prester John. Similar to these in ritual, but quite different in color, are the Jacobites, who are white. Others are called Armenians, named after the part of the world that they inhabit; these are a good-looking and very pious people. Others are Georgians, who are wealthier than the rest. In the Church of the Sepulcher, these have control over the place where the Lord was crucified. For the church comprises that part of Calvary where Jesus was crucified and the part of the Garden where the tomb was hewn from rock; the most important place is entrusted to these prominent Georgians and to other wealthy persons. They also have many places, churches, houses, and estates in Jerusalem and its environs. These are indeed the ones about whom we have learned from reliable, elder priests, that the five kings of this race are not inferior, as we have said, to the Sultan. In addition to these, there are the Syrians and Maronites, of whom there are not many currently in Jerusalem. The Maronites inhabit Mt. Lebanon and the surrounding areas; they elected the Franciscan friar Gabriel,[33] a man skilled in languages, as their bishop, and he has kept them in obedience to the Roman Church. These are the six nations we mentioned, and if we add the better-known Greeks, we will have seven eastern and southern Christian nations, as we said. Those, however, who are counted as Greeks and who observe the rite of the Church of Constantinople number more than one hundred households in Jerusalem and do not accept the customs of the Roman Church. There are virtually countless others of this nation who live throughout Greece and in the whole region of the Turks and Moors.

What these nations have in common, however, is that they do not belong to the Roman Church; they either do not know the Roman Pontiff

---

33   Gabriel ibn al Qila'i (1450-1516) was a Maronite Franciscan, the first Maronite to study in Venice and Rome. He returned to Lebanon, becoming an important scholar. He became bishop of Cyprus In 1507.

[661] cognoscere,[50] aut omnium Ecclesiarum, quae in universo sunt orbe, Caput nequaquam existimare; Petrum, non Principem Apostolorum, sed unum de numero aliorum credere; earum ecclesias, quas a Iacobo, a Bartholomaeo a ceteris Apostolis constitutas autumant, Beati Petri Ecclesiae, Romanae scilicet Sedi, non inferiores, sed aequales esse: sed et praeter haec, Christianae Religionis Evangelicae, Apostolicaeque doctrinae mores, ac ritus hae singulae perfectius puriusque, quam reliquae omnes, observare credunt; cum tamen magnopere in suscipiendis Ecclesiae Sacramentis, aliisque ritibus servandis inter se invicem, et a nobis quoque discrepent. Sunt enim, qui aquae et ignis baptismum suscipiunt, quamquam aquae necessarium ad salutem, ignis vero nequaquam necessarium, sed ad melius esse institutum aiunt. Altaris Sacramentum in fermentata bucella conficiunt, et infantibus quoque fere omnes ministrant. In Matrimonio alii repudium admittunt: alii secundas nuptias non suscipiunt.

Quae quidem omnia, dum ipsi consideramus, et praeter haec singulas has nationes, circa mores peculiares quosdam ritus habere, et in his quae credimus, non eadem nobiscum, neque eadem omnes sentire, quamquam non satis aperte omnia eorum placita, ob linguarum diversitatem intellegere potuimus, neque etiam definire, si de his, in quibus a nobis dissentire videntur, necessarium sit pro eorum salute aliquid opinari; de omnium salute valde dubitamus, timemusque, ne membra haec ab eorum Capite penitus divisa, sic a fide, et a vita sint aliena, ut nulla salutis spes sit reliqua, nisi Capiti suo coniungantur, Romanaeque Ecclesiae mores, ritus, caeremonias, fidem, placita, decretaque omnia, quantum ad salutem necessarium esse creditur, suscipiant. Quoniam vero haec suscipere, nisi illis tradantur, nequaquam possunt; tradi autem, nisi a Te uno, aut per Temetipsum, aut per alios, qui a Te potestatem acceperint, omnino non valent: magna Tibi, Beatissime Pater, necessitas incumbit, postquam pastoralem hanc dignitatem suscipiens omnium quoque humanarum creaturarum, maxime vero Christianorum hominum regimen suscepisti. Si salutem itaque tuam penitus non vis neglegere, harum nationum, quae sub Christiano nomine vivunt, maximam curam, diligentissimamque sollicitudinem Te suscipere oportet, ne pereuntibus illis, secundum Propheticam sententiam, sanguis eorum de manibus tuis requiratur, qui tunc solum

---

50   cognoscere MS, *Barletta*: cognoscunt ED

[661] or do not believe that he is the head of all the Churches in the
world. They believe that Peter was not the prince of the apostles, but
simply one among their number; they hold that the Churches that
were founded by James, Bartholomew, and the other apostles are not
inferior, but equal to the Church of St. Peter—that is, the Roman
Church. Moreover, they believe that they observe the customs and
rites of the Christian religion of the Gospels and Apostles more
purely and perfectly than all the rest, even though they differ greatly
among themselves and from us in the reception of the sacraments
and in other rites. There are some who receive a baptism of water and
fire, although, they say, the baptism of water is necessary for salvation
and that of fire is not necessary, but has been instituted for an
increase of well-being. They perform the Sacrament of the Altar in
the form of leavened bread, and practically all of them give it even to
infants. In the matter of Matrimony some allow divorce, while others
do not accept second marriages.

When we consider all these things, and the fact that these nations
have their own rites and customs and do not believe the same
things that we do or even agree among themselves, we are very
doubtful about their salvation—although it was impossible for us to
understand their views plainly, because of the diversity of languages,
and to determine whether salvation depends on a certain view
regarding the matters in which they seem to differ from us. We
also fear that these members who are divided from their head are
so alienated from the Faith and from Life that there is no hope for
their salvation, unless they are joined to their Head and accept the
customs, rites, ceremonies, faith, beliefs, and decrees of the Roman
Church, insofar as these are thought necessary for salvation. They
cannot accept these things, however, unless they receive them, and
they cannot receive them except from you alone, either directly or
through others who have received the power from you. And so, Holy
Father, a great obligation falls upon you, since by undertaking this
pastoral office you undertook the government of all creatures and
especially of Christians. If you do not wish to neglect your salvation
altogether, it behooves you to assume with all diligence and solicitude
the care of these nations, which live with the title of Christians, lest
they perish and their blood, as the Prophet says, should be required
of your hands (Ezek 3:16). It will not be required of you,

[662] requiri non poterit, cum Tu, quantum in Te erit, non laboribus parcens, non expensis, omni studio, ac diligentia curaveris, has nationes ad Ecclesiae Romanae gremium, oboedientiam, unitatem, conformitatemque reducere; quod Domino Iesu Christo auxiliante facile fieri posse credimus, si modo sapientia illa, pietasque animi tui hoc in Domini Iesu Christi gratiam efficere proposuerit. Neque enim rei novitate, neque regionum longinquitate, neque nationum diversitate, neque alia ulla difficultate invincibilis illa virtus tua superari poterit; quae si semel hoc tam sanctum, tam Deo placitum opus inceperit, nunquam desistet, nisi et ipsum perficiat.

Perfici vero posse de Domini misericordia, deque tua Sapientia, ac Pietate confisi, facile existimamus. Multa enim in eis cognovimus, quae nos facilem eorum conversionem sperare docent.[51] Sunt enim fere omnes illarum nationum viri, quos cognovimus, tantum naturali quadam bonitate praediti, tanto Fidei, quam recte sentire arbitrantur, zelo succensi, tantum Christiani nominis, Christianaeque religionis studiosi, ut erubescere nos omnes Europae Christiani merito possemus,[52] si intueri vel semel datum esset, quanta reverentia sancta illa loca venerentur; quanta veneratione Christianum nomen prosequantur; quam in omnibus vitae officiis modesti, quam benigni. Quae omnia saepius considerans, memini me in haec verba saepius prorupisse: hi Christiani vere sunt, nos Semipagani. Ne vero illos tantum, qui Ierosolymis degunt, huiusmodi esse, sed omnes illarum nationum populos existimemus, illud nobis argumento est, quod audivimus, quotannis instantibus Sacrae Passionis, Resurrectionisque Dominicae diebus, quamplurimos ex singulis illis nationibus, longissimis, difficillimisque itineribus superatis, ad sancta ea loca visenda, venerandaque, Ierosolymam summa Fidei devotione venire.

Sed et erga Apostolicam Beati Petri Sedem ita recte affectae sunt singulae nationes, ut interrogantibus ex tot Christianorum nationibus, quinam illi sint, qui rectius, puriusque Christianam custodiunt pietatem, primo quidem loco singuli seipsos ponant; secundo autem omnes communi responsione, Petri et Pauli Ecclesiam constituant. Quod magnam esse rectae institutionis nostrae approbationem optime novit Beatitudo tua. Meminit enim non aliter potuisse olim peritissimorum illorum Statuariorum imagines, quaenam perfectior esset, iudicari, singulis suam ante alias laudantibus,

---

51   docent *Barletta*: decent MS, ED
52   possemus *Barletta*: possimus MS, ED

[662] however, if you are able, without regard for the labor and expense involved, and with all zeal and diligence to bring these nations back to the lap of Mother Church and to obedience, unity, and conformity with her. We believe that this can easily be done with the help of the Lord Jesus Christ, once you have determined in your wisdom and generosity to accomplish this for our Lord Jesus' sake. Neither the novelty of the situation, nor the distances involved, nor the diversity of nations, nor any other difficulty can overcome your invincible virtue, and once you have begun this holy work, so pleasing to God, you will not cease until you have finished it.

That it can be finished we have no doubt, trusting as we do in the mercy of God and your wisdom and generosity; for we recognize many qualities in these people that teach us to hope for their conversion. Practically all the men of those nations that we have met are so endowed with natural goodness and so ardent with zeal for their faith—which they believe to be the true one—and so zealous for the Christian religion that we European Christians might all blush for shame, if given the chance just once to observe the reverence that they have for those sacred places and the veneration they give to the title of Christian, and how modest and kind they are in all the duties of life. As I continually pondered these things, I recall that I often exclaimed, "These are real Christians, and we are semi-pagans." And lest we should think that only those who live in Jerusalem are such, and not all the peoples of those nations, I have heard that every year, around the time of the Lord's Sacred Passion and Resurrection, many people from those nations come to Jerusalem, after long and difficult journeys, to see and venerate these holy places with the greatest faith and devotion.

Moreover, these nations are individually so well disposed to the Apostolic See of St. Peter that if you ask them which, of all Christian nations, observes the Christian religion in the purest and most correct manner, they will list themselves first, but in the second place they all agree in placing the Church of Peter and Paul. In this way, as Your Holiness knows well, they show their great esteem for our orthodoxy. For you remember that in ancient times the statues of the most skilled sculptors could not be ranked otherwise than as follows: though each sculptor praised his own work before the others,

[663] nisi quam secundo loco laudandam esse, plures eorum dixissent, eam absolutiorem iudicassent. Sed praeter haec illud multum prodesse ad has nationes Sanctae Romanae Ecclesiae copulandas poterit, quod certissime cognovimus; singulas scilicet earum nationum Novi Testamenti, neque plures, neque pauciores, quam nos Libros habere. Magno enim, memini, gaudio afficiebar, cum volumina eorum, quae legere nesciebam, evolvens, quid quoque volumine contineretur, interrogans, apertissime cognoscebam, nihil a nostris eorum Scripturas discrepare. Quattuor habent Evangelia, eo, quo nos, ordine disposita, Matthaei, Marci, Lucae, et Iohannis. Et quod maius est, singula eorum in totidem Capitulis divisa, quot sunt apud nos. Epistolas Pauli tresdecim, quarum, quae ad Romanos est, primo loco, et ceterae deinceps non alia serie, quam apud nos ordinatae. Post haec Apostolorum actus, et totidem, quot habemus nos, Apostolorum Epistolas, quae canonicae appellantur; postremo vero loco Ioannis Apocalypsim. Spem enim maximam concipiebam easdem, quas nos Scripturas habentes facillime posse ex eisdem scriptis veritatem Fidei edoceri. Quippe quoniam, quantum nos cognoscere potuimus, et prompti, paratique sunt ad audiendum, et faciles ad aliorum sententias suscipiendas; Graecos dumtaxat ex omnibus excipimus, qui pertinaci quadam superbia, crassiorique ignorantia, neque audire facile acquiescunt, neque audientes rationibus cedere consueverunt; qui etiam ab omnibus aliis nationibus communi consensu, postremo loco inter omnes Christianos statuuntur, difficiliorque certe unius istius nationis, quam ceterarum omnium simul cura a nobis existimatur. Cum tamen et Graecos ipsos, si Tu modo volueris, corrigibiles satis esse credamus, has septem nationes Domino lucrifacere, Ecclesiaeque Romanae coniungere, Te magis optare, quam septem qualescumque sint, Civitates, septemve terrena imperia Beatorum Apostolorum Patrimonio addere certissimi sumus.

Quare maiori cura sollicite perquirere cor tuum credimus, quos ad singulos harum nationum Oratores, quos Sacrarum Litterarum Doctores mittere possis, quam quos exercitus, quos Duces ad tuendas, aut expugnandas aliquas Civitates mittere debeas. Novit enim Beatitudo tua nulla alia ratione facilius has Christianorum nationes ad unitatem, veramque subiectionem Romanae Ecclesiae attrahere posse, quam si ad singulas

[663] the one that most of them deemed worthy of second place they judged to be the best.[34] In addition to these facts, we know for certain one other thing that will greatly aid us in joining these nations to the Holy Roman Church: they have the same number of books in the New Testament, neither more nor less than we have. I recall that I was filled with joy when I handled their books, which I could not read, and when I asked what each volume contained I learned clearly that they differed not at all from our Scriptures. They have the four Gospels in the same order that we use, namely Matthew, Mark, Luke, and John; what is more, each of these Gospels is divided into the same number of chapters as in our version. They have the thirteen epistles of Paul, of which the Epistle to the Romans occupies first place, and the others follow in the same order that we observe. After these come the Acts of the Apostles and the same number of apostolic epistles, which are called canonical, that we possess; in the last place is the Apocalypse of John.[35] And so I conceived the greatest hope that, since they have the same Scriptures that we do, they can easily be taught the truth of the Faith from them. From what we could tell, they are ready and eager to hear, and quick to understand, the views of others—with the exception of the Greeks, who from a stubborn pride and a more inflexible ignorance are not very willing to listen or, when they do listen, to yield to reason. By the common consent of all the other nations, these occupy the last place among Christians, and thus the care of this one nation will be, in our estimation, more difficult than that of all the others combined. Since we believe, however, that even the Greeks will not be incorrigible if you are willing to correct them, we are confident that you are more interested in gaining these seven nations for Christ and joining them to the Roman Church than in adding seven cities and seven realms, of whatever sort they are, to the patrimony of the Apostles.

Thus, we believe that you will choose the spokesmen and the doctors of Sacred Scripture that you will send to these nations with greater care than the generals or armies you would send to take various cities. For Your Holiness knows that the easiest way to attract these Christian nations to unity with the Roman Church and to true submission to her is to send

---

34 Pliny the Elder (23 CE- 79), *Naturalis historia*, 34, 19, 53.
35 This is the sequence of the books of the New Testament, namely, with the Acts of the Apostles between Jude and Revelation, the sequence given in a decree from the Council of Florence, February 4, 1442. The Vulgate's order appears in all modern translations, the order given in Eusebius (260-340).

[664] earum maximos Sapientia, et Dignitate, ac singulares Doctrina viros miseris, ut illi auctoritate, isti autem doctrina eos ad salutem animarum suarum hortari, atque persuadere valeant. Si autem ad eos huiuscemodi viros miseris, et aliquos ex illarum gentium numero Episcopos, ac Sacerdotes ad Te, ad Concilium Lateranense advocaveris, tuaque Sapientia eorum conversionem non neglexerit, futurum facile speramus, ut nobilissima haec Christianae Reipublicae membra, quae dissipata nunc, ac disiecta, veraeque Fidei vita privata iacent, reviviscant, et Capiti suo uniantur. Quod sane magis futurum Ecclesiae lucrum est, quam si mille insignes Civitates tuae subiicerentur potestati. Tantum igitur Sanctae Ecclesiae lucrum posse Te minoribus curis impeditum neglegere, nos certe existimare non possumus; sed iam videre nobis videtur, Te nobilissimos Oratores, dignissimosque Legatos ad harum nationum Reges, Principes, populosque mittere, et una cum illis Christianae veritatis praedicatores, doctoresque dirigere, Episcopos praeterea earum nationum (habent enim et suos illi populi Episcopos, Archiepiscopos, ac Patriarchas) ad Lateranense Concilium vocare, ad Ecclesiae unitatem omnibus artibus revocare, in Ecclesia Romana aliquas illis dignitates concedere. Neque enim bene Tibi cum Patrefamilias futurum aperte intellegis, si hos populos, qui sane maior pars commissarum Tibi ovium sunt, ad verum Ecclesiae, unicumque Ovile reducere neglexeris. Prodesse vero, et multum quidem ad infidelium expugnationem Tibi poteris, si has populorum nationes Sanctae Ecclesiae coniunxeris; si enim Te cum infidelibus pugnante, illi communes Fidei Christianae hostes a tergo adorientur, quaenam via salutis infidelibus relinquetur? Si vero haec, quae diximus, minus prodesse cognoveris, non deerunt Sapientiae tuae alia, atque alia opportuna remedia, quibus languescentibus istis Sanctae Ecclesiae membris, mederi possis. Nunc enim Te ad Ecclesiam suam vocavit Dominus, cum maxime medico egere visa est.

Nos vero, quoniam illis paucis, quae diximus, argumentis, Domino Iesu favente, omnes illas nationes, praeter Graecos, ad Ecclesiae unitatem, subiectionemque redituras certissime speramus, plura alia, quae tentari in huiusmodi negotio possent, consulto scribere praetermittimus. Graecis vero, tamquam iis, qui gravius laborant, potentiora sunt medicamenta praeparanda. Cum enim alii vel ignorantia, vel neglegentia

[664] men who are foremost in wisdom and rank and conspicuous for their learning. The former by their authority, and the latter by their learning will be able to urge and persuade them for the salvation of their souls. If you send such men to them, and also invite some of their bishops and priests to the Lateran Council and do not neglect their conversion, we have good reason to hope that these noble members of the Christian Commonwealth, which now lie scattered and severed from the life of the true Faith, will come back to life and be united with their head. This, indeed, will be a greater gain for the Church than if a thousand noble cities should be subjected to her power. Thus we cannot imagine that you, because you are hindered by lesser cares, will neglect such a gain for the Church; rather, it seems to us that you are already looking into sending the best spokesmen and the worthiest ambassadors to the kings, leaders, and people of those nations, and with them preachers and doctors of Christian truth, and that you will invite the bishops of those nations—for they have their own bishops, archbishops, and patriarchs—to the Lateran Council and will use every means to bring them back to the unity of the Church, and will grant them some marks of distinction in the Roman Church. Indeed, you clearly understand that the Master of the house will not be pleased with you if you fail to restore these peoples, who are such a large part of the sheep entrusted to you, to the one, true Flock of the Church. You will profit greatly, however, and particularly in your effort to conquer the Infidels, if you join these nations to the Holy Church; for if those common enemies of the Christian Faith are attacked from the rear, while you are fighting with them in front, what escape will be left for the Infidels? If, however, you find the suggestions that we have made less effective, your wisdom will not fail to discover other appropriate remedies for the healing of these languishing members of the Church. God calls you to his Church at precisely the moment that it most seems to need a physician.

Now, since we have the greatest hope that these nations, apart from the Greeks, will be convinced by the few arguments that we have mentioned and will return to the unity and obedience of the Church, we are deliberately omitting many other arguments that could be tried in this matter. For the Greeks, however, as for those who are more gravely ill, stronger medicines must be prepared. While others are separated from the Roman Church by a sort of ignorance or negligence

[665] quadam a Romana sint Ecclesia divisi, Graeci soli sunt, qui
non ignorantia solum, sed pertinaci etiam impietate tantum a
Romana dissentiunt Ecclesia, ut Romanum Pontificem, omnesque
illi subiectos populos malos Christianos, Haereticosque appellare
non formident. In illis enim Graeciae civitatibus, in quibus permixti
Graeci, Latinique vivunt, Latinam uxorem vir si ducat Graecus, aut
Latino viro Graeca si nubat mulier, Graeco instituto vivere, iurare,
ac vovere Latinus cogitur. Filios cum suscipiunt, parens Graecus ad
Presbyteros Graecos, Latina autem mater ad Latinos, unus clam
alio ad baptizandum portat, ita ut multi sint, quibus bis baptizari
contigit. Ad Altare, supra quod Latinus sacra ministeria Sacerdos
celebraverit, Graecus non accedit, nisi prius multis vicibus illud ablui
curaverit. Haec, multaque alia his deteriora, quae his oculis vidimus,
his auribus audivimus, perversitatis eorum magna nobis sunt argumenta, non tamen eorum salus desperanda est, sed quantum gravius
laborare creduntur, tantum diligentius pietatem tuam studio salutis
eorum incumbere decet. Non enim sanarum tantum, sed infirmarum
quoque ovium curam suscepisti. Quoniam autem nulla infirmitas
tam gravis est, quae facile sanari non possit, si eius origo, causaque
prius percipiatur, cogitare Sapientiam tuam credimus, quomodo
factum sit, ut post Florentinum Concilium, in quo omnis, quae inter
Graecos, Latinosque esse videbatur discordia, sopita omnino, atque
amputata est, iterum Graeci a Romana tantum Ecclesia discesserint,
ut legitimum eius Pastorem haereticum audeant appellare. Quis vero
impius ille fuerit, qui a Concilio illo discedens iratus, quod Cardinalatus non fuerit dignitate decoratus, omnem Graeciam falsis ru-
moribus conturbaverit, auctoritatemque Concilii illius fregerit, tuam
latere Sapientiam non potest. Eo vero discordiarum sparso semine,
quanta contra Latinos orta sit odiorum seges, vix existimare ullus
posset, qui Graeciae loca non adiisset. Quantum vero in dies crescat,
nullus omnino est, qui pro merito dicere valeat. Dum enim populorum ignorantia a Sacerdotum temeritate, impudentia vero et audacia
Sacerdotum a plebis inscitia continue fovetur, ad id ventum est, ut
Graecus palam Latinum, tamquam Ethnicum et publicanum habere
affirmet. Concepit enim semel plebs ignara a Romana dissentire Ecclesia, unde eos eleemosynis et beneficiis omnibus largius Sacerdotes
prosequuntur,

[665], the Greeks alone dissent from the Church not only from ignorance, but also with a certain tenacious disrespect, so that they do not scruple to call the Roman Pontiff and all those who are subject to him "bad Christians" and "heretics." In those Greek cities in which Greeks and Latins live together, if a Greek man marries a Latin woman, or if a Greek woman marries a Latin man, the Latin partner is forced to swear to live according to the Greek rite. When they have children, a Greek father takes them to Greek priests and a Latin mother to Latin priests, each without the other's knowledge, to be baptized; thus many happen to have been baptized twice. A Greek will not approach an altar on which a Latin priest has celebrated the sacred rites unless he has carefully purified it many times. These and many other things that we have seen with our own eyes and heard with our own ears are great proofs of their perversity. And yet we must not despair of their being saved, but the more they seem to be ailing, the more it falls to your kindness to labor diligently for their salvation. You have undertaken, after all, the care not only of healthy sheep, but also of the infirm. And since no infirmity is so great that it cannot easily be healed if its origin and cause is first discovered, we are confident that your wisdom is pondering how it happened that after the Council of Florence, in which all apparent discord between the Greeks and Latins was put to rest and eliminated, the Greeks once again withdrew from the Roman Church, to the extent that they dare to call its legitimate Pastor a heretic. Your wisdom cannot fail to identify that impious man who departed from the Council in anger, because he had not been dignified with the title of Cardinal, and who disturbed all Greece with false rumors and wrecked the authority of the Council.[36] Once the seed of discord has been sown, scarcely anyone can appreciate how great a crop of hatred has risen against the Latins, unless he has been to Greece himself; and how much this hatred daily increases, no one can really say. As the ignorance of the people is nourished by the temerity of priests, and the audacity of priests is nourished by the simplicity of the people, the point has been reached that a Greek publicly compares a Latin to a pagan or a publican. Once the ignorant people have thus determined to dissent from the Roman Church, they more generously reward with alms and benefices those priests

36 Mark Eugenicus (1392-1445), metropolitan of Ephesus, a major Greek speaker at the Council of Florence, vehemently opposed the proposal for union between Rome and the Greek Orthodox bishops. When the decree passed anyway, he left the council, returned to Greece and preached against the decree until the faithful rejected it outright.

[666] qui audacius ac promptius contra loqui Ecclesiam non formidant. Ipsi vero Sacerdotes, qui non solum communi cum plebe ignorantia, sed inopia etiam maxima laborant, ut populorum subsidia aucupent, ea dicere de Latinis audent, quae de Iudaeis, aut Mahumetanis vix nos dicere auderemus. Inopia vero Sacerdotibus omnibus illis tanta inest, ut aliter, quam ex populorum eleemosynis, vivere nequaquam valeant.

Hanc, Beatissime Pater, cum Tu infirmitatis eorum causam ignorare non possis, salutifera illis remedia adhibere facillime poteris. Si enim populorum ignorantiam, multis missis ad eos praedicatoribus imminuere, audaciam vero auctoritate, severitateque pastorali compescere curabis, Sacerdotumque inopiam ex eorum locorum Ecclesiis, quae Latinis Praelatis subditae sunt, illis portionem aliquam, qua vivere possint, concedendo, levare non pigebit, aliquosque eorum ad aliquam Ecclesiae Romanae dignitatem promovere statueris, facillime fiet, ut tanta erroris impietate dimissa ad cor redeant, et Romanam Ecclesiam, quam nunc, quantum possunt, infamare, deprimereque non cessant, venerari incipiant; illique, a qua maxime divisos esse nunc gaudent, coniungi cupient. Nihil enim est, quod magis animos ad concordiam, benevolentiamque alliciat, quam oblata non petentibus beneficia. Illi enim, qui a Romanis Pontificibus neglectos esse molestissime ferunt, si a Te foveri se senserint, facile ex odio ad amorem, ex discordia ad concordiam, unitatemque convertentur. Meminimus, olim de hoc Graecorum hominum schismate multos sermones cum Reverendissimo Episcopo Cremonensi habuisse, qui certe, Pater Beatissime, vir est Religionis Zelo, Doctrina, Moribusque, ac alia omni virtute nihilo sanctis illis antiquioribus Ecclesiae luminibus inferior, qui multos annos apud Graecos commoratus, miseras horum populorum infirmitates optime novit, cui, si Tu negotium hoc tantum commiseris, pro sua erga Romanam Ecclesiam observantia atque pietate, pro magna animi eius prudentia, atque doctrina, rem pro votis Beatitudinis tuae conficiet: mores enim eorum non ignorat, Linguam optime callet, infirmitates, ac remedia, quae illis prodesse valeant, cognoscit; labores, ac pericula pro Christiana pietate subire non formidat; et ut postremo hoc etiam adiiciamus, si auctoritatem a Te Pontifice Summo omnium haberet, Graecos omnes ad Ecclesiae Romanae concordiam, unitatem, veramque

[666] who do not hesitate to speak more boldly and readily against the Church. The priests, for their part, who suffer not only from the ignorance they share with the common people, but also from great poverty, so that they depend for their livelihood on the people's support, dare to say things about Latins that we would scarcely dare to say about Jews or Muslims. So great, indeed, is the poverty of their priests that they cannot survive except by the alms-giving of the people.

Since you know the cause of their infirmity, Holy Father, you will easily find healthy remedies for it. If you take care to diminish the people's ignorance by sending them many preachers and to curb their audacity with your authority and pastoral firmness, and if you do not stint to alleviate the poverty of their priests by conceding a portion of funds from the churches which are subject to Latin prelates, and if you determine to promote some of them to an office in the Roman Church, they will promptly abandon their impious error and experience a change of heart, and they will begin to revere the Roman Church, which they currently slander and defame at every opportunity, and will wish to be united with the very Church from which they now rejoice to be divided. Nothing attracts souls to concord and benevolence as much as kindnesses offered to those who do not seek them. Those who most bitterly resent being neglected by the Roman Pontiff will easily be converted from hatred to love and from discord to concord, if they feel that they have your favor. We recall that we once had many conversations about the schism of the Greeks with the most Reverend Bishop of Cremona,[37] who is surely, Holy Father, not inferior to the ancient luminaries of the Church in religious zeal, learning, manner of life, and every other virtue, and who has lived among the Greeks for many years and knows the pitiful infirmities of this people very well. If you commit to him this undertaking, he will, in keeping with his respect and love for the Roman Church and his great prudence and learning, handle the matter just as Your Holiness would wish. For he knows their habits, he speaks the language fluently, and he understands the remedies that will help them; he is not afraid to undergo labor and danger for the sake of Christian charity; and in conclusion, if he has the authority from you, the Supreme Pontiff,

---

37 Girolamo Trevisan was a Cistercian monk, who became abbot of the monastery di Borgognoni (Torcello, Venice) and was later made bishop of Cremona in 1475. He died February 24, 1523. Both Giustiniani and Querini held him in high esteem.

[667] subiectionem, parvo temporis spatio se posse reducere non dif-
fidit. Nec vir est, qui temere aliquid suscipere auderet, qui quorsum
tendere posset, quemque finem habiturum esset, non prudentissime
praevidisset. Utinam multos tales Romana haberet Ecclesia. Utinam
iste, quem nos satis cognovimus, aliique huic persimiles, quos Sapientia tua Te cognovisse credimus, in his operibus exerceantur. Messis
quidem multa multos operarios Te optare admonet. Cum vero messis
multitudine omnino pauci ipsi sint operarii, illos quotquot sunt, mitti
in messem Domini optamus.

Cumque a nullo, nisi a Te, qui Patrisfamilias vices geris, mitti
possint, Te per sacra Domini Nostri Iesu Christi vulnera rogamus,
ut quoscumque habere potes operarios, illos ad messem Domini
dirigere non neglegas, ut undecumque ex Iudaeis, ex Idololatris, et
Mahumetanis, ex aliis Christianorum diversis nationibus, ex Graecis, ex omnibus denique hominum conditionibus fruges quamplures
in horreis Domini congregentur, ne forte super Te, qui messoribus
omnibus praepositus es, illa in novissimo die cadat confusio, quae
per Ioelem Prophetam pronuntiatur; Confusi enim, ait ille, sunt
Agricolae, quia periit Messis agri. Quoniam vero in Domo Domini
magna, non solum sunt vasa aurea, et argentea, sed et lignea, et fictilia, quaedam scilicet in honorem, ad utile, dignumque ministerium;
quaedam autem in contumeliam, ad viliora, abiectioraque opera sub-
eunda; et in uno corpore multa sunt membra, neque omnia eundem
actum habent, sed alia quidem nobiliora, perfectioraque in nobile
ministerium, alia autem ignobiliora, atque infirmiora, vilioribus
utique officiis inservientia, non incongruum nos facturi arbitramur,
si pro multitudine messis Te multis operariis egere existimantes, nos,
qualescumque sumus, non tamquam aurea, aut argentea vasa, sed ut
fictilia, confractaque, et paene omnino perdita, non tamquam oculi,
aut manus, sed tamquam pedes, et si quod pedibus etiam ignobilius,
infirmiusque membrum est, Tibi Beatissime Pater nosmetipsos offe-
ramus. Et quamquam ad omne inutiles ministerium nosmet cognoscamus, pro Christi tamen nomine, pro Fidei nostrae zelo, pro nostra
in Te observantia, atque veneratione, nullum tam vile, tam abiectum
ministerium est, quod suscipere erubescamus, nullum periculorum,
aut quorumcumque discriminum tam plenum, ut illud subire timea-
mus, nullum tam arduum, tam difficile,

[667] he is confident that he will be able in a short time to bring back all the Greeks to the concord, unity, and true obedience of the Roman Church. He is not a man to undertake something rashly, without having clearly foreseen where things are tending and what the end of them will be. Would that the Roman Church had many such men! May he, whom we know well, and others like him whom Your Holiness surely knows, be exercised in such works! A great harvest obliges you to wish for many workers. But since, given the size of the harvest, the workers are indeed few, we pray that as many as we have will be sent to the harvest of the Lord.

And since they can be sent by no one but you, who take the place of the Head of the household, we beg you by the sacred wounds of our Lord Jesus Christ to send as many workers as you possess to the harvest of the Lord, so that as much fruit as possible may be gathered into the granaries of the Lord from among the Jews, Pagans, Muslims, from other Christian nations and from the Greeks, and indeed from every class of men, lest on the last day that confusion fall upon you, who have been put in charge of all the harvesters, which was foretold through the prophet Joel: "The husbandmen are ashamed, because the harvest of the field has perished" (Joel 1:11). But because in the great house of the Lord there are not only vessels of gold and silver, but also of wood and clay, and some are made for honor, use, and worthy service, while others are made for contempt and the performance of base and humble tasks, and since in one body there are many members, which do not all have the same function, but some are more noble and perfect for noble service, while others are ignoble and weak and serve in a baser capacity, we think it is not inappropriate for us, considering your need for many workers in so great a harvest, to offer ourselves to you, holy Father, such as we are, not as golden or silver vessels, but as earthen and broken ones, practically worthless, and not as eyes or hands, but as feet or whatever member is humbler and weaker than feet. Although we know that we are useless for every ministry, nevertheless, for the sake of Christ's name, and for zeal for our faith, and for our respect and reverence for you, no work is so base and lowly that we blush to undertake it, or so full of perils and dangers of all sorts that we fear to undergo it, or so arduous and difficult

[668] quod Te iubente, et Domino Iesu auxiliante, perficere non
confidamus. Parati enim sumus pro Christi nomine viliores omnibus hominibus fieri, nulla unquam difficultate terreri, nullisque
laboribus frangi, manifestissima denique pericula omnia, et mortem
etiam ipsam intrepide subire, ut Christo Domino nostro in Caelis, et
Tibi eius vicem gerenti in Terris, quamquam ad omne opus inutiles,
utcumque possumus, serviamus.

[Part V]

Haec omnia, Pater Beatissime, quae scripsimus, de tribus illis
hominum conditionibus, qui intra Ecclesiae gremium non plene[53]
continentur, minus fortasse prudenter, nimiumve prolixe dicta sunt.
Nunc autem ultimo loco non multa de his, qui intra Matris Ecclesiae
sinum obsequentissimi filii continentur, dicere nos tuae Sanctitatis
indulgentissima benignitas tanto libentius permittet, quanto apertius
intellegere potest, quod ea, quae hucusque diximus, de his, qui Tibi,
quasi Reipublicae partibus optimo Reipublicae Patri et Conservatori
subiacent, dicta sunt. Quae autem dicenda restant, ea de familia, cui
Tu optimus Paterfamilias praepositus es, dicenda videntur. Memi-
nitque Beatitudo Tua ab Apostolo pronuntiatum, quod qui domui
suae praeesse nescit, Ecclesiae Dei diligentiam, atque sollicitudinem
habere non novit. Et certe sicut quisque diligentior familiae suae,
quam Reipublicae Procurator esse solet, ita Te, Beatissime Pater, eorum, de quibus nunc dicere aggredimur, quasi propriorum filiorum,
domusque tuae familiarium, maiorem quandam, ac diligentiorem
curam habere oportet; idque Te minime latere credimus. Quemadmodum enim orbis terrarum, omnisque humani generis universitas,
Respublica illa est, cui Tu Princeps designatus es, ita certe Christiani
hi populi, qui fideliter Romanae Ecclesiae adhaerent, subiectique
sunt, domus illa est, cui Tu Paterfamilias es institutus, et eorum, qui
in ea sunt, diligentissimam Te curam suscipere oportere, ille satis effi-
caciter admonere potuit, qui ait: Si quis suorum, et maxime domesti-
corum curam non habet, fidem negavit, et est infideli deterior.

Cum enim omnibus, quemadmodum in principio diximus, debitor
sis, dum tempus, facultasque suppetit, Te non deficiens bonum operari oportet, ad omnes quidem, maxime autem ad domesticos fidei;
Fidei autem domestici illi certe credendi sunt, qui verae Fidei vestigiis
inhaerentes, Ecclesiae Romanae humiliter, fideliterque adhaerent.
Magna

---

53   plene MS: plane ED

[668] that, at your command and with the help of the Lord Jesus, we are not confident that we can perform it. For the name of Christ we are prepared to become baser than all men, to be deterred by no danger, to be broken by no labors, and boldly to undergo the most evident perils and even death itself, so that we, useless as we are for any task, may nonetheless serve Christ our Lord in heaven, and you his Vicar on earth, in so far as we are able.

[Part V]

All that we have written, Holy Father, concerning the three conditions of men who are not fully contained in the bosom of the Church, has perhaps been less prudent and more prolix than it should have been. Now, however, we ask Your Holiness' kind permission to conclude with a few words about those who are obedient sons in the lap of Mother Church. This you will grant all the more readily, because you understand that what we have said so far pertains to those who are subject to you in the manner of citizens to the rulers of states; for you are the great father and conserver of the Commonwealth. What we have to say now, however, concerns the household over which you have been placed as the great *paterfamilias*. Your Holiness recalls what the Apostle said, that anyone who does not know how to rule his own house cannot have the necessary care and solicitude for God's Church (1 Tim 3:4). Just as any man is a more diligent manager of his own household than of the state, so it behooves you, Holy Father, to be more diligent and careful concerning the things that we are about to say, as if they pertained to your own children and to the members of your household, as you well know. For just as the whole world and the entire human race are the Commonwealth over which you have been appointed ruler, so too the Christian peoples who faithfully adhere to the Roman Church and are subject to her are the household of which you have been made the head, and you must undertake the greatest care of those who are in it. This was made sufficiently clear by the One who warned, "But if any man has not care of his own, and especially of those of his house, he has denied the Faith, and is worse than an infidel" (1 Tim 5:8).

Since you are indebted to all, as we said in the beginning, it behooves you, while you have the time and ability, to perform unfailing good works for all men, but especially for the householders of the Faith. Those are surely to be regarded as such who, walking in the footsteps of the true Faith, humbly and faithfully adhere to the Roman Church. Practically all of Europe is one great house

[669] domus Europa fere universa: multi familiares omnis vere
Christianorum hominum multitudo; Tu vero Paterfamilias a Domino constitutus, et magna animi virtute, et Sapientiae abundantia
his omnibus multum profecto maior es. Et ita ad hanc regendam
familiam Christianam natus esse videris, ut nemini certe melius,
quam Tibi, potuisset haec cura demandari. Quis enim diligentius
Christianae huius familiae diversitates omnes comprehendere, quis
singulorum membrorum infirmitates sapientius cognoscere, quis
singulis infirmitatibus propria remedia diligentius inquirere, facilius
invenire, aut maiori pietate apponere potuisset?

Existimamus enim nos, Beatissime Pater, Te, cum primum ad
hanc sublimitatem Apostolicae Sedis pervenisti, inde, tamquam ex
eminentissima quadam specula, omnem Christianam familiam, uno
quasi intuitu mentis tuae acie comprehendisse. Si enim nihil aliud
Episcopus est, quam speculator, Tu Episcoporum Episcopus effectus,
super omnes speculatores diligentissimus speculator in eminentissima specula constitutus, perspicacissimo lumine intueri iam potuisti,
familiam hanc tuam multas, magnasque continere hominum diversitates. Alii namque sunt in ea, qui, quoniam hoc saeculum, hanc
vitam, quam in terris agimus, mente transcendere nequeunt, neque
caelestia, aeternaque noverunt terrenis his, et caducis rebus praeponere, saeculares appellantur. Alii vero, qui, propterea quod Deo,
a quo fragilitate, imbecillitateque humanae huius naturae saepius
discedunt, per Divini cultus frequentiam, per mandatorum observantiam, per terrenarum rerum despectum, per sui ipsius denique
abnegationem, continue se coniungere, ac relegare contendunt, Religiosi appellari soliti sunt. In utroque vero genere magnae diversitates.
Saecularium enim hominum, alii nobiles sunt, qui scilicet aliqua
ceteris dignitate praecellunt; alii autem inferiores, ut vulgus; Religiosorum consimili, eademque omnino ratione, alii sunt, qui superiorem
locum, eminentiorem dignitatem, regendi potestatem tenent; alii vero
inferiori sunt loco constituti, qui si recte conditionis suae servant
instituta, pro maxima dignitate ducunt, omni carere dignitate. Haec
maiora quaedam sunt totius Ecclesiae membra, quae tamen multas in
se diversitates continent. Sicut enim totum corpus in multa maiora
membra dividimus, ipsaque deinceps singula membra, diversa alia
minora membra obtinent; sic sane haec ipsa, quae numeravimus
Ecclesiae membra,

[669], and the entire multitude of Christians amounts to many householders; but you, whom the Lord has established as the head of this house, with your great virtue and abundant wisdom, are much greater than these. You seem to have been born for the task of ruling this Christian family, so that surely no one other than you could have been asked to undertake this office. Who could better have comprehended all the varieties of this household, or more wisely diagnosed the infirmities of its individual members, or more diligently sought, more easily found, and more tenderly applied the remedies proper to each?

We believe that when you first ascended the apostolic throne, you could perceive with one glance of the mind's eye, as if from a lofty vantage point, the entire Christian household. Indeed, if a bishop (*episcopus*) is really an Overseer, then you, as the Bishop of bishops, being established on a lofty vantage point as the most diligent overseer over all overseers, can already perceive with the clearest sight this household of yours, which contains such a great diversity of people. In it there are some who, because they cannot transcend this world and the life we live here, and do not know how to place celestial and eternal things before those that are earthly and corruptible, are called men of the world (*saeculares*). There are others who often withdraw from God through the weakness and fragility of human nature, but endeavor to reunite and reconnect (*relegare*) with him by assisting in divine worship and observing the commandments,[38] by contempt for earthly things and self-denial; these are called "religious." In both classes, however, there is a considerable variety. For among men of the world, some are noble—those who excel the rest in social position—while others are inferior, the common crowd. Among religious, by a similar reckoning, there are some who hold a higher place and a more elevated station with the power to govern, while others are placed in an inferior position, and who, if they rightly observe the rules of their state, consider it the greatest dignity to be without dignity. These are, as it were, the greater members of the whole Church, but they contain many varieties within themselves. For just as we divide the whole body into many larger members, which themselves possess other, smaller members, so too the members of the Church that we have just listed contain

---

38 "The work of obedience will bring you back to him from whom you had drifted by the sloth of disobedience," Rule of St. Benedict, Prologue.

[670] singula multa, infinitaque minora ab invicem diversa membra continere, Tuam latere Sapientiam non potest, quae per singula recensere laboriosum sane esset, et minus fortasse ad curationem necessarium. Si enim totius huius infirmi corporis maiora, potioraque haec membra congruis, ac salutaribus appositis medicamentis convalescent, et minora etiam illa omnia, quae illorum partes quasdam esse constat, sanitatem consequentur. Has, Beatissime Pater, familiae tuae diversitates, quasi magni cuiusdam Corporis membra, Sapientiae Tuae oculis conspiciens, singulorumque varios languores considerans (in nullo enim plena sanitas est) magnae illius pietatis Tuae abundantia omnibus Te iam praeparare saluberrima medicamenta non dubitamus, singulisque pro singulorum necessitate, atque opportunitate, Te ministrare, atque inservire paratum credimus. Aliter enim neque illum imitari velle videberis, qui non ministrari, sed ministrare se advenisse aiebat, neque nobilissimum illud nomen, quo, qui Summi Sacerdotii dignitate decorantur, appellari solent, merito Tibi vindicare poteris. Omnibus enim Christi membris languescentibus, nisi singulis pro singulorum necessitate inservire studueris, Servus Servorum Dei dici quidem poteris, esse autem non poteris.

Cum vero non omnes uno morbo teneantur, non uno omnes languoris genere laborent, sed multiplicibus, variisque infirmitatibus premantur, considerasse Beatitudinem Tuam diligentissime, omnibusque aliis perfectius persensisse credimus, alias graves esse totius Christiani populi infirmitates, quibus praesentis vitae statum minus quiete, minusque placide agere permittitur; alias vero his multo graviores, quibus ad aeternae vitae felicitatem via nobis praecluditur, aditusque denegatur; et sicut duo sunt haec infirmitatum genera, ita duplici ex fonte haec eadem in Christianos populos derivari[54] Tibi incognitum esse non potest. Sentis enim, Beatissime Pater, illa omnia, quae Christianum populum minus quiete, minusque tranquille, hanc peregrinationis humanae vitam ducere permittunt, in omnibus Christianis hominibus ex paucorum Regum, Principum, Potentiorumque regnandi libidine, dominandi ambitione, avaritiaque, et aliis huiuscemodi vitiis derivantia reperiri; illa vero, quae perveniendi ad Beatae Patriae veram tranquillitatem, viam, aditumquae praecludunt, ex Religiosorum hominum ignorantia, superstitione, aliisque his non

54   derivari MS: derivare ED

[670] many individual parts. This Your Holiness knows quite well, and it would, perhaps, be tedious to list them, and unnecessary for their proper care. If one applies appropriate and salutary remedies to the greater and stronger members of a sick body, and these get better, all those smaller parts, since they belong to the larger, will also become healthy. And so, Holy Father, as you cast a wise glance upon the diversity of your household, like the members of a great body, and consider the infirmities of each one—for none is completely healthy—we are counting on the great abundance of your kindness to prepare healthful remedies for all and to administer and attend to them according to the special requirements of each. Otherwise, you will not show your willingness to imitate the One who said he had come not to be served, but to serve (Matt 20:28), nor will you earn the noble name by which we call those are invested with the office of Chief Priest. For if all the members of Christ are languishing and you fail to attend to the needs of each, you may be called "Servant of the Servants of God,"[39] but you will not be so in fact.

Since, however, they are not all gripped by the same disease, nor suffer from the same kind of weakness, but are oppressed by many and various infirmities, Your Holiness has no doubt carefully considered and most clearly perceived that some grave infirmities afflict the whole Christian people, allowing it to enjoy this present life less quietly and peacefully, while others are much more serious, since they bar access to the joy of eternal life. Moreover, just as there are these two sorts of infirmities, there are likewise two sources, as you know well, from which Christians derive them. You observe, Holy Father, that all the things that prevent the Christian people from making this life-long pilgrimage more quietly and peacefully derive from the ambition and lust for power of a few kings, princes, and rulers, while those that bar access to the true peace of our blessed homeland spread among the people

---

39   Pope Gregory the Great was the first to use this phrase for himself. Many popes have followed the practice.

dissimilibus malis in omne Christianum vulgus,

[671] quasi ex fonte diffundi, aut ex radice ortum suum habere.
Quare si Sapientia, Pietasque Tua paucorum Potentiorum regnandi,
iniusteque rapiendi libidinem coercere, et male Religiosorum hominum vitia emendare studuerit, facillime certe toti populo Christiano
pacem, tranquillitatem, et unanimitatis Caritatem in hac vita reddes,
et ad aeternae tranquillitatis, et pacis fruitionem in Beata illa Caelorum Patria aditum reserabis, et totum hoc Christianae Reipublicae
corpus, quod languidum, infirmumque, et morti vicinum, Tibi,
tamquam peritissimo Medico, a Domino commissum est, sanitati,
salutique restitues, et antiqui decoris, et pulchritudinis eius stola
ornatum ostendes; ut qualem fuisse in primordiis Fidei, Christianae Religionis pietatem, puritatem, simplicitatemque in plerisque
legimus, talem in hoc postremo saeculorum fine intueri, Te auctore,
immo Te ministro, valeamus. Bonorum enim omnium unus auctor
Deus ipse Optimus Maximus est; Creaturae vero omnes non solum,
quae in terra, sed quae in Caelis etiam sunt, si boni aliquid operari
videntur, ministri, et instrumenta summae illius Bonitatis, et Potenti-
ae existimari debent.

Tu vero, Beatissime Pater, secundum Apostolicam admonitionem
ministerium tuum implebis, si ante omnia Christianorum Regum,
Principum, et Potentiorum hominum miseram bellorum rabiem,
qua sibi ipsis imprimis, et omni deinceps Christiano populo pacem,
tranquillitatem adimunt, sedare, atque reprimere curabis, et arma
ipsa, quae contra semetipsos Christiani quasi in propriis visceribus
saevientes, praeteritis annis exercuerunt, et nunc ad eundem usum
parata habent, contra saevissimos Christiani nominis, Christianae
Fidei, Christianaeque libertatis hostes moveri, exercerique pro
Tua Sapientia, et auctoritate persuadere, atque imperare non dissimulabis; et quod peritiores Medicorum facere consueverunt, si hos
crudiores, iniquioresque odiorum humores, ampliandique Regni
ambitiones, quae non facile extrahi, consumi, evacuari, regularique
possunt, ex nobilioribus membris ad aliam quandam ignobiliorem
partem, ubi aut minori, aut nullo penitus cum sanitatis discrimine,
futuri sint, divertere tentabis. Pacem vero ante omnia Te Christianis
populis dare velle ideo credimus, quoniam eius Tu in Terris locum
tenes, qui oriendo ex alto, pacem in Terris attulit, qui vivendo, pacem
habendam docuit, qui ascendens ad Caelos, pacem nobis quasi propriam hereditatem reliquit

[671] like water from the fountain, or grow like a plant from the root, of ignorance, superstition, and other similar vices of religious. And so, if you apply your wisdom and goodness to constrain the lust for rule and for unjust seizure of those few powerful men and to emend the evil vices of religious, you will surely and easily restore peace, tranquility, and the charity of heartfelt unity to the Christian people in this life, and you will open the way to the enjoyment of eternal peace and tranquility in that blessed land of Heaven. By the same token, you will restore health and well-being to this body of the Christian Commonwealth, which the Lord has entrusted in its weakened, diseased, and moribund condition to you as to a skilled physician, and you will display it clothed in its ancient beauty and splendor, so that in these latter days we shall see the original piety, purity, and simplicity of the Christian religion, about which we read, and this will be thanks to your initiative—or rather, to your service. For the sole author of all good things is God, the Greatest Good, and all creatures in heaven as well as on earth, if they seem to do any good, must be regarded as the servants and instruments of that supreme goodness and power.

But you, Holy Father, will fulfill your ministry according to the apostle's exhortation if, above all things, you work to calm and suppress the wretched madness of war among Christian kings, princes, and leaders, by which they deprive themselves as well as the Christian people of peace and tranquility, and if you sincerely persuade and command these Christians—who in recent years, like madmen, have trained arms against themselves as if against their own breasts, and who now hold them ready for the same use—to turn and train those arms against the savage enemies of the Christian faith and Christian liberty. Thus, you will be acting as a skilled physician, if you divert the crude and impure humors of hatred and the ambition for extended rule—humors which cannot easily be extracted, consumed, evacuated, or regulated—from the higher members to some lower part, where they will do less harm, or indeed no harm, to the health of the body. We have confidence in your intention to bring peace to the Christian peoples because you are taking the earthly place of the One who, as the Orient from on high (Luke 1:78), brought peace on earth, and in his life taught the obligation of peace, and when he rose to heaven left us his peace as his peculiar legacy, as it were,

[672] et Deus Pacis saepius ab Apostolo suo appellari voluit. Scisque praeterea, quod si pacem familiae tuae, Christiano scilicet populo dederis, cum pace bona omnia dabis. Sine pace autem, etiamsi multa alia dare coneris, nihil omnino dedisse videberis, quoniam sine pacis bono, nihil omnino est, quod bonum esse existimari possit. Et vere, nisi ante omnia Christianos Principes ad pacis iura conciliare Tibi a Domino permissum fuerit, nihil est, quod in hoc Tuo Pontificatus officio Deo gratum, aut hominibus utile Te facere posse sperandum sit. Pace autem confecta, nihil tam magnum, tamque arduum est, quod non facillime Te consequi posse, sit apertissimum.

Pacem autem Christianis omnibus reddere poteris, si proposita contra Turcas expeditione, eos in omnes Fidei nostrae hostes arma convertere persuadebis, si ex Romanorum Cardinalium numero ad Hispanos, ad Gallos, ad Britannos, ad Helvetios, ad Pannones, ad Venetos, Tua,[55] Apostolicaeque Sedis auctoritate Legatos pro pace conficienda destinaveris; si priusquam ipsi ad proprias Legationes accedant, pluribus privatis internuntiis, nunc minis, nunc blandis pollicitationibus Christianorum Principum animos ad eas suscipiendas, quas pro Sapientia Tua pacis conditiones proposueris, persuadere curabis. Tanta enim apud omnes Christianorum nationes Pontificis semper fuit auctoritas, quod Te (si haec omnia feceris) aut ad pacem, aut ad indutias, propositis quibuscumque conditionibus, conducere posse, nequaquam desperamus. Et quamquam Christiani Principes omnes universum Italiae Imperium, aut ex animo optare, aut suasionibus quibusdam sperare videantur, si tamen ditiora, et ampliora Europae, Asiaeque Imperia ipsis proposueris, si huius sanctae expeditionis facilitatem declaraveris, nemini dubium esse posse credimus, hos omnes pacis, indutiarumque conditiones suscipere velle, et arma contra impios Fidei nostrae inimicos convertere. Tu modo, quod Tuum est, Pater Beatissime, in expeditione proponenda, in Legatis destinandis, in Christianorum Principum animis disponendis, prius omnia consulendo, et de Domini Iesu Christi auxilio nequaquam diffidendo, nulla interposita mora adimpleas.

Quoniam autem vera pax esse non poterit, ubi iustitiae aequitas defuerit, ideo iustitiam paci coniungere Te curaturum speramus, ut in diebus tuis ortam esse iustitiam, pacisque abundantiam dicere valeamus. Iustitiae autem munera cum multa sint, ea Te

---

55   Tua MS, *Barletta*: Tuae ED

[672] and who willed that his Apostle should often call him "the God of peace" (Rom 15:30, 16:20; Phil 4:9). You know, moreover, that if you give peace to your household, which is the Christian people, you will give them all good things along with it. Without peace, however, even if you try to give them many other things, you will seem to have given them nothing; for without the good of peace, nothing can be considered good. Truly, unless the Lord permits you before all else to reconcile Christian princes to the laws of peace, you cannot hope to do anything in your pontificate that is pleasing to God and useful to men. When peace has been achieved, however, there will clearly be nothing too great or arduous for you to accomplish, and that with ease.

Now, you will be able to bring peace to all Christians if you propose an expedition against the Turks and persuade them to turn their arms against all the enemies of our Faith. You will accomplish this if you send Roman Cardinals as peacemakers on behalf of yourself and the Holy See to the Spaniards, the French, the Britons, the Swiss, the Hungarians, and the Venetians, and if, before these have reached their embassies, you try to persuade Christian princes through private communications, using both threats and enticing promises, to accept the terms of peace which you in your wisdom will propose to them. For such is the authority of the Pontiff among all Christian nations that you will surely be able to bring about either a peace treaty or a truce with any terms you propose. While it is true that all Christian princes seem inwardly to desire, or from the persuasion of others to hope for the control of all Italy, nevertheless, if you set before them richer and ampler realms in Europe and Asia, and make clear to them the ease of this holy expedition, no one can doubt that they all will be willing to accept terms of peace and truce and turn their arms against the impious enemies of our Faith. As for you, Holy Father, only fulfill your part at once in proposing the expedition, choosing your ambassadors, and rightly disposing the minds of Christian princes, by planning everything first and never despairing of the help of our Lord, Jesus Christ.

Since true peace cannot exist, however, where justice and fairness are absent, we hope that you will take care to combine justice with peace, so that we can say that in your days, "Justice sprang up and an abundance of peace" (Ps 72:7). Since the obligations of justice are many, however,

[673] potissimum servare velle existimamus, quae Ecclesiae, Christianorumque populorum omnium libertatem respiciunt. Si enim Christianis Principibus, et aliis Civitatum Rectoribus prohibueris, Ecclesiasticas Personas Decimis, aut exactionibus quibuscumque onerare, si nullo modo permiseris homines cuiuscumque Dignitatis fuerint, aut Virorum collegia, aut etiam Respublicas ad Ecclesiasticarum dignitatum electionem procedere; si perversam consuetudinem, quae in plerisque locis invaluit, ut ad possessionem Ecclesiarum capessendam armati homines accedant, tua fregeris auctoritate, et his similia multa, quae res Christiana postulare videtur, et Tu melius omnibus cognoscere poteris; si opportuna facere remedia non dissimulabis, Ecclesiae libertatem, quod iustitiae maximum munus est, conservabis. Si vero Christianos populos a Potentiorum oppressione liberare cupiens, violentas cuiuscumque generis exactiones, iniqua, et multum ab aequitate aliena pedagia ex omnibus Christianorum civitatibus, aut auferre, aut moderari pro Tua auctoritate curabis; si usurarum pessimum crimen, quo Potentiores sanguinem pauperum exsorbent, delere volens, Iudaeis foenerari nullo modo permittes; Christianos vero a faeneratione, sub quocumque velamine fieri soleat, mortis poena proposita, deterrebis; si litium, causarumque longa dispendia abstuleris, omnemque controversiam, non ad libelli examinationem, sed ad summariam aequitatis definitionem deduxeris; si Iudicum quoque, et eorum, qui Iudiciis inserviunt, avaritiam tuo moderamine temperabis; si appellationes, quae nimium certe ab ea, propter quam institutae sunt, semita aberrarunt, ad legitimum usum revocabis; si Hospitalium bona usurpari, quemadmodum nunc sit a Potentioribus, non permittes, sed Apostolica auctoritate ad eos usus, in quos relicta sunt, converti curabis; si tertiam partem bonorum singularum Ecclesiarum, secundum sacras Canonum definitiones, in pauperes erogari imperabis; si piratis, ac praedonibus neque portum concedi, neque ea, quae victui, aut navigationi necessaria sunt, ministrari, anathematis poena proposita, mandare volueris; si alia huiuscemodi plurima, quae quantum sint Christiano populo necessaria, optime nosti, facere Beatitudinem tuam non pigebit, Christianorum populorum commodis optime consuluisse videberis.

Quae ideo sunt a Te, Beatissime Pater, amplius appetenda, ardentiusque aggredienda, quoniam, dum

[673] we suppose that you will wish to fulfill those which particularly relate to the liberty of the Church and Christian peoples. You will preserve the liberty of the Church, which is the greatest requirement of justice, if you forbid Christian princes and all leaders to burden ecclesiastical persons with tithes and other exactions; if you refuse to allow men of any rank or associations of men or indeed entire states to become involved in the awarding of ecclesiastical honors; if you use your authority to break the perverse custom, which obtains in many places, whereby armed men take possession of churches; if you boldly uncover many other opportune remedies, which the interests of Christianity evidently require and which you know better than anyone. You will seem to have attended to the needs of Christians very well indeed, if you are willing to free the Christian people from the oppression of powerful men, and to use your authority either to remove or to control violent exactions of every sort and unfair and unjust taxes in all Christian states; to erase the wicked crime of usury, by which the powerful soak up the blood of the poor, to prohibit Jews from lending at interest and to deter Christians from making interest-bearing loans under any pretense, on penalty of death; to eliminate the huge waste of court cases and lawsuits, and to resolve every dispute not by examining legal briefs, but by a summary statement of fairness; to temper with your moderation the avarice of judges and other officers of the law, and to recall the appeal process, which has certainly strayed from the path on which it was established, to its proper use; to prevent the endowments of hospitals from being usurped, as they currently are, by powerful individuals, and to exercise your authority so that they revert to the uses for which they have been left; to command that a third part of the goods of churches,[40] in accordance with the Holy Canons, be spent on the poor; to stipulate, on pain of excommunication, that neither harborage nor any supplies or equipment be given to pirates or thieves; and boldly to undertake many other such measures, which, as Your Holiness knows quite well, are necessary for the Christian people.

These measures, Holy Father, should be all the more aggressively pursued, since

---

40   Gratian (12th century) in his *Decretum* records, on the basis of traditions going back to the end of the fifth century, that one fourth of the churches' resources be given to the poor. The canonists in the Middle Ages sometimes cited one third as the amount for the needy.

[674] his artibus pacis tranquillitatem, iustitiaequae aequitatem et
huius vitae commoda pauperibus, et populis Christianis dare conaris,
Potentioribus non minus, ac divitibus viam aeternae felicitatis Te
aperire cognoscis. Dum enim Potentiores quosque ab iniustitiis, et
rapinis compescere studes, una et subditorum tranquillitati, et commodo consulis, et aeternae Potentiorum saluti Te consulere certum
est; qui dum tranquillitatem, et vitae commoda[56] populis auferunt,
ipsi sibi ante omnes aeternae salutis felicitatem adimunt; cum vero
pacis tranquillitatem, iustitiaeque aequitatem Christiano populo reddideris, omnia huius terrenae vitae incommoda, perturbationesque
omnes certissime abstuleris.

Haec enim potissima, solaque illa sunt, quae si desint, humanum
genus non secus ac navis sine gubernatoribus in saevissimo pelago
variis ventis commota, omnibus perturbationibus, incommodis,
miseriisque in hoc mare magnum, et spatiosum huius vitae agitatur;
si vero adsint, omnem humanae vitae cursum, tranquillitatis, iucun-
ditatisque plenissimum reddunt, et ad instar caelestis illius felicissi-
mae vitae hanc terreni incolatus nostri vitam effingunt, ita ut, si haec
duo, pacem scilicet, et iustitiam Christianis hominibus reddideris,
in his, quae ad hanc vitam pertinent, omnia certe reddidisse videberis, nihilque Tibi reliquum futurum est, nisi ut perfectam Religionis Christianae observantiam, per quam futuram vitam acquirere
possumus, instituere, immo reparare, atque instaurare satagas, ut
scilicet Religiosorum hominum ignorantia, superstitione, avaritia,
aliisque huiuscemodi Religioni contrariis vitiis depulsis, quae et illis
ipsis Religiosis hominibus, et prorsus omni populo Christiano viam
aditumque aeternae Beatitudinis praecludunt; Tu Religionis perfecta
observantia instaurata, erroribusque omnibus expulsis, viam ad aeternae Beatitudinis felicitatem ostendas, et aditum beatae, caelestisque
vitae omnibus pariter Christianis aperias. Et vero vitia, quae puram
Religionis Christianae observantiam perturbant, Christianaeque
simplicitatis, et perfectionis mores corrumpunt, et proinde viam,
aditumque aeternae Beatitudinis praecludunt, sicut omnia a Religiosis hominibus oriri certissimum est, ita notum est, quaedam ex illis
esse, quae a Religiosis in populorum vulgus derivant, quae scilicet
non secus, quam saevissimae viperae illos ipsos, a quibus oriuntur,
Religiosos viros ante alios miserrime perimunt, totumque deinceps
Christianum

---

56 commoda MS: commodum ED

[674] you know that by endeavoring to bring the tranquility of peace and the standard of fairness along with the good things of life to the poor and common Christian peoples, you are opening the way of eternal beatitude to the rich and powerful, as well. Indeed, it is certain that when you restrain the powerful from injustice and depredation and attend to the tranquility and comfort of their subjects, you are also looking after the salvation of the powerful, who deprive no one so much as themselves of the joys of eternal felicity when they rob their people of the enjoyment of life. When, however, you restore the tranquility of peace and the standard of justice to the Christian people, you will certainly eliminate all the miseries and disturbances of this earthly life.

These two are the main things, indeed the only things, without which the human race, driven like a ship without a helmsman by contrary winds on violent waves, is tossed about by troubles, suffering and misery on the great and spacious sea of this life. When these two are present, however, they fill the entire course of human life with tranquility and joy, and make this earthly life of our sojourning like that blessed life of heaven. And so, if you give these two gifts, peace and justice, to Christians, you will seem to have given them everything that pertains to this life, and there will remain nothing for you to do but to establish, or rather to repair and restore the perfect observance of the Christian religion, through which we can acquire the life to come. When you put down the ignorance, superstition, avarice, and other vices contrary to religious profession that one finds in religious, and which block for them and for all Christians the way to eternal blessedness, and when you restore the perfect observance of religious life and eliminate all error, you will have shown the way to eternal beatitude and will have opened for all Christians the door to the blessed life of heaven. Indeed, the vices that disturb the true and pure observance of the Christian religion, which corrupt the practices of Christian simplicity and perfection, and which block the way to eternal blessedness, all arise from the religious. It is well known, moreover, that some of them flow from the religious into the common people and, like ferocious vipers, first kill the religious from which they originate, and then infect the entire Christian people

[675] populum venenis omnibus inficiunt, et quasi communis pestis
nemini omnino parcunt; quaedam autem, quae ab ipsis Religiosis
orientia, et in illis ipsis cotidie crescentia, quasi infestissimi vermi-
culi, et mordacissimae tineae totum Religionis corpus consumunt, et
Christianae Fidei puritatem, decorem, pulchritudinemque corrumpunt. Haec autem mala omnia, quae in Christiana Republica pestes
quasdam, seu Christianae Religionis hostes appellare possumus,
multa varia, ac innumerabilia paene sunt. Eorum autem maxima, ac
saeviora haec nos esse existimamus, ignorantia, superstitio, dissensio,
ambitio, avaritia, divitiarum abundantia, et propriarum regularum,
professionumque minor, quam deceat, observantia, quorum superiora duo a religiosis hominibus initium sumentia illis, populisque
omnibus communia sunt; reliqua vero illis ipsis, a quibus oriuntur, si
ad aeternae vitae acquisitionem spectes, peculiaria mala existimantur,
quoniam Christiano populo aeternae vitae aditum non praecludunt,
praesentis tamen vitae tranquillitatem saepissime, et gravissime
perturbant. Tu vero, Beatissime Pater, solus es, qui quasi peritissi-
mus medicus a Domino ad familiam suam curandam vocatus, has
a Christiana Tibi commissa Republica pestes amovere potes; et qui
solus hos Christianae fidei hostes, quasi saevissimos intra Dominicum Tibi commissum ovile ab adversario immissos lupos, non sicut
mercenarium fugere, sed debellare, et ad nihilum reducere debes,
si veri, legitimique Pastoris, non nomen tantum, sed munus in hac
peregrinatione implere, et praemium in aeterna patria possidere
desideras.

Horum autem, quae numeravimus, maximum et malorum omnium
caput, causamque ignorantiam esse, nemo est, qui possit ambigere;
quae quidem tanto gravior, periculosiorque infirmitas est, quanto
magis in illis vigere comprehenditur, qui non solum scire ipsi debuerant, sed ad alios docendos, et instituendos ordinati esse videntur.
Nulla enim paene salutis spes reliqua existimatur, ubi medici, qui
languentes alios curare habeant, eadem ipsi infirmitate gravissime
laborent.[57] Quanta autem, qualisve nunc in Ecclesia Dei in religiosis
hominibus omnibus ignorantia sit, sicut neminem prorsus latere
potest,[58] ita nullus omnino est, qui pro merito valeat explicare. Milia
multa religiosorum hominum invenies, qui neque legere quidem,
neque scribere mediocriter sciunt. In omni autem tam numerosa
Religiosorum multitudine vix duo ex centum, aut decem

---

57   habeant...laborent: habebant...laborant MS, habebant...laborent ED
58   potest MS: poterit ED

[675] with their venom, and like a common plague show mercy to no one. Other vices, however, which originate and daily grow among people in religious life, are like foul worms and hungry maggots, which consume the entire Christian body and corrupt the purity, seemliness, and beauty of the Christian Faith. These ills, which we may call the plagues and enemies of the Christian Commonwealth, are many, varied, and almost beyond reckoning; but the greatest and most harmful of them are, in our opinion, ignorance, superstition, dissension, ambition, avarice, abundant wealth, and the inadequate observance of one's own rules and profession. Of these, the first two originate among religious, but are the common ills of all people, while the rest are peculiar to those among whom they arise, if you consider the goal of acquiring eternal life. They do not prevent the Christian people from reaching eternity, but they frequently and seriously disturb the tranquility of the present life. You, Holy Father, are the only one who, like a skilled physician summoned by the Lord to treat his household, can remove these diseases from the Commonwealth entrusted to your care, and the only one who, when faced with these enemies of the Christian Faith, which the enemy has sent like savage wolves into the sheepfold that the Lord has entrusted to you, will not flee like a hired hand, but can overcome and annihilate them—if indeed you wish to play the part of a true and authentic shepherd in fact, and not merely in name, and to obtain your reward in our eternal home.

Now, the greatest and chief of the evils that I have listed and the cause of them all is ignorance, no one can doubt. This infirmity is all the graver and more dangerous when it flourishes among those who not only should possess knowledge themselves, but have been appointed to teach and inform others. For there is obviously no hope left when physicians, who have the job of caring for others in their sickness, are seriously afflicted with the same illness themselves. Now, the magnitude and quality of the ignorance that can be found among religious in God's Church is as difficult to explain as it is obvious to all. You will find many thousands who can neither read nor write even passably well. Moreover, in this vast multitude of religious, you can find scarcely two out of ten or ten

[676] e mille reperies, qui tantum Latinae linguae addiscerint, ut
quae Latino sermone conscripta cotidie in Ecclesiis legunt, plane
valeant intellegere; ex his vero, qui intellegunt, paucos admodum
invenies, qui ulterius ad aliquam disciplinarum, atque scientiarum
cognitionem progressi sint; ex paucissimis vero illis, qui litterarum
studiis incumbere quoquo modo videntur, rarus quippe est, qui non
Poetarum potius mendacia, aut Philosophorum impietatem, quam
Christianam pietatem amplexus sit; ex rarissimis vero illis, qui veram,
solamque Philosophiam, Christianam Disciplinam sequuntur, vix
unum, aut alterum invenies, qui non inanissima recentiorum Scriptorum argumenta, simultatum sane, odiorumque irritamenta, potius
quam Sacrarum Scripturarum, antiquaque Patrum documenta
sectetur; qui non inanibus quaestionibus, quae ad nihilum quidem
utiles sunt, potius quam Sanctorum Evangeliorum lectionibus occupetur; qui denique non illam potius vanam, quae inflat, quae extollit,
disputativam disciplinam, quam illam sanctam, puram, castamque
Sacrarum Scripturarum, quae inflammat, et humiliat, doctrinam
sequatur. Et si unum, aut alterum huiuscemodi reperire fortasse
poteris, numquid tantum profecisse ullum omnino invenies, ut in
tota Ecclesia Dei hoc saeculo aliquem unum habeas, quem possis
cum antiquioribus illis Patribus, quibus Graeca, et Latina Ecclesia
praeteritis saeculis abundavit, comparare. Tanta vero cum sit religiosorum ignorantia, quanta ceterorum hominum inscitia existimanda
sit, quilibet facile elicere potest. Unde certe dolere magis, admirari
vero minus decet, si multi errores, ac falsae plurimae opiniones a fidei
veritate alienae, et multa Religioni,[59] Christianaeque pietati adversa
religiosos ipsos[60] homines, et Christianam plebem occupent, oppri-
mantque, et miserabiliter per ignorantiae caecitatem, ad aeternarum
tenebrarum miseriam ducant. Dum enim caecum vulgus caecum
religiosorum ordinem sequitur, illud evenit, quod a Domino in Evangelio dictum est, ut ambo in aeternae perditionis, et miseriae foveam
simul dilabantur, et cadant.

Huic tamen magno malo, malorum, aut omnium, aut certe plurimorum origini sapientiam Tuam multa iam, efficacissimaque remedia
excogitasse credimus, ut depravata nunc omnium litterarum studia
rectius instituantur, neglegentiores quique ad studia provocentur,
studere volentibus commoda, in studiis vero proficientibus praemia

---

59   Religioni *Barletta*: religiosi MS, Religionis ED
60   ipsos MS: istos ED

[676] out of a thousand who have learned enough Latin to understand clearly the texts that they read in church. Of these, you will find fewer still who have made any progress in the knowledge of the arts and sciences, and among the very few who seem to have given any study to letters, rare indeed is the man who has embraced Christian piety rather than the lies of poets and the impiety of philosophers. Finally, among that rare breed of men who devote themselves to the one true philosophy and to Christian learning, you will find scarcely one or two who do not pursue the empty arguments of modern writers and their disturbing quarrels and disagreements, in preference to the teaching of the Holy Scriptures and the ancient fathers; who are not occupied with empty and utterly useless questions, rather than the reading of the Holy Gospels; who, finally, do not pursue the art of disputation, which elates men's souls and puffs them up, rather than the holy, pure, and chaste teaching of the Holy Scriptures, which kindles their souls and makes them humble. And even if you can find one or two such men, you will never find anyone in the entire Church of God in this age who has progressed to the point that he can be compared to the ancient fathers, of whom the Church, both Greek and Latin, once had a surplus. Now, if such is the ignorance of religious, one can readily calculate that of other men. Thus, one has more cause to grieve than to wonder that many errors and countless false and extraneous opinions and other obstacles to religious life and Christian piety are taking hold of religious and the entire Christian people, and, sadly, are leading them through blind ignorance to the misery of eternal darkness. For when the blind crowd follows the blind order of religious, the Lord's saying in the Gospel is fulfilled (Matt 15:14): both slip and fall into the pit of eternal perdition and wretchedness.

Nevertheless, your wisdom has no doubt come up with many efficacious remedies for this great evil, which is the origin of all, or at least of most evils, so that the study of letters, which is now debased, will be rightly established, and that those who neglect their studies will be brought back to them, and that advantages will be given to those who wish to study and prizes offered to those who make progress.

[677] proponantur; nemo enim est, qui depravata, contaminataque,
et corrupta penitus studia emendare, recte instituere possit, nisi Tu
unus, Beatissime Pater. Quae quidem reparari, et meliorem familiam
instruere poterunt, si praeter eos, qui Gentilium litteris incumbunt,
Dialecticorum cavillationes, ingeniorum certe depravationes, quae
sophistica ars appellari solet, in qua sine aliqua utilitate iuniores
et tempus, et ingenium conterunt, Te iubente, ita prohibeantur, ut
nullus sit, qui deinceps eam valeat publice profiteri; si tot modernorum hominum commentaria, quae nihil aliud sunt, quam illa, quae
a veteribus auctoribus diligentissime conscripta sunt, novis voluminibus deterius explicata, in ea potissimum disciplina, quae per
quaestiones traditur, locum omnino habere non permittantur; sed et
veteribus auctoribus, his scilicet, qui legitime res ipsas pertractant,
aliquis locus, honorque concedatur, si nemini, non dicam scribere,
sed edere scripta liceat, nisi ea fuerint ab aliquibus doctioribus, qui
a Te instituti sint, approbata, atque digna, ut edantur iudicata; si in
omnibus studiis non expositores auctorum, sed ipsi auctores potius
legantur. Mirum enim est, et miserabile, quantum temporis consu-
mimus, dum expositores omnes perquirimus, et nihil addiscimus de
his, quae facilius addiscere poteramus, si in auctorum potius, quam in
expositorum lectione insudare voluissemus.

Haec, Sanctissime Pater, aliaque huiuscemodi plurima, quae Tua,
omnibus prudentius, excogitare sapientia potest, si institueris,
Gentilia etiam ipsa studia multum iuvare poteris, quamquam nisi
ad divina studia, et ad sacras litteras haec Gentilia studia dirigantur,
nihil omnino curiosius, nihil vanius, nihil sine fructu laboriosius,
nihil denique a Christianis hominibus magis alienum existimari
debet, quam haec ipsa Poetarum, Oratorum Gentiliumque auctorum studia; unde tunc maxime recte studia instituere Te iudicabi-
mus, cum pueris et ipsis, pro Gentilibus Oratoribus, pro Gentilibus
fabulis, Christianam veritatem, Christianosque Scriptores proponi
iusseris. Habent enim et suos Christiani historiographos, habent
et suos Oratores, quos in utraque pariter lingua, Graeca scilicet, et
Latina cum Gentilibus conferre non erubescimus. Si enim hoc a Te
iussum fuerit, incipient Christiani homines, non linguis addiscendis
sine aliquo alio fructu aetatem omnem conterere, sed et linguam
Graecam, et Latinam, ac Christianam simul disciplinam addiscere.

[677] No one but you, Holy Father, can repair and restore the studies that have been thoroughly corrupted, debased, and contaminated. They can be repaired, however, and can produce a better instructed household, if, apart from the study of pagan literature, you abolish the dialectical quibbles and the perversion of intelligence that we call the "sophistical" art, in which young men uselessly squander their time and intelligence, and you see to it that no one dares to teach it publicly; if all those modern commentaries, which are nothing other than inferior explanations of the careful investigations of the ancients, are abolished, especially in subjects organized around controversial topics; if the place of honor is given instead to ancient authors who correctly treat the matter at hand; if no one is allowed to publish—I will not say, to write—anything that has not been approved and judged worthy of publication by more learned men, whom you have appointed; if, in all one's studies, one reads not the expounders of authors, but the authors themselves. Indeed, it is amazing and regrettable how much time we spend going through all the commentators, while we learn nothing that we might not have gained more easily by pouring over the original authors.

If you take these steps and others that you will have discovered in your superior wisdom, you will do much for the study of the classical authors, as well. Nevertheless, if studying the classics does not lead to divine subjects and sacred literature, there can be nothing more trivial, empty, fruitless, and inappropriate for Christians than the study of pagan orators and poets. Accordingly, we believe that you will put education on the best footing when you order that, in the place of pagan orators and fables, children should be taught Christian truth and Christian writers. Christians have their own historians and orators in both languages, Greek and Latin, which we do not blush to compare with the pagans. If you give the command, Christians will no longer spend their whole lives learning languages with no further benefit, but will acquire Greek and Latin and Christian learning at the same time.

[678] Proderit ad hoc, si antiqua illa Sanctorum Patrum, Sacrorumque Canonum Decreta instaurari curabis, quibus cautum est, ut in locis, ubi studia litterarum vigent, sint semper, qui Christianam Theologiam, non hanc Parisiensium cavillosiorem disciplinam, sed puram illam Sanctarum, Canonicarumque Scripturarum Doctrinam doceant; qui scilicet antiquae legis, et Prophetarum obscura dilucident; qui Sacrum Evangelium, Apostolicasque Scripturas declarare non erubescant.

Cum vero omnis Christiana Disciplina duplex sit; alia; in qua ea, quae nos credere, quae sperare, quae amare debeamus, doceri possumus; alia vero, in qua quid agere, quid evitare conveniat, unusquisque instituitur; et illa quidem Theologia usitato vocabulo, haec vero Canonici Iuris Doctrina appellari consuevit; non satis Beatitudini Tuae videri posse existimamus, nisi utraque earum rectius a Te fuerit instituta. Decet enim Summum Pontificem et veram illam iamdiu neglectam Christianam Theologiam, cavillationibus, inutilibusque modernorum Scriptorum quaestionibus expulsis, et antiquioribus tam Graecis, quam Latinis Christianis auctoribus introductis, ornare atque illustrare, et aliam Christianae Disciplinae partem, eam scilicet, quae ad Ecclesiasticum ius pertinet, emendare, atque in melius reformare. Satis vero partem hanc in melius reformatam fore aliqui existimant, si, Te iubente, iura ac leges non canonicae modo, sed civiles etiam sine ullo commento, absque omni interprete, in publicis Scholis a Doctoribus legantur, et pure sincereque, ut sonant, intellegantur, interpretenturque. Obscura vero, et dubia si qua in eis inveniantur, ad Pontificis sententiam sine ulla prorsus disputatione deducantur. Tibi vero, Beatissime Pater, qui perfectam in omnibus plebis tuae reformationem desideras, hoc fortasse satis futurum non est, sed ipsa Decretorum, Decretalium, Sexti, et Clementinarum volumina (quoniam quaedam in se aut contraria, aut diversa, quaedam saepius repetita, et superflua omnino, quaedam pro temporum conditione saepius immutata habere videntur) reformari, instaurarique curabis; et non necessariis titulis amotis, eadem, quantum brevius, lucidiusque fieri potest, unico volumine redigenda sapientioribus, doctioribusque mandabis, ut his omnibus tam multis, tamque perplexis, quae nunc habemus, cum omnibus expositoribus suis amotis, Christianus populus quid agere, quid evitare debeat, unico volumine instruatur.

[678] To this end, you may also endeavor to restore the decrees of the Holy Fathers and the Sacred Canons, so that, where learning flourishes, there will always be men who will teach Christian Theology and the pure doctrine of the Holy Scriptures and Canons rather than the over-subtle learning of Parisian dons, and who will elucidate the obscure parts of the ancient law and the prophets and will not be ashamed to proclaim the Holy Gospel and Apostolic writings.

Now, there are two parts to Christian education: one, in which we learn what we should believe, hope for, and love, and another, in which we are taught what to do and what to avoid. The first is customarily called Theology, and the latter, Canon Law, and we do not believe that Your Holiness will be satisfied until you have rectified both. It surely befits the Supreme Pontiff to adorn and illuminate true Christian Theology, which has been too much neglected, by expelling the subtle and useless controversies of modern writers and introducing the ancient Greek and Latin authorities. It also befits him to repair and reform the other part of Christian learning, which relates to ecclesiastical law. Now, some believe that you will have done enough to reform this second part if both canon and civil laws and statutes are read and taught in public schools without any commentary or interpreter and are understood and interpreted straightforwardly and integrally, just as they are written. If any obscure and dubious points are found in them, they may be referred to the Pontiff's judgment without any further argument. But since you, Holy Father, desire the perfect reformation of your people, you may not consider this sufficient. In that case, you will take care to reform and restore the books that contain the Decrees and Decretals, the Liber Sextus and the Clementine Constitutions.[41] For they seem to contain things that are contradictory or at variance with each other, or which are needlessly repeated and superfluous or frequently altered by the conditions of the times. After removing all unnecessary headings, you may appoint wise and learned men to collect all the laws in a single volume, which will be as clear and as brief as possible. Thus, having dispensed with the many and complex points that we currently have, along with all their expositors, we may teach the Christian people from a single volume what they should do and what they should avoid.

---

41   Liber Sextus is the name given to the collection of church laws, namely, the five book of the decretals of Gregory IX in 1234 and the sixth added in 1298 under Pope Boniface VIII. The Clementine Constitutions are from 1313 under Pope Clement V. These were among the forerunners of Code of Canon Law. Two twentieth century revisions of the Code were in 1917 and 1983.

[679] Super quod nemini liceat expositiones, interpretationes, aut
alias quasvis glossulas, nisi de permissione tua, aut scribere, aut scripta habere, aut ullo pacto edere.

Proderit etiam ad hoc tam magnum, lateque diffusum ignorantiae
morbum aut curandum, aut mitigandum, si, Te ita instituente, nemo
Monachi habitum, nemo sacros aliquos ordines suscipiat, nisi Latinae
linguae ita sit eruditus, ut quae in Ecclesiis leguntur, aperte intellegat,
nisi sacram paginam,[61] vetus scilicet, novumque Testamentum semel ad
minus legerit. Nam indecens, indecorumque est, multos esse in Ecclesia
Dei religiosos, multos presbyteros, qui nunquam sacram Evangelii His-
toriam, quae admodum brevis est, legerint; cum tamen fabulas multas,
inanesque plurimas perlegerint quaestiones; si nemo, neque in saeculari,
neque in Monachi habitu[62] sacrum Sacerdotis characterem accipiat,
nisi sit in Sacrarum Scripturarum Doctrina, in Sanctorum Doctorum,
Gregorii scilicet, Ambrosii, Augustini, Hieronymi, et aliorum scriptis
vel mediocriter eruditus; si nullus ad curam aliquam animarum, nullus
ad episcopalem dignitatem promoveatur, nisi et Sacrae Scripturae,
et Sacrorum Ecclesiasticorum Canonum, non tam doctoratus, quam
recte doctus esse inveniatur. Turpe enim, et indecens est aliquem ad
animarum languentium curam advocare, qui artem illam, qua possint
animae curari, non noverit. Haec autem facilius fient, si nemini, qui religionis habitum, aut sacri alicuius Ordinis formam susceperit, ulterius
liceat Gentilibus disciplinis, nisi pro linguarum erudimentis addiscendis, ullo modo vacare; si Sacerdotes curam animarum habentes singulis
Dominicis diebus praecepta Decalogi, articulos Fidei, Symbolum,
Dominicam Orationem, et alia de Evangelio, et Apostolorum Epistolis
ad salutem pertinentia,[63] aut praedicando, aut docendo, populis, com-
missaeque sibi plebi proponere cogantur; si nemo ad audiendas peccatorum confessiones, nemo ad verbum Dei praedicandum accedere audeat,
nisi Sacrorum Canonum et Sacrosanctae Theologiae studiis operam
dederit, atque in illis fuerit approbatus; aut si nemo sine Tua, Beatissime Pontifex, concessione, quam diligens inquisitio de viri sufficientia
praecedat, aut peccatorum confessiones audire, aut publice praedicare
praesumat; si praedicatoribus omnibus praecipiatur, ut non quaestiones,
non proprias opiniones, non diversas Doctorum sententias, quas non
veritatis amore, sed vincendi libidine obstinatius, quam

---

61   sacram paginam MS: sacras paginas ED
62   habitu MS, *Barletta*: habitum ED
63   ad salutem pertinentia MS: pertinentia ad salutem ED

[679] Moreover, let no one be allowed to write, publish, or keep explanations, interpretations, or glosses of any kind on this volume, except with your permission.

To cure this great and widely diffused disease of ignorance, it will also help if you allow no one to assume a monk's habit or holy orders unless he has learned enough Latin to understand what is read in church, and has read the Holy Scriptures—that is, the Old and New Testaments—at least once. For it is neither seemly nor appropriate that many religious in God's Church and many priests have never read the narrative of the Gospel, which is quite brief, though they have read many fables and empty treatises. Further, let no one, either in the religious habit or in secular garb, receive the sacred character of the priesthood unless he is at least somewhat versed in the teaching of the Holy Doctors—that is, in the writings of Gregory, Ambrose, Augustine, Jerome, and others. Nor let anyone be promoted to the care of souls or to the rank of bishop unless he is found to be not a doctor, but a man truly learned (*doctus*) in Sacred Scripture and the Holy Canons of the Church. Indeed, it is unseemly and shameful to call someone to the care of languishing souls who is ignorant of the very art by which they may be cured. These principles will be implemented more easily, if those who take the habit or receive holy orders are allowed to spend no more time reading pagan authors than is necessary to become proficient in the languages; if priests entrusted with the care of souls are required on Sundays to preach and to teach their people the Ten Commandments, the articles of faith, the Creed, the Lord's Prayer, and other things from the Gospels and Epistles that relate to salvation; if no one presumes to hear confessions or preach the word of God unless he has studied the Holy Canons and Sacred Theology, and has been tested in them; if no one is allowed to hear confessions or preach without your approval, Holy Father, after a diligent inquiry into the man's qualifications; and if all preachers are forbidden to proclaim their own views or the various opinions of learned men—which they defend too obstinately, not for love of the truth, but from a desire to win arguments—

[680] deceat, aliquando defendunt, sed sacram veteris, novique Testamenti Scripturam, Sanctos Ecclesiae Doctores, illa scilicet, quae ad salutem animarum apertissime pertinent, praedicent, atque declarent, Gentilium Philosophorum rationibus, modernorumque Scriptorum cavillationibus penitus dimissis. Haec si a Te, Beatissime Pater, et alia huiuscemodi contra ignorantiae malum instituantur, facilius, quam cogitari possit, eveniet, ut religiosi homines ea, quae ad Christianam pietatem pertinent, cognoscere, et alios docere valeant.

Proderit etiam non minus ad Christianorum hominum miseram inscitiam delendam, si Tu vanas, impiasque divinandi artes, per astra scilicet, aut per quaevis somnia, aut signa, et huiusmodi plurima, in quibus multi hominum, et tempus amittunt, et ingenium corrumpunt, et sibi ipsis, aliisque multis salutis aditum praecludunt, ita penitus damnabis, ut omnes harum impiarum, et vanarum artium libri, quorum magna nunc ubique copia est, comburantur; si ex numerosa Ecclesiasticorum librorum copia, qui sine ullo discrimine boni, malique promiscue leguntur, qui digni sunt, in Ecclesia legantur, et a Te approbentur; qui autem minus digni sunt, improbentur; illi maxime, in quibus Sanctorum historiae, antiquorum Patrum vitae a veritate alienae describuntur. Dum enim nunc falsa multa pro veris, perversa pro rectis, a Fide etiam quaedam dissentientia pro rectae fidei institutis in ipsis Christianorum Ecclesiis, in religiosorum hominum conventibus saepius leguntur, fit, ut non ignorantia solum, sed perversa quadam contra veritatem Christianam obstinatione multi laborent; si quattuor universalium Conciliorum, Nicaeni scilicet, Constantinopolitani, Ephesini, et Chalcedonensis volumina, in quibus nostrae Fidei exordia, et fundamenta continentur, quae Beatus Gregorius non semel, tamquam quattuor Evangelia suscipere, et venerari profitetur; quippe quod supra illa, quasi supra quattuor firmissimas columnas omnis Christiana institutio in aedificium consurgat; si haec, inquam, aliaque Concilia, Te iubente, ex Bibliothecis Tuis, in quibus ea contineri existimamus, in manus Christianorum hominum impressa exeant. Si enim quasi quattuor Evangelia a tantae auctoritatis viro existimantur, quantum Christianus populus detrimenti de eorum Conciliorum privatione patiatur, facile considerare Beatitudinem Tuam posse credimus.

Multa paene, ac innumerabilia sunt, quae contra huiusmodi

[680] and are commanded to preach instead the Old and New
Testaments and the Holy Doctors of the Church—in short, the
things that clearly relate to the salvation of souls—and to put
away, once and for all, the subtleties of pagan philosophers and the
logic-chopping of modern writers. If you take these and other such
measures, Holy Father, against the evil of ignorance, one can hardly
imagine how easily religious will come to know and be able to teach
the things that relate to Christian piety.

An equally helpful means of eliminating the wretched ignorance of
Christians will be to condemn those vain and impious techniques of
divination by stars, dreams, signs, and other such things, in which
many people waste their time, ruin their talents, and create obstacles
to the way of salvation both for themselves and many others, and
to burn all the books of their impious and vain arts, which are now
everywhere in great supply. Moreover, a vast number of ecclesiastical
books are read without any distinction between the good ones and
the bad; of these, you should approve those which are worthy of
being read in church, and condemn those which are not—especially
those which contain inaccuracies about the lives of the saints and
the ancient Fathers. For when many false statements are taken as
true and crooked things are accepted as straight, when teachings at
variance with the Faith are taken as orthodox, and when these are
read in Christian churches and the houses of religious orders, many
people are harmed not only by ignorance, but also by a perverse
stubbornness toward Christian truth. Moreover, you would do well
to publish the books of the four Ecumenical Councils—Nicaea,
Constantinople, Ephesus, and Chalcedon—which contain the
beginnings and foundations of our faith, and which Blessed Gregory
more than once professed to take up and venerate in the same way
as the four Gospels; for upon these Councils, as upon four steady
columns, rests the entire edifice of Christian teaching. Accordingly,
as we said, let editions of these and the other councils be made from
your library, which surely contains them, and let them be put into
the hands of the faithful. If a man of such authority regarded these
documents as comparable to the four Gospels, Your Holiness can
surely estimate the damage that the Christian people suffer when
they are deprived of them.

There are many—indeed, there are virtually countless such remedies
that can be devised against the

[681] ignorantiae potestatem excogitari remedia possunt; unum tamen est, quod etsi superioribus contrarium esse videatur, patienter tamen Te audire, Beatissime Pater, optamus, quod (quoniam omnium efficacissimum, communeque omnibus tam religiosis, quam ceteris omnibus hominibus censemus) ultimo loco dicere voluimus. Cogitavimus enim saepius, nihil magis omnes homines de Divinis, humanisque rebus instruere posse, quam Sacrosanctam veteris, novique Testamenti Scripturam, quae ideo in Ecclesiis cotidie legi ab antiquioribus Patribus instituta est, ut maxima Christianorum pars, qui propter alias vitae occupationes, aut propter legendi imperitiam, seu etiam propter librorum penuriam (non enim tunc abundabant, sicut nunc, Christiani voluminibus) minus haec domi legere poterant, ad Ecclesiam convenientes, ibi verbum Domini audirent, quo multum proficere in rerum cognitione, et morum emendatione possent. Legebanturque, quemadmodum credimus, primis illis Fidei temporibus in Ecclesiis Hebraica, seu Graeca lingua Divinae Scripturae. Inter Hebraeos enim Hebraice, inter Graecos Graece legi congruum erat. Immo neque aliter legi poterant, cum totum vetus Testamentum Hebraeo, novum vero, praeter Matthaeum, et unam Pauli Epistolam, Graeco sit sermone conscriptum. At postquam multiplicari ex Romanis, Latinisque hominibus credentium numerus coepit, et maior iam fidelium pars Hebraeum, Graecumque sermonem nesciret, nihilque prodesse Sancti Patres intellexerunt, si Scripturae in Ecclesiis legerentur, a populo autem minime intellegerentur; temporum ratione hoc postulante, Scripturae in Latinum sermonem versae sunt, et Latine in Ecclesiis legi coeperunt. Cum autem nunc ex multis milibus populorum, et magna Sacerdotum, religiosorumque hominum multitudine pauci admodum, rarique sint, qui Latinam linguam intellegant, quid, quaeso, prohibet, antiquiorum Patrum mores imitari, et ex minus noto ad notiorem sermonem sanctam ipsam Scripturam convertere? Et sicut illi iam ex Hebraeo et Graeco sermone, in quo conscripta fuerat, in Latinum verterunt, ut Christianus populus, qui Latina utebatur lingua, divina posset praecepta, dum legerentur in Ecclesiis, intellegere; ita nunc ex Latino in vulgarem sermonem conversas Scripturas ad populorum aedificationem legere. Aliter enim quid prodest cotidie Sanctorum Evangeliorum, Apostolicarumque Epistolarum portiunculas in Ecclesiis,

[681] power of ignorance. Nevertheless, there is one that we earnestly beg Your Holiness to consider, even though it may seem contrary to those previously mentioned. Since we regard this remedy as the most efficacious both for religious and for all other men, we wish to speak of it last. We have often thought that nothing can better instruct men concerning divine and human things than the Holy Scriptures of the Old and New Testaments. The ancient Fathers established the custom of reading these in church, so that the majority of Christians, who could not read them at home because of life's occupations or their inability to read or the lack of books—since Christians did not have as many books then as they do now—could come to church and listen to the word of God, and thus make progress in their understanding and the amendment of their lives. In that first era of the Faith, the Scriptures were read in church, we believe, in Greek or Hebrew—in Hebrew among the Hebrews, as is fitting, and in Greek among the Greeks. Indeed, it could not have been otherwise, since the entire Old Testament was written in Hebrew, and the New Testament, except for Matthew and one letter of Paul, was written in Greek.[42] But as the number of faithful among the Romans and Latin-speaking peoples increased, and since most of these were ignorant of Greek and Hebrew, the Fathers realized that there was no profit in reading the Scriptures in church if the people did not understand them. And so, as the times required, the Scriptures were translated into Latin, and one began to read them in Latin in the churches. Now, however, when very few among the many thousands of laymen and the vast multitude of priests and religious can understand Latin, what prevents us, indeed, from imitating the custom of the ancient Fathers and translating the Holy Scriptures from a less intelligible language to a more familiar one? Just as they translated the Scriptures from the Hebrew and Greek in which they were written into Latin, so that the Christian people who used Latin might understand the divine precepts as they were read in Church, the Scriptures today could be read translated from Latin into the common tongue for the edification of the people. Otherwise, what is the point of chanting portions of the Holy Gospels, Apostolic Letters and Psalms in churches every day,

---

42 Parts of the Old Testament were written in Aramaic and Greek. In the New Testament, Matthew was composed in Greek as well as the Letter to the Hebrews.

[682] psalmosque decantare, si neque, qui legunt, neque qui audiunt, quae dicantur,[64] intellegunt? Abhorrere vero, ut quidam, qui se peritissimos solos credunt, ab hac conversione sanae mentis neminem decet; quoniam si rem ipsam, vimque rationis, potius quam vanam quamdam opinionem inspicimus, eadem omnino est sapientia, eademque doctrina, quae in Evangelio, et ceteris Scripturis continetur, sive Hebraeo, sive Latino, sive Graeco, sive vulgari sermone scripta sint. Ad linguarum vero diversitatem si quis inspicere velit, unamque alia digniorem linguam existimare, apertissime videri potest, quod multo magis abhorrere ab ea translatione debuissent Christiani, qua[65] ex Hebraeo, et Graeco fonte, ubi primum omnia scripta sunt, ad Latinum sermonem, in quo nihil penitus ex Canonicis Scripturis traditum est, conversa sunt omnia.

Quod si illi Sanctissimi Patres, qui ante nos fuere, populorum utilitatem, non inanitatem opinionis respicientes, non abhorruerunt, ex propriis linguis sacras paginas ad peregrinum sermonem convertere, minus certe nos abhorrere debemus, ex una peregrina lingua ad peregrinam aliam transferre. Sicut enim divinis eloquiis peregrinum vulgarem sermonem non dubitamus, ita Latinum peregrinum eloquiis illis penitus esse certissime intellegimus. Si igitur, Te auctore, quae in Ecclesiis leguntur, quae psalluntur, aut ubique, aut in aliqua saltem regione, vulgari sermone legantur, atque psallantur iubeatur, mirum in modum prodesse ad cognitionem divinorum praeceptorum, morumque emendationem posse existimamus. Cogitet Sanctitatis Tuae Sapientia, quam multa milia sanctarum Monialium sint, ut religiosorum virorum transeamus innumerabilem multitudinem, quae cotidie ex Scriptura psalmos, lectionesque legunt, et nihil omnino intellegunt; quantum proficerent, si quae legunt, intellegerent! Omnis enim Scriptura, Apostoli testimonio, utilis est ad docendum, ad instruendum, intellegentes quidem, non autem eos, qui non intellegunt. Cogitet pietas Tua, quanto magis, quam nunc, sancta a populis frequentaretur Ecclesia, quantum fructum divina frequentantes officia ex Ecclesia Domini reportarent, si divina, quae ibi leguntur, verba intellegerent! Utinam de hac tantum re nobis apud maiestatis Tuae sublimitatem sermo habendus esset. Nunc autem quoniam rudis sermonis prolixitate offendere amplitudinem Tuam timemus, multa praetermittimus, quae ostendi[66] manifestissime possent,

---

64   dicantur: dicunt MS, ED
65   qua *Barletta*: quam MS, ED
66   ostendi MS: ostendere ED

[682] if they are understood neither by those who read nor by those who listen? No sane person should recoil from this change, as do some who fancy that they alone are learned. If we look at the matter itself and the force of reason, rather than our own empty opinions, we find that the same wisdom and the same doctrine are contained in the Gospel and other writings, whether they are written in Latin, in Greek, or in the common language. If one wishes, on the other hand, to consider the diversity of languages and to regard one of them as more worthy than the others, it will be clear that Christians should have been far more reluctant to translate the Scriptures from Hebrew and Greek, in which they were first written, into Latin, a language in which none of the canonical texts had been transmitted.[43]

If, then, the Holy Fathers who came before us, considering the utility of the people rather than empty opinion, did not hesitate to translate the Holy Scriptures from their original languages into an alien tongue, we should be even less reluctant to translate them from one alien tongue into another. If we boldly insist that the common language is alien to the word of God, we must surely suppose that Latin is foreign to it, as well. Thus, if you command that what we read and sing in Church should be read and sung in the common language, if not everywhere, at least in some regions, we believe that you will have done much to help the people understand the commandments of God and amend their ways. Let Your Holiness ponder how many thousands of holy nuns there are—not to mention the countless multitude of religious men—who daily read Psalms and lessons from Scripture with no comprehension, and who would benefit if they understood what they read! All Scripture, as the Apostle testifies (2 Tim 3:16), is profitable to teach and instruct— but only to those who understand it, not to those who do not. Consider how many more people will come to church than currently do, and how much profit they will bring home after assisting in divine services, if they understand the godly words that are read there.[44] If only we might converse with Your Holiness about this matter alone! Now, however, since we fear that we are offending Your Holiness with an abundance of uncultivated speech, we will omit many clear proofs

---

43 The earliest pieces of Latin translation, called the Vetus Latina, date from the second century C.E.

44 Vatican Council 2 (1962-1965) allowed for the use of the local language in all forms of worship.

[683] nihil in tota Ecclesia magis necessarium esse, nihil utilius omnino futurum, nihil magis decorum, atque secundum Sanctorum Patrum disciplinam institui posse, quam haec Sanctarum Scripturarum, quae in Ecclesia leguntur, ex Latino in vulgarem sermonem permutatio, de qua nunc haec dixisse sufficiat. Alias vero, si benignitatis Tuae magnitudo permiserit, plura fortasse dicturi sumus.

Quod autem de divinis Scripturis diximus, idem de omnibus aliis conventionibus, venditionibus, emptionibus quae inter Christianos homines fiunt, intellegi cupimus. Prodesse enim multum ad instruendos de rebus suis homines, ad [...] miseram[67] tollendam posse existimamus, si Notarii et Tabelliones ea, quae rogant, et quae stipulari consueverunt, materna lingua scribere aperte et clare iubeantur; ut qui contrahunt, et qui testes adhibentur, plene omnia intellegant. Haec, quae multi, qui latinae linguae peritia gloriantur, graviter audiunt, clementiam, sapientiamque Tuam benigne suscepturam non dubitamus. Intellegit namque Beatitudo tua, ex iis, quae diximus, quam pium sit, ut Deus, qui tot linguarum diversitate in universo orbe laudatur, hac etiam nostra lingua incipiat laudari. Sciat praeterea Sapientia Tua, quod omnes illi, quos superius nominavimus, Christiani populi, qui Asiam, Africamque incolunt, et aliqui etiam, qui in Europae ambitu continentur, materna propria lingua in Sacris Missis, et Divinis Officiis utuntur. Neque frustra institutum id esse credimus a Sanctis Patribus, qui ante Te Petri Sedem tenuerunt, ut Bulla, quae in Cena Domini legitur, non Latino tantum, sed vulgari etiam sermone ad populi eruditionem quotannis legatur. Si enim ex parvo non exigui instructionis fructus colliguntur, ex maximo quanta colligi messis possit apertissime quisque intuetur.

Ex hac ignorantia malorum omnium matre superstitio exoritur, ex iniqua Matre nequior filia. Sicut enim nihil in humana vita recta religione sanctius, nihil omnino melius, ita certe superstitione, quae vitium contra religionem esse a peritioribus definitur, nihil deterius, nihil penitus magis impium, atque nefarium est. Tot autem, tantae, ac tam perversae hac tempestate vigent inter Christianos populos superstitiones, ut nemo sane aut sermone comprehendere, aut pro merito deplorare valeat. Quidquid enim vanarum superstitionum orbis olim universus habuit, nunc ad Christianos populos fluxisse videtur. Divinationes per astrorum motus, dierum observationes,

---

67   [...] miseram: Latinum miseriam MS, Latinam miseriam ED

[683] that nothing is more necessary and nothing will be more useful, fitting, and in accordance with the discipline of the Holy Fathers, than the translation of the Holy Scriptures which are read in church from Latin into the common tongue; let what we have said suffice. Perhaps we shall say more, if it pleases Your Holiness, at another time.

What we have said about the Scriptures, however, should also be taken as relating to all other agreements, sales, and purchases among Christians. For we think it would be conducive to the knowledge of one's own affairs and the removal of the pitiful Latin if notaries and clerks were required to write their questions and stipulations clearly and openly in their mother tongue, so that those who make contracts and give testimony may understand everything fully. We are confident that Your Holiness will lend a kindly ear to all these suggestions, which disturb many who glory in their knowledge of Latin. For you understand, from what we have said, how fitting it would be for God, who is praised throughout the world by such a diversity of languages, to be praised in our own language as well. You also know that all the Christian peoples named previously who dwell in Asia and Africa, and some who are contained within Europe, use their own language in the Holy Mass and divine offices. Nor do we believe that your predecessors in the See of Peter acted in vain when they fixed the custom of reading the annual announcement on Holy Thursday not only in Latin, but also in the common tongue for the edification of the people. For if a small thing produces such a harvest of instruction, it is obvious how much can be gathered from a great one.

Now, from ignorance, which is the mother of all evils, rises superstition; thus from a wicked mother comes a daughter who is worse. And just as nothing in human life is better and more sacred than true religion, nothing is worse, or more impious and wicked, than superstition, which learned men have defined as the vice contrary to religion. Indeed, so many great and perverse superstitions now thrive among Christians that no one can justly describe or adequately deplore the situation, and all the vain superstitions that ever existed in the world now seem to have infiltrated Christian nations. Fortune-telling by the motions of the stars,

[684] somniorum interpretationes, omnium generum vanissimas praedictiones, Chiromantias, Hydromantias, Pryomantias, Geomantias, aliaque huiuscemodi tam multa, tam vana, ut neque genera singula facile sit numerare. Quis enim numero aliquo comprehendere poterit innumerabiles paene execrabiles superstitiones, quae contra religionis Christianae puritatem pro futuris cognoscendis, pro amovendis, aut auferendis infirmitatibus fiunt? aut quae sub devotionis, ac religionis umbra impia, saeva, ac nefanda perpetrantur? Nam, ut singula quaeque perstringamus, omnis potissimum ad harum trium artium imitationem refertur superstitio; ad Divinationem, ad Medicinam, et ad affectatam Caeremoniarum Religionis nostrae observantiam. Nulla enim est civitas, si Christianos nunc populos respicimus, nulla domus, nulla paene hominis mens est, quae aliqua ex his tribus generibus superstitione non laboret; et quod dolendum magis est, palam nefandissima multa fiunt, eaque a Christiana veritate ita diversa, ut adversa penitus sint. Et nemo ex tanto Episcoporum numero obstat, ita ut, quod sine lacrimis scribere non possumus, vix aliqua religionis, Christianae veritatis, ac puritatis apud Christianos populos forma reliqua sit, dum nulla publica, nulla privata, nulla profana, nulla sacra actio sit, quae superstitione foedata non appareat. Sed haec ipsa longiori volumine et deplorare, et impugnare instituimus. Nunc vero per Christi Iesu caritatem Te orare volumus, ut quemadmodum perversa haec emendare solus potes, et ex officii tui munere debes (si Christianae Fidei, Christianae puritatis, ut Christi Vicarium decet, zelum habes, ut Te habere non ambigimus) sic velis, et studeas haec ipsa emendare atque corrigere. Excita, pientissime Pater, contra has impias superstitionum foeditates, quae Christianum Tibi commissum populum iam paene ad apertam Gentilitatem, et Idolorum servitutem deduxerunt, quasi Phinees alter, zelum iustae indignationis Tuae, et Astrologorum libros, qui ad divinationem pertinent, ab Ecclesia, a Sanctis Conciliis, Sanctisque Patribus damnatos omnes combure; Astrologosque ipsos, et omnes, qui per astrorum inspectionem, aut per quascumque alias observationes, futura praedicere audent, qui ab aliis Principibus foveri solent, Tu Dei zelo, et magna in populum Tuum pietatis forma, non spirituali modo, sed temporali etiam gladio, nisi ab impietate sua resipiscant, ad mortem

[684] the reckoning of days, the interpretation of dreams, and vain prognostications of all kinds, chiromancy, hydromancy, pyromancy, geomancy, and so many other similar, foolish practices have arisen that it is difficult to list individual types. Who indeed can keep track of the virtually countless execrable superstitions that exist, contrary to the Christian religion, for predicting the future or repelling and curing illnesses? Who can count the many impious, savage, and nefarious things that are done under the cover of devotion and religion? If we touch on them singly, however, every superstition can be classified under one of these three arts: divination, healing, and the abuse of religious ceremonies. There is no city—taking into account the Christian peoples—no house, and practically no human mind that does not suffer from one of these three kinds of superstition. More regrettable still is the fact that many of the wickedest things are done openly, and that these things diverge from true Christianity to the point of being completely opposed to it. Yet not one of our many bishops objects to it, with the result—which we weep to set on paper—that scarcely any shape of religion, Christian truth, and purity remains among the Christian peoples, while no public, private, profane or sacred action appears free from the taint of superstition. We have decided, however, to deplore and attack these things in a longer work. For the moment, we simply wish to implore you, for the love of Christ, since you alone can rectify this perverse situation, and since you are obliged to do so by your office—if indeed you are as zealous for Christian faith and Christian purity as the Vicar of Christ ought to be, which we do not doubt—willingly and eagerly to amend and correct these faults. Stir your righteous indignation, kindly Father, against these impious and foul superstitions, which have brought the Christian people, who have been committed to your care, to the point of open paganism and slavery to idols. Be a second Phinehas (Num 25:7-13; Ps 106:30) and burn all the astrological books that relate to divination, which have already been condemned by the Church, the Holy Councils, and the Holy Fathers. As for the astrologers themselves, and all who dare to predict the future by gazing at the stars or by any other kind of observation, and who often find favor with other princes, pursue them, out of zeal for God and kindness for your people,

[685] usque percute. Tot somniorum interpretationes, quae ut facilius incautam plebem decipiant, sub Danielis, sub Salomonis nomine,
magnis impressas voluminibus habent; tot vanarum, atque impiarum
artium publice venales libros, si pietas, sapientiaque Tua inter Christianorum manus ulterius versari sustinebit, quo confugere valeat, a
quo auxilium petere Christiana pietas possit, non videmus. Perquirat
Sanctitas Tua illicitarum artium impressa volumina, et inveniet sane
tam multa, tam varia, quam vana et impia sint, ut neque credere
facile, neque cogitare antea potuisset. Quae nihil aliud sunt, quam
multarum animarum venena, ac laquei inextricabiles, quibus tanto
facilius, liberiusque Christianos populos in miseram captivitatem re-
tinere Diabolus solet, quanto haec a Christianis Pontificibus admitti,
et aliquando etiam suscipi videntes, ac si mala non essent, Christiani
populi talia non evitare, sed prosequi potius assueverunt.

Perquirat pietatis Tuae zelus alterius generis, earum scilicet, quae ad
medicinam referri videntur, vanissimas, scelestissimasque superstitiones, attendatque, quot ab omnibus Christianis hominibus huiusmodi
fiant; et inveniet sane, nullam infirmitatem esse, nullum infortunium,
quod non propriis execrabilibus superstitionibus mederi atque vitari
posse credatur. Quae enim infirmitas est, quae non a quibusdam
philateriis, brevibus, characteribus, suspensionibus, carminationibus,
execrationibus, vanissimisque verbis, aliisque artibus, quae non secundum medicorum doctrinam sunt, curari posse credant. Sunt, qui
audent harum artium publicas officinas habere. Sunt, qui non timent
execrabilia haec populis in plateis civitatum vendere. Sed cum Te ad
sublimitatem Apostolicae Sedis sublevatum videmus, cui nihil magis
curae[68] est, quam Christianam pietatem omnibus modis fovere, speramus, impia haec, et Christianae Fidei inimica nunc demum finem
habitura. Non enim Te permissurum credimus a Sacris Canonum
Decretis prohibitas ligaturas, breves, suspensiones, incantationes,
aliaque huiusmodi paene infinita Christianum ulterius populum cor-
rumpere, Christianam Religionem destruere; sed praeter ea,[69] quae
Medicorum ars comprobat, nihil omnino pro infirmitatibus curandis
neque sumere, neque suspendere, aut alligari, neque ullo modo uti
permittes. Nam certum est, quidquid aliud, quam quod secundum
naturam suam sanitatem inducere valeat, tenetur id superstitiosum,
et proinde impium ac

---

68   curae *Barletta*: cura MS, ED
69   praeter ea MS: praeterea ED

[685] even to death, unless they repent of their impiety, using not only your spiritual sword, but the temporal as well.[45] If Your Holiness allows so many books of dream-interpretation—which, to deceive an unwary public more easily, are printed in great volumes under the names of Daniel and Solomon—and books of other vain and impious arts to be sold and read by Christians, we do not see to whom Christian piety can flee, or with whom it may seek refuge. If Your Holiness should seek out the printed books of the illicit arts, you would find them more numerous, varied, empty and impious than you could have believed or even imagined. These are nothing other than the poison of many souls and the inescapable snares with which the Devil keeps the Christian peoples in wretched captivity. He does so with the greater ease and freedom, as Christians, seeing that their bishops allow these practices and sometimes even take them up, become accustomed not to avoiding these things, but to pursuing them.

If Your Holiness should also zealously inquire into the second category of empty and wicked superstition, which speciously relates to healing, and should consider how many of these superstitions are observed by Christians, you would find that there is no infirmity or misfortune that they do not believe can be cured or avoided by means of execrable superstitious practices. Indeed, what infirmity is not thought to be curable by phylacteries, tickets, characters, amulets, charms, curses, empty words, and those other techniques that do not come under medical science? There are some who dare to maintain public shops for these arts. There are others who do not fear to sell these accursed objects to the people in the streets of cities. But when we see that you, to whom nothing is more important than to encourage Christian piety in every way, have been raised to the Holy See, we are hopeful that these impious practices, which are the enemy of Christian faith, will finally come to an end. Indeed, we cannot believe that you will permit these bindings, tickets, amulets, charms, and countless other such things, which have been condemned by the Sacred Canons, any longer to corrupt the Christian people and destroy the Christian religion; nor will you permit one to consume, bind, or suspend anything for the cure of infirmities except that which is approved by the physicians' art. For it is certain that whatever does not induce health according to its own nature is superstitious, and is therefore impious and criminal.

---

45 The medieval doctrine of the two swords (Luke 22:38) held that the church possessed both swords, i.e., spiritual power and worldly power.

[686] criminosum esse.

Sed praeter haec tertium omnium detrimentum, superstitionum impiarum genus destruere non dissimulabis; non poterit enim recta fidei, et pietatis Tuae regula perversa multa, quae sub devotionis, religionisque umbra fiunt, dissimulando sustinere, sed cum viderit tot vanas, non ab Ecclesia institutas caeremonias, insanias sane, et praestigia in omni actione observari; cum adverterit Orationes omnes fore execrationes effectas, dum vanissimis loci, temporis, numeri, modique dicendi observationibus dicuntur; dum hanc, si stans, illam, si prostratus quis dixerit, propriam gratiam vel sanitatis, vel consolationis, vel cuiuscumque infortunii liberationem afferre existimant; dum hanc ab igne, alteram a ferro, tertiam ab inimicis liberare, singulis proprias virtutes tribuentes, affirmant; non poteris certe, non poteris, Sanctissime Pater, has nefandissimas contra veram Religionis puritatem observationes sustinere. Illud etiam forsitan Tibi placere non poterit, quod humana curiositas adinvenit. Nunc enim singulis Sanctis pro singulis infirmitatibus vota fiunt, quasi Sanctorum in Caelis distributa unicuique propria sint officia, et singulis singula humana membra tradita sint curanda; unde Dominus omnium creaturarum Pater, omnium infirmitatum solus curator minus invocari consuevit.

Atque haec cum aliis emendare pro Tua Sapientia curabis. Neque omnino id, quod deterius certe est, et nostris temporibus inter plebeios homines maximum iam locum habet, ulterius procedere permittes. Multorum enim nunc populorum opinio est, multique firmissime credunt, hanc tabellam, in qua Christi, vel Beatae Virginis aut Sanctorum quorundam imagines depictae sunt, si ad eam recurrant, infirmitatem hanc, illam vero aliam infirmitatem curare existimant; si per civitatem deferatur, pluvias inducere, grandines amovere, serenitatem adducere, aliam, si domi habeatur, fulgura dissipare, nonnullas greges, aut boves fecundare, ut penitus a diversis Ecclesiis, a diversis imaginibus, diversas gratias reportare posse omnis populus credat. Haec autem qualia sint, nunc dicere omittimus, quoniam sapientiam Tuam latere non potest, haec ipsa Gentilitatem, idololatriamque manifestissime sapere, et a Christiana pietate quammaxime esse aliena. Ad haec vero omnia emendanda, Beatissime Pater, prodesse multum posse confidimus, si praestigiatores, circulatores, maleficos, magicisque artibus deditos, divinantes,

[686] Beyond these, there is a third class of impious superstitions, equally harmful, which you will not hesitate to destroy; for your correct rule of faith and practice will not tolerate the many things that are done under the false pretense of devotion and religion.

For indeed, Holy Father, when you see the observance of so many vain and foolish ceremonies which have not have been instituted by the Church, and such scruples in every kind of behavior; and when you observe that all prayers have become curses, since they are recited with a pointless regard for place, time, rhythm, and pronunciation, and that one supposes that if this prayer is said while standing, and that prayer while lying down, one will obtain the specific favor of health, consolation, or freedom from some misfortune, and that one prayer frees a person from fire, and another from the sword, and another from one's enemies, each with its own power; you will surely not tolerate these wicked practices, which are opposed to true purity of religion. Nor can you be pleased with this additional invention of human curiosity: prayers are now made to particular saints for particular infirmities, as if each of the Saints in heaven had his own assignment, and particular human limbs were entrusted to the care of particular saints. As a result, the Lord, the Father of all creatures and the only healer of all infirmities, is now less commonly invoked.

These things, and all others, you will correct in your wisdom. Nor will you permit the following vice, which is surely worse, and which is now very widespread among simple people, to continue any longer. Many are now of the opinion, and firmly believe, that one tablet, on which the image of Christ or the Blessed Virgin or certain saints is painted, can cure one kind of infirmity, while another tablet cures another, if one has recourse to it; or that one image will cause rain or avert hail or bring good weather if it is carried through the city, and that another, if it is kept home, will divert lightning, or fecundate the flocks or cattle; thus the people believe that various graces can be obtained from various images and churches. What sort of things these are, we forbear to say, since Your Holiness knows well that they smack of paganism and idolatry, and are altogether foreign to Christian piety. We are confident that you will make great progress in correcting these abuses, if you decree with pious zeal that magicians, quacks, potion-makers, and practitioners of the occult arts, as well as diviners,

[687] quosque manuum inspectores, carminatores, somniorum interpretes, et similium omnium impietatum inventores omnes, magno
pietatis zelo (si penitus has omnes superstitiones non abnegaverint)
vivos etiam cremandos esse statueris, et illos, qui eos in domum suam
pro huiusmodi impietatibus exercendis adduxerint, aut artes illas
in se operari permiserint, facultatibus omnibus expoliari, perpetuo-
que propriae patriae exilio mulctari decreveris, et illorum imprimis
destruere, atque delere genus curaveris, qui sub B. Pauli nomine fal-
lacibus, diabolicisque artibus cum serpentibus civitates circumeunt,
vendereque, non sancti Pauli gratiam, qua carent omnino, et quae
vendi nequaquam potest, sed diabolicam quamdam artem consue-
vere, et dum corporibus contra venenosorum animalium morsus
oblatis curationem promittunt, populorum animas pestiferis venenis
inficiunt; si psalmos, picturas, characteres, phylacteria, pittaciola,
breves deferri nullo pacto permittes; si neminem ad aegros curandos,
qui medicinam professi non sint, accedere imperabis, nihilque pro
quavis infirmitate apponi constitues, quod non secundum propriam
naturam, et secundum medicorum rationes curare posse existimetur;
si nullas orationes neque deferri, neque scribi neque dici consenties,
nisi quae a sancta Ecclesia, a sanctis ab Ecclesia approbatis doctoribus sunt institutae, et quae falso Sanctis adscribuntur (plurima
enim huiusmodi sunt) cremanda omnino esse curabis; si illas omnes
praecipue manifesto edicto condemnabis, quae propriis titulis,
seu rubricis hanc aut illam sanitatis, aut consolationis gratiam, aut
infortunii liberationem promittunt; si peculiares, votivasque missas,
in quibus mille superstitionum genera exercentur,[70] absque Episcopi
concessione, neminem celebrare posse institues; si ea omnia caeremoniarum genera, quae a sancta Ecclesia instituta non sint, diabolicas
esse observationes declarabis; si huic vel illi imagini tabellas pro
votis, statuasque apponere non permittes; haec enim et Gentilitatem
sapiunt, et vana cum sint, religiosorum hominum mentes ad avaritiam procliviores facilius corrumpunt; si nullam imaginem pro peste
amovenda, pro pluvia, aut serenitate impetranda deferri patieris; haec
enim quantum a rectae fidei semita, a Christianae puritatis calle multos aberrare faciant, non Te latet. Dum enim haec fieri permittuntur,
eo iam deventum est, ut picta tabella, in qua Sancti alicuius imago sit,
maiori honore, atque

---

70   exercentur *Barletta*: exercent MS, ED

[687] palm-readers, charmers, dream-interpreters, and all who devise similar impieties, if they refuse to abjure these superstitions, should be burned alive, and that those who receive them into their homes to practice these impieties or permit these arts to be practiced on themselves should be deprived of all faculties and punished with perpetual exile from their homeland; if you destroy those in particular who, on the authority of St. Paul, practice their deceitful and diabolical arts by going around cities with serpents, and sell not the grace of St. Paul—which they lack altogether, and which cannot be sold—but the devil's art, and while they promise to cure bodies that have been exposed to the bite of venomous animals, they infect the souls of the people with a truly mortal poison; if you forbid the carrying of incantations, pictures, marks, amulets, patches, and tickets, and forbid anyone to heal the sick who is not qualified in medicine, and stipulate that nothing may be applied to any sickness that is not consistent with its own nature, and is considered by physicians to have curative powers, and that no prayer may be carried, written, or spoken, except those which have been composed by the Church and by the holy doctors whom the Church has approved; if you also take care to burn prayers that have been falsely ascribed to the saints—and there are many of these; if, moreover, you manifestly and publicly forbid all prayers that promise in their titles or rubrics a particular grace of health or consolation or freedom from misfortune, and should allow no one to celebrate masses for special intentions—in which a thousand kinds of superstition are practiced—without the permission of a bishop; if you declare that all ceremonies which have not been established by the Church are diabolical rites, and forbid the placement of votive tablets and figurines before this or that image—since these things smack of paganism, and, because they are useless, easily corrupt the minds of religious who are especially prone to avarice—and allow no image to be carried for the sake of removing plague or obtaining rain or fair weather—for you know how far these practices stray from the path of Christian purity, but as long as they are permitted, practically everyone pays greater honor and respect to a picture of some saint

[688] reverentia a multis et fere omnibus suscipiatur, venereturque, quam ipsum Domini Iesu Christi Sacratissimum Corpus; si vota Domino potius fienda, reddendaque esse, Christianam plebem docere[71] volueris; si quicumque fuerint, qui ad alliciendos populos miracula cuiuscumque imaginis finxerint, praedicaverint, fallaciisque huiusmodi, et mendaciis in ignarum vulgus invexerint, qui semel, atque iterum admoniti ab his non destiterint, acerbo quovis mortis genere, Te iubente, e medio tollantur; si in Ecclesiis, aut alibi a religionis hominibus spectacula quaecumque seu Gentilia, seu Christiana fieri nullo pacto permittantur; si haec omnia superstitiosa, vana, impia, a Christianae fidei veritate aliena, et Christianae puritati adversa, diaboli laquei, animarum perditiones, quae tot tam varia, tam multiplicia sunt, ut neque numerari quidem facile possint, a Te cum eorum auctoribus, cum libris, cum his, qui ea aut exercent, aut in se exerceri permittunt, magna severitate condemnabuntur; si Episcopi, qui in suis civitatibus haec locum habere patiuntur, dignitate priventur; aliter enim tam magnum, tamque in omnes fere diffusum, ulteriusque continue serpentem superstitionis morbum tollendum esse non existimamus.

Duo haec mala, de quibus locuti sumus, ignorantia scilicet, et superstitio, et a religiosis[72] hominibus initium capiunt, et ex illis a quibus curari habebant, in Christianos populos derivant. Religiosorum enim opus fuisset, nisi ipsi eadem infirmitate laborarent, populorum ignorantiae subvenire, eorundemque sane munus esset, superstitiones omnes amovere, nisi perversa consuetudine instituere potius, ac eas fovere didicissent. Nunc vero, peccatis nostris sic facientibus, non religiosos solum homines hae duae pestes, sed omnem penitus Christianum virorum, et mulierum, nobilium, et ignobilium populum corrumpunt, et utraque earum, non secus ac letalis cancer, quantum ab origine sua longius serpit, tantum saevior, magisque incurabilis efficitur. Illa autem, de quibus dicere secundum ea, quae proposita sunt, nobis superest, religiosorum hominum magis propria mala esse existimantur, quam quae diximus; non quod similibus infirmitatibus et qui religiosi non sunt, et ipsi religiosi non laborent, sed quoniam infirmitates istae ex religiosis ad saeculares homines, aut non penitus derivant, aut si aliquo modo pertingunt, religiosos ipsos magis, quam alios inficiunt atque gravius corrumpunt. In his autem

---

71 docere MS, *Barletta*: decere ED
72 religiosis MS: religionis ED

LATIN TEXT WITH ENGLISH TRANSLATION   181

[688] than to the Sacred Body of our Lord Jesus Christ; if you are
willing to teach the Christian people that vows are to be made and
paid only to the Lord; if those who deceive the people by inventing,
proclaiming, and falsely popularizing miracles associated with
some image, and who refuse after one or two warnings to desist, are
removed at your orders by some harsh form of mortal execution;[46]
if you forbid religious to engage in performances, either pagan or
Christian, in church or anywhere else; if all these superstitious,
empty, and impious practices, which are foreign to the truth of the
Christian Faith and opposed to pure Christianity, which are the
snares of the devil and the ruin of souls, which are so various and
numerous that one can scarcely count them, are condemned by
your command along with their authors, their books, and those
who practice them or allow them to be practiced; and if bishops
who allow these things to take place in their cities are deprived
of their office. For otherwise, we do not believe that the disease
of superstition, which is so great, so widely diffused, and which
continues to spread, can be destroyed.

The two evils of which we have spoken, ignorance and superstition,
originate among religious, and from those who ought to have the
cure they spread to the people. It should have been the task of
religious to heal the ignorance of the people, had they not all been
infected with the same infirmity, and it would have been their job to
eliminate all superstitious practices, had not perverse custom taught
them to establish and foster them instead. Now, however, on account
of our sins, these two plagues are corrupting not only religious, but
practically the entire Christian people, men and women, nobles and
commoners; and each of these plagues, like a lethal cancer, becomes
more malignant and less curable, the further it travels from its source.
Nevertheless, the matters that we have yet to discuss are considered
peculiar to religious—not because religious and non-religious do not
suffer from similar infirmities, but because these ailments either do
not spread from religious to seculars, or, if they do affect the latter
somehow, cause greater harm to religious than to others. Among
these,

---

46   The execution of wizards and witches is found as early as the Code of Hammurabi
(1700 B.C.E.). Exod 22:18 echoes it; the New Testament alludes to it: Rev 21:8.
A major witch-hunting period in Europe and North America occurred from about
1350 to about 1750.

[689] primas partes tenent dissensiones, discordiae, divisiones, schismata, separationes. Non enim possumus nunc dicere, quod multitudinis credentium sit anima una, et cor unum, neque etiam una vivendi ratio, neque una de sacris humanisque rebus opinio; sed, ut exteriora etiam, qualia interiora sint, ostendant, neque habitus forma, neque color unus, neque sacrorum officiorum, atque caeremoniarum idem ritus, ac norma; quae quidem divisiones, ac diversitates, partim ex animorum dissensionibus oriri, partim vero easdem ipsas animorum discordias parare, atque fovere existimamus. Has autem delere Tibi perfacile futurum est, Beatissime Pater, si ad haec intendere aliae minus fortasse necessariae, aut minus certe pastoralis curae dignae occupationes Tibi permittent. Si enim omnes Clerici, Monachi, Sanctimoniales, aliique cuiuscumque conditionis viri, qui divina officia celebrare aut professione tenentur, aut devotionis gratia volunt, uno tantum modo, unica tantum forma divinas laudes persolvant, Missas celebrent, aliasque caeremonias observent; si omnis Ecclesia una Dei eiusdem semper Sancti memoriam non dispari celebritate concelebret, illis exceptis, in quorum titulis Ecclesiae erectae sunt, in quibus festivitatis, celebritatisque dissimilitudo conceditur; si de religionis huius, vel illius praestantia, excellentia, ac puritate, de Sanctorum, a quibus institutae sunt, aut qui in eis[73] floruere, dignitate, et gloria, omnis disputatio, ac controversia sub anathematis poena amoveatur, in quibus miseris contentionibus eo humana pervenit audacia, ut non formidet hunc, vel illum religionis institutorem tantum aliis Sanctis hominibus praeponere, ut Christo Domino, magnis impressis voluminibus, comparare, et comparando aequare, immo potius praeferre praesumat; et qui fidei propugnatores esse gloriantur, dum hoc dissensionis spiritu misere agitantur, his et huiusmodi vanitatibus omnem fidei pietatem corrumpunt; si quoties ad rogationes publicas religiosi ordines procedunt, non aliqua dignitatis ratione, sed sorte potius, quae per Episcopos mittatur, modo hic, modo ille ordo praecedere incipiat instituatur;[74] si nullus ordo, nulla congregatio sit, quae amplioribus, dignioribusve, quam reliquae omnes, apostolicis, atque aliis gaudeat privilegiis, sed omnibus et in confessionibus audiendis, et in praedicando, et in aliis religiosis officiis obeundis aequalia munera concedantur, singulis sane secundum proprias institutiones; si omnes sub

---

73   eis *Barletta*: ea MS, ED
74   instituatur: instituat MS, ED

[689] the foremost are dissension, discord, division, schism, and separation. Indeed, we cannot now say that the multitude of faithful has one mind and one heart, one manner of living, or one opinion about sacred and human affairs.[47] Exterior marks reveal the interior, for there is no single color and form of habit, nor a common rite and norm of sacred offices and ceremonies. We believe that these differences and divisions stem partly from a dissension of minds, but we also think that they create and foster mental discord. We trust that you will easily destroy these divisions, Holy Father—provided that other concerns, which are perhaps less necessary, and certainly less pastoral, do not prevent you from attending to them—if all clerics, monks, nuns, and men of any condition who are bound by profession or who desire out of private devotion to celebrate the divine offices use the same method and form when singing the divine praises, celebrating Mass, and performing other ceremonies; if the entire Church celebrates the memorial of the same saint on the same day with comparable solemnity—excepting the titular feasts of particular churches, in which a disparity of celebration and festivity is allowed; if you abolish, on pain of excommunication, all argument and controversy regarding the superiority of this or that religious order, or about the dignity and glory of the saints who founded them or flourished in them—for in these wretched controversies human audacity has gone so far in exalting, in huge printed volumes, this or that religious founder above all other saints as to compare him, and thus to equate or even prefer him, to Christ the Lord; thus the ones who glory in being champions of the Faith, when they are miserably preoccupied by these and similar vanities, actually corrupt all genuine faith and piety; if religious orders walking in a public procession proceed not according to rank, but according to lots drawn by the bishop on each occasion, and no order or congregation enjoys wider and higher privileges, Apostolic or otherwise, than the other orders, but each of them is assigned an equal share in the task of hearing confessions, preaching, and performing other religious duties, in keeping with their proper institutes; if all

---

47   This is the definition of friendship of Cicero (106-43 B.C.E.), *De Amicitia*, 6, 20.

[690] Sancti Benedicti regula militantes habitum formae colorisque
eiusdem ferre cogantur,[75] eademque denominatione, sancti scilicet
Benedicti, Monachi appellari iubeantur, ut tot habituum diversitates,
tot variae denominationes amoveantur, si hoc idem ab illis, qui sub
B. Augustini, aut Francisci, aut aliorum Sanctorum regulis professi
sunt, observari instituatur, si disputationes de B. Virginis Concep-
tione, de Christi Sanguine, an in terra aliquid eius remanserit, et de
his similibus, quae inter diversos ordines obstinatius, quam deceat,
agitantur, ita amoveri penitus statuatur, ut de illis vel loqui, vel
scribere, vel quovis modo disputare, anathema censeatur; si in his, in
quibus Iohannes Scotus Beato Thomae contradicit, aut alii similiter
Doctores ad invicem dissentiunt, in illis dumtaxat, quae ad fidem
spectare videntur, cuiusnam sententia sit ab Ecclesia suscipienda, ita
definiatur, ut opposita omnino damnabilis iudicetur; si omnes, qui
sub eadem regula pertinent, in victu, vestitu, et aliis omnibus vitae
muneribus, eandem formam, modumque eundem tenere cogantur; si
declinantes Monachi, aut religiosi quique viri ad aliquod Monasterium, quamdiu in illo fuerint, hospites licet censeantur, fratrum tamen
ibidem commorantium more vivere, et omnia munera obire teneantur; si omnium religiosorum cuiuscumque ordinis bibliothecae ita
omnibus religiosis communes efficiantur, ut in eas omnibus ingredi
liceat, et ex eis, chirographo, pignoreque pro librorum existimatione
relicto, libros quoslibet asportare, et statuto tempore pro librorum
magnitudine eos apud se habere; si ambulantibus simul, aut navi-
gantibus vel ad quodcumque hospitium diversantibus diversorum
ordinum fratribus, communis semper, eademque, Te iubente, sit
mensa; si religiosus, cuiuscumque ordinis sit, qui suum ordinem, aut
monasterium scriptis, aut verbis aliis praeferre, aut aliquem alium
calumniari, atque damnare religiosum ordinem, aut monasterium
praesumpserit, excommunicationis sententiam incurrat, aut alteri
gravi poenae subiaceat; nulla tamen fortasse congrua magis videri poterit, quam si ex eo ordine, quem aliis praeferre ausus fuerit, ad illum,
quem damnare non timuerit, ita transire cogatur, ac si speciali voto
eum professus ordinem fuisset; si alia de causa, aut ex nullo ordine ad
alium ordinem, aut ex omnibus ad omnes transire religiosis permittatur; si qui reformari ad veram observantiam ordines non possunt,
omnino destruantur, et loca

---

75   ferre cogantur: ferre cogant MS, forte gerant ED

LATIN TEXT WITH ENGLISH TRANSLATION

[690] who follow the Rule of St. Benedict are required to wear a
habit of the same color and form and are called by the same name
(i.e., Monks of St. Benedict), so that we may abolish such differences
of habit and so many different names; if those who observe the rule
of St. Augustine, or Francis, or the rules of other saints do likewise;[48]
if disputes about the Conception of the Blessed Virgin[49] or the
Blood of Christ—whether some of it remained on earth—and so
forth, which are waged among the religious orders more heatedly
than they should be, are thoroughly abolished, so that even to speak,
write, or dispute about them is punishable by excommunication; if
the Church defines which view must be accepted when Duns Scotus
contradicts Blessed Thomas and when other doctors disagree among
themselves, at least in those matters which pertain to the Faith,
and if she condemns the opposite opinion; if all who belong to the
same rule are compelled to keep the same manner and form in diet,
clothing, and all other departments of life, and if traveling monks or
religious or others who become guests at a monastery are obliged,
although they are guests, to live in the same way as the brothers
who dwell there and to perform the same tasks; if the libraries of
religious in any order are shared in common with all others, so that
anyone may enter and, after signing for the books he requires and
leaving a deposit commensurate with their value, may take them
away and keep them for a set time, in keeping with their size; if the
brothers of different orders who are traveling or sailing together or
who are lodging at an inn are commanded to share the same table; if
a religious of any order who presumes in speech or writing to prefer
his own order or monastery to others or to slander or condemn
another religious order incurs a sentence of excommunication, or is
subject to another heavy penalty—none would seem so appropriate
as to compel him to leave the order he dared to prefer, and to join
the one that he presumed to condemn, as if he had made a special
profession in the latter; if, for some other reason, religious are not
permitted to pass from any order to another, or permitted to pass
from all orders to all others; and if orders that cannot be reformed
and brought to a true observance are destroyed

48 The confusion caused by the variety of religious orders in the Church was discussed at Lateran Council IV (1215) and continued to be discussed in the sixteenth century.

49 The Immaculate Conception (being conceived without original sin) of Mary was
debated among theologians in the Middle Ages, with many Franciscans arguing for
the position and many Dominicans maintaining doubts. In 1854, Pope Pius IX
declared the doctrine to be part of the Catholic faith.

[691] eorum observantibus cedant; si haec inquam, aut his similia, quae aut a Sapientia Tua prudentius, saniusque cogitabuntur, aut ab aliis, qui rectius, quam nos haec iudicare possunt, Tibi suggerentur, apostolicis firmissimis definitionibus, gravissimisque animadversionibus decernantur, ac statuantur, omnes inter religiosos homines dissensiones, discordiae, ac schismata e medio facile ita auferentur, ut non multi ac paene innumeri, ut modo sunt religionis ordines, congregationesque, sed unus omnium ordo, unaque congregatio, et omnium cor unum, et anima una, sicut una fides, esse videbitur.

Tu vero, Beatissime Pontifex, et Domini[76], qui Te ad hanc dignitatem vocavit, et hominum expectationi, hoc etiam munere satisfacies, neque invicta illa animi Tui fortitudo, quae difficillima, et ardua quaeque superavit, in hoc postremo, quod facillimum esse credimus, deficiet, sed omnia perficies, quae ad singulos Ecclesiae ordines ad puram conversationis sanctitatem ac regularis observantiae probitatem reducendos, opportuna, ac necessaria esse cognoveris, et quasi bonus agricola, postquam ex agro Dominico, cui colonus es constitutus, vitiorum spinas, malarumque consuetudinum sentes avulseris, ac eradicaveris, tunc demum virtutum semina sparges, et optimorum quorumcumque morum surculos plantabis, irrigabisque continue; quibus certe Deum incrementum postmodum daturum speramus, ut ex tuis laboribus, et in hac vita, et in futura quoque beatitudine fructum amplius etiam quam centuplum recipias.

Quoniam autem novit Beatitudo tua, nullum decretum, nullam legem tantum valere ad subditorum emendationem, quantum optimi Principis sanctissimos mores (Principum enim exempla magis multo, quam leges movere animos solent). Ideo a Temetipso incipies, relictaque malarum consuetudinum ab aliquibus praeteritis Pontificibus nimium attrita via, ad rectam semitam pontificalis dignitatis ordinem reduces. Neque enim aliter Te facere posse ullo modo credimus. Qui enim ad pastoralem amplitudinem, eo ordine venisti, quo veniendum esse ille optimus Pastor Beatissimus Gregorius descripsit, et primam pastoralis regulae eius partem optime implesti, et reliquas etiam implere Tibi curae futurum existimamus. Neque enim Tibi satis esse ullo modo poterit, rite, recteque ad pastoralem apicem ascendisse, nisi in eo Tu recte vivas, et alios recte vivere, aut praedicationibus, aut exemplo,

---

76   Domini MS: Domino ED

[691] and yield their place to observant ones. If these and similar measures, which Your Holiness will devise with greater soundness and prudence, or which will be suggested by others with better judgment than ours, are established with the firmest Pontifical pronouncements and the most serious penalties, all the dissensions, discord, and schisms among religious will vanish. Then we shall see not many and countless religious orders and congregations, such as now exist, but one order and one congregation of all, and there will be one heart and one mind, just as there is one faith.

But you, Holy Father, will no doubt satisfy both the expectation of the Lord, who called you to this office, and that of men. Moreover, the unconquerable fortitude of your mind, which has overcome the most arduous and difficult challenges, will not be found wanting in this final task, which we think will be very easy, but will accomplish everything you deem timely and necessary for restoring the various orders of the church to a pure and holy manner of life and a correct observance of their rule. When, like a farmer, you have pulled up and removed the thorns of vice and the brambles of bad habit from the Lord's field, you will sow the seeds of the virtues and plant the shoots of good habits, and you will water them continually. To these we hope that God will give increase, so that from your labors you shall reap, both in this life and in the blessedness to come, a harvest of a hundred-fold.

Your Holiness knows, however, that no decree or law can improve the moral habits of subjects as much as the godly conduct of a good prince; for the example of princes tends to make a stronger impression than laws. You will begin, then, with yourself, and by leaving the path of bad habits, which has been too much traveled by some previous Pontiffs, you will bring the office back to the straight path of Pontifical dignity. We believe that you cannot do otherwise, for you came to your pastoral office by the route that Saint Gregory, the greatest of pastors, recommended, and you have laudably fulfilled the first part of his pastoral rule.[50] Thus, we are confident that you will also take care to fulfill the others. Nor will you ever be satisfied merely to have assumed your office in the correct and proper manner, but you will desire also to live in it properly, and to teach others—by preaching, example,

---

50 Pope Gregory the Great (540-604) divided his *Regula Pastoralis* into four parts: a religious leader must have qualifications, the interior life must not be lessened by excessive action, the variety of individuals must be sensitively cared for, and, finally, when all that is successful, the leader must be humble, thanking God.

[692] aut optimis institutionibus doceas, et Te demum cognoscere velis. Haec enim quattuor illa sunt, quae pastoralis regula adimplenda esse admonet. Quae cum[77] Tu ad unguem observanda tibimetipsi proposueris, iamque universo paene terrarum orbe testimonium perhibente, ad pastoralem dignitatem rite, recte, ac legitime ascenderis, primum perfectissime implevisti; reliquum itaque erit, ut et tres alias huius magni muneris Tui partes adimpleas, recte scilicet vivere, ad bene beateque vivendum, aut verbo, aut exemplo, aut rectis optimisque institutionibus reliquos instruere, et temetipsum demum cognoscere; et sic qualis esse debeat optimus pastor, Te abundantissime praestabis. Dimittimus necessarias Pontificis virtutes recognoscere, quae Te saepius legisse credimus, memoriaeque non solum mandasse, sed et ad[78] eas etiam vitae integritate, morumque sanctitate perfectissime attigisse.

Neque tamen hoc Tibi satis esse potest, nisi Romanam Curiam, omnes Cardinalium, Episcoporum, et Clericorum ordines, universas Religiosorum virorum ac mulierum congregationes, quaslibet Christianorum populorum multitudines, Tuo exemplo, Tuis admonitionibus, praedicationibus, institutionibusque eadem, quae Tu sapere, eadem facere, eodemque modo vivere doceas, et quamquam per Temetipsum, incumbentibus Tibi maioribus negotiis, Verbum divinum praedicare non possis, Tui tamen candidissimi mores, Tua Sanctissima Decreta pro magna, efficacique praedicatione habenda sunt, Tuaque illa recte censeri praedicatio potest, quae, Te iubente, per alios impleatur. Cum enim Tu omnium sis fidelium caput, et omnes Christianae Religionis ordines, nonnisi quaedam huius capitis membra esse videantur, quidquid per quoscumque alios facis, per Temetipsum facere videris. Haec igitur Tibi, Beatissime Pater, potissima semper cura futura est, sollicite scilicet curare, ut singuli Ordines sua munera impleant, singula membra suas legitimas, propriasque operationes habeant, et nulla sit Christianorum hominum conditio, quae non propriam vivendi regulam, propriam institutionis normam diligenter custodiat, quoniam, sicut quidquid in tota Ecclesia, Te moderante, boni efficitur, illud Te fecisse, bonique illius operis mercedem expectare non ambigimus, sic sane quodlibet cuiuscumque ordinis peccatum ad Te attinere existimamus; non enim culpae expers caput esse potest, ubi membra ipsa, quae capitis imperio subiecta sunt, proprias institutiones

---

77   cum MS: enim ED
78   ad MS: *om.* ED

[692] or the best arrangements—to live rightly, and finally to examine yourself. These are the four obligations that the *Pastoral Rule* requires. Having determined to observe these to the letter, you fulfilled the first of them, as practically the whole world bears witness, when you assumed your pastoral office in the correct and legal manner. It remains, then, for you to fulfill the other three parts of your great responsibility: to live properly, to teach others to live well—by your words, example, and good and proper arrangements—and to examine yourself. Thus you will clearly show yourself to be the kind of man the best pastor ought to be. We forbear to list the virtues required of a Pontiff, since we assume that you have often read them and have not only committed them to memory, but perfectly attained them by the integrity of your life and the purity of your manners.

You will also not be satisfied unless you teach the Roman Curia, the orders of cardinals, bishops, and clergy, the orders of religious men and women, and the multitudes of Christian people, by your example, advice, preaching, and regulation, to think and act as you do and to live in the same way. Although your great responsibilities prevent you from preaching the word of God in person, your shining conduct and godly decrees will serve as a great and efficacious kind of preaching, and that preaching will rightly be considered yours which others fulfill at your command. Since you are the head of all the faithful and all the branches of the Christian people are but members of this head, whatever you do through others, whoever they may be, you evidently accomplish yourself. And so, Holy Father, it will always be your greatest care that the various branches fulfill their duties and the particular members have their proper and legitimate work to do, and that there is no class of Christians that does not keep to its own rule of life and its own customary norms. Indeed, we know that whatever good is done in the entire Church under your direction is done by you, and that you can expect the reward of that good work; by the same token, any sin of any order belongs to you, for the head cannot be exempt from fault when the members, which are subject to the head's authority,

[693] non recte servant; neque illi, qui aliis praepositus est, satis
esse potest, se immaculatum ab omni peccato custodire, nisi et illos,
quibus pro tempore praeest, propria quaeque instituta servare magna
satagat sollicitudine; quoniam qui subiectorum errata corrigere, atque
emendare neglegit, et consentire, et peccata aliorum consentiendo
propria facere, et viam delinquendi indulgentia aperire videtur; et
cum miserum omnino sit propriis peccatis aeternae felicitatis beatitudine privari, miserrimum sane erit, non propriis, sed aliorum vitiis
aeternae damnationis poenam subire.

Cum igitur temetipsum, Sanctissime Pater, secundum interiorem, ex-
terioremque hominem, iam multo tempore ita formaveris, ut Deo per
interiorem pulchritudinem placere, hominibus vero per exteriorem
virtutem optimorum exemplorum lumen ostendere possis, reliquum
est, ut ad aliorum vitas diligentissime considerandas, et exactissime
corrigendas convertaris. Quid enim Episcopi nomen importet,
nequaquam Te latere credimus, et Bernardum, non Eugenium modo,
sed omnes in Eugenio Pontifices admonere nosti, ut non se tantum,
sed et quae circa se, et quae sub se sunt, considerare diligentissime
velint. Dimittimus ea, quae supra nos sunt, quae quarto ab eo loco
annumerantur, recensere; quoniam de his non attinet nunc aliquid
dicere; sed illud nunc agimus, ut Te summis laudibus extollamus, qui
non solum talem temetipsum, qualem optimum Pontificem Maximum Christi Vicarium, bonumque Pastorem decet, omnibus Christianis praestas, sed maximas curarum sollicitudines subire paratus es,
ut possis omnes Dominicas oves per quaecumque devia aberrantes,
ad viam sanctae conversationis, et Christianae puritatis adducere, et
parare Domino plebem perfectam, et Christianam, cui praees, Ecclesiam universam virginem castam exhibere Christo; quod te minime
facere posse credimus, nisi sic omnium in universum curam suscipias,
ut[79] singulorum ordinum, et singularum personarum non minor Tibi
sit sollicitudo; sic singulos quoque ordines, singulos quoque homines
corrigendos, emendandos, instruendosque Tibi proponas, ut universorum cura nequaquam imminuatur; oportet enim (credimus)
Pontificem summum, Deum Optimum Maximum imitari, qui sic et
universis hominibus providet, et singulis studet, ut omnium optimus,
et singulorum pientissimus Pater esse cognoscatur. Quod cum Tu,
quantum humana conditio patitur,

---

79   ut: et MS, ED

[693] do not rightly keep their rule of life. The man who has authority cannot be content if he keeps himself unstained by sin, but fails to guarantee that those who are temporarily placed in his charge preserve their way of life entire. Whoever fails to correct and amend the errors of his subjects is viewed as consenting to them; by consenting he makes them his own errors, and by his indulgence he opens the way to wrongdoing. While it is a sad thing to be deprived of eternal blessedness by one's own sins, it is surely most regrettable to pay the price of eternal damnation for others' vices, rather than one's own.

And so, Holy Father, since you have formed yourself in both the inner and the outer man in such a way as to please God with your interior beauty, and to set a shining example to others with your exterior virtue, it remains for you carefully to examine and diligently to correct their lives. We have no doubt that you know that the word "bishop" means "overseer," and that St. Bernard warned Eugenius— and every other Pope, by extension— to examine not only himself, but also everything around him and beneath him. We omit to mention the things above, which he counts in the fourth place, since they do not concern us here. Rather, our present object is to extol you with the highest praise, since you are not only showing yourself to be what the Supreme Pontiff, the great Vicar of Christ, and a good shepherd ought to be, but you are prepared to take the greatest care to lead all the Lord's sheep, no matter where they stray, to the path of holy living and Christian purity, to prepare for the Lord a perfect people, and to present the entire Christian Church, over which you preside, as a chaste bride to Christ. We do not believe you can do this unless you undertake the care of all persons together in such a way that you show equal concern for each and every estate and person within the Church, and set yourself to correct, amend, and instruct individual classes of men and individual persons in such a way as not to diminish the care of all. In our opinion, it behooves the Supreme Pontiff to imitate God, the Greatest Good, who so provides for all men collectively and for each person individually that he is recognized as the best father of all and the kindest father of each. Since you desire to fulfill this role, insofar as the human condition allows,

[694] implere desideras, omnes ecclesiasticos ordines ante mentis Tuae oculos statuisti, et singulorum errata considerando, magnae illius sapientiae et pietatis Tuae institutione, et omnibus et singulis saluberrima remedia praeparare non dissimulabis.

Cardinalium ante omnes ordo sese Tibi offert, qui non solum sub Te, et circa Te, sed intra Te quodammodo esse videntur; fratres enim eos Tuos appellas, et sunt, cum quibus pontificalis curae onera dispertiri mos est. In horum ordine, si quid aut temporis iniuria, aut aliquorum pontificum indulgentia, ne incuriam dixerimus, vitium inolevit; si propter maximam, quam post Te iste ordo auctoritatem ac potestatem habere videtur, ad aliquam peccandi libertatem delapsus est; si sint ex eo numero aliqui, quibus quaecumque libuerint, eadem sibi licere videantur; si ad illud aliqui forte pervenerunt, ut dum neque peccare erubescunt, et Dominum offendant, et hominibus scandali ruinaeque occasionem praebeant; nihil enim magis Divinae Maiestatis bonitatem spernere, magisque irritare existimamus, quam illorum peccata, qui alios a peccatis coercere deberent; nihil magis hominibus peccandi occasionem praestare censemus, quam maiorum exempla virorum, et eorum maxime, qui ideo a Domino super ecclesiasticae dignitatis candelabrum erecti sunt, ut quasi ardentes lampades per bonorum operum lumen omnibus, qui in hac universae ecclesiae domo sunt, lucentem suo exemplo verae religionis et pietatis semitam demonstrent; si non maiora crimina, sed vel minima aliqua macula hunc dignissimum praestantissimumque ordinem deturpet; quoniam in tam excellenti ordine minimum esse nihil omnino potest; peccata namque etiam ipsa, quae in humili abiectoque homine parva existimari solent, in his, qui sublimiores sunt, maxima reputantur, et quanto aliis dignitate antecellunt, tanto eorum turpiora[80] atque deformiora sunt vitia. Si aliquid huiusmodi hic Celsitudini Tuae proximus Ordo patitur, Tu vero, quae patitur,[81] non intelligis, timendum sane est, ne pro maximo Tibi a Domino peccato imputetur, quod pretiosa haec Domini Iesu membra, nobiliorem Ecclesiae partem, sublimiorem ordinem, Tibique viciniorem vel tantillum dedecoris pati permittas, Tu, quem in Pastorem et[82] Episcopum animarum suarum elegerunt, si aliqua parte laborantem, minimeque sanum ordinem neglegas,[83] Tu temetipsum alienum a culpa existimare vix poteris. Si enim eos, qui a Te solo

---

80   turpiora *Barletta*: turpia MS, ED
81   quae MS: si quae ED
82   et MS: *om.* ED
83   si aliqua parte laborantem minimeque sanum ordinem neglegas: si aliqua parti laborantem minimeque sanum ordinem negligas ED, haec minime sanitas si autem aliaque parte laborare sentis et curare negligis MS

[694] you have placed all the ecclesiastical orders before your mind's eye, and as you consider the errors of each, in keeping with your customary wisdom and kindness, you will not hesitate to prepare the most salutary remedies for all.

The first to come before you are the cardinals, who, evidently, are not only below you and around you but are, in a sense, within you. You call them "brothers," and by custom you share with them the burdens of the Pontifical office. And so, if some vice has grown among them, either through the injury of time or the indulgence—not to say carelessness—of Pontiffs; if this class, because of the authority and power it clearly enjoys, which is second only to yours, has lapsed into a certain liberty to sin; if there are some in this number who think that they may do whatever they please;[51] if some have come into this office who do not blush to sin, who offend the Lord, and who cause an occasion for scandal and ruin for other men—for nothing, in our opinion, amounts to a greater rejection and insult of God's goodness than the sins of those who ought to keep others from sin, and nothing produces a greater occasion for sin in others than the bad example of great men, especially those who have been set upon the lamp-stand of ecclesiastical office, and who, like burning lamps, ought to shine the light of their good works and show the entire family of the Universal Church the shining path of true religion and piety; if not only great crimes, but even the least defilement has stained this worthy and distinguished order—for in such an excellent order there can be no minimum, and even sins regarded as small in a humble and lowly man are considered very great in the more exalted, and to the degree that such men excel others in status, their vices are more ugly and shameful; if the order closest to Your Holiness suffers in this way, but you do not understand what it suffers, there is good reason to fear that the Lord will lay great blame upon you, since you have allowed these precious members of the Lord Jesus, the nobler part of the Church, its more exalted branch and the one closest to you, to suffer even the slightest disgrace. If you, whom they elected as Shepherd and Overseer of their souls, neglect the infirmity and sickness of this order in any part, you will scarcely be able to hold yourself free from blame.

---

51 Giustiniani employs the well-known Latin pun on licet (permitted) and libet (pleasing). This pun is also used by Dante in Italian in Inferno 5:56.

[695] curandi instruendique sunt, quippe, qui alium, praeter Te,
in terris superiorem non habent, aut gratia, aut amore, aut timore,
trepidationeve aliqua, aut alia quavis ratione curare dissimulabis, illi
a quo curabuntur? Et quinam futuri sunt, qui curae Tuae pietatem
aut sentire possint, aut sperare audeant, si viscera ipsa Tua, fratres
Tuos, quos cotidie vides, cum quibus communi labore omnia Ecclesiae sanctae Dei negotia tractas, quos aut Tu tibi elegisti, aut illi Te in
Pastorem et Principem delegerunt, si forte, quoniam et ipsi homines
sunt, aberrare quoquomodo eos contingat, ad congruam dignitatis
eorum sanctitatem deducere, non omni cura et sollicitudine invigiles
et labores? Quomodo, qui et dignitatis ratione et officiorum diversitate et locorum distantia ita a Te longe absunt, ut paene extranei
dici possint, licet nullus omnino Christiani nominis, nullus humanae
naturae particeps a Te extraneus sit, suorum errorum correctionem
sperare poterunt?

Quoniam autem hunc Cardinalium ordinem nimio beneficiorum
honore et onere, rerumque omnium affluxu et abundantia, si quid
aberrant, aberrare credimus, eorum saluti maxime conducere existimamus, si firma irrefragabilique sanctione decreveris, Cardinalibus
nullum deinceps beneficium, eorum titulis dumtaxat exceptis, confer-
ri posse. Et ne a Te summo eorumdem pontifice debitis pro suprema
Cardinalatus dignitate stipendiis defraudentur, consulentes Tuae et
eorum utilitati, valde congruum fore iudicamus, si certis pensionibus,
nequaquam imminuto publico aerario, omnes alantur; quas pen-
siones Tu, Beatissime Pater, beneficiorum omnium habita ratione,
quotannis diligentissime exigendas curabis. Haec autem, Beatissime
Pater, per excessum quemdam illius caritatis, quae modum aliquem
servare nescit, nos dixisse, Beatitudinem Tuam existimare putamus;
non quod in praestantissimo Eminentissimoque hoc Cardinalium
ordine minimum aliquid minus rectum, aut minus decens inesse
suspicemur. Non enim nostrum est, sinistrum aliquid de tanti ordinis
maiestate suspicari, sed quoniam, si fortasse macula aliqua in tanta
dignitate esse contigerit, Te, Sanctissime Pater, vigilem, sollicitum,
magnanimum, intrepidum, magno caritatis zelo succensum, in
eorum quamvis minimo errore correctorem optamus. Tu, quoniam
ex horum paucorum vivendi rectitudine, universae Ecclesiae salus
pendet, Tu, quem nihil

[695] Indeed, if you hesitate out of favor, love, fear, or some scruple to care for those whom you alone must care for and instruct, since they have no other superior on earth but you, who else will care for them? Who will feel your kindly attention or hope for your favor, if even your inward parts, your brothers, whom you see every day, with whom you share all the business of the holy Church of God, and whom you personally appointed or who elected you as Shepherd and Prince, should happen to stray somewhat—for they too are men—and you should fail to watch with all care and to work with all solicitude to bring them back to the holiness that befits their office? How then will those who by virtue of their rank or various duties or distance from Rome are so far removed from you that they can be called strangers—although in fact no Christian and no member of the human race is really a stranger to you—hope to obtain the correction of their errors?

Since, however, we believe that the order of cardinals, if it errs at all, errs through the excessive granting of the honor and burden of benefices[52] and the acquisition and abundance of all sorts of goods, we think it would be most conducive to their salvation if you would decree, with firm and unquestionable sanctions, that cardinals may receive no benefice otherwise than from their titular churches. But lest you, the Supreme Pontiff, deprive them of a just recompense in keeping with the high rank of cardinal, we think it would be best for your good and theirs to support them with fixed pensions, without diminishing the public treasury. They would receive these pensions every year from you, Holy Father, after you have taken account of their benefices. In any case, you surely recognize that we have made these suggestions through an excess of that charity which knows no bounds, and not because we suspect that there is anything at all crooked or indecent in that illustrious and eminent order of cardinals. For it is not our part to entertain dark suspicions about this majestic order; rather, we simply wish you, Holy Father, to be a watchful, careful, magnanimous, fearless, and zealous corrector of any error on their part, however small. Since the health of the entire Church depends upon their rectitude of life,

---

52   The pun here is one used by St. Jerome: honoris (honor) and onoris (burden). It occurred earlier in the Libellus in 627 and 696

[696] utilius illis facere posse sentimus, neque quam maiorem illis gratiam referre valeas, qui te in Pontificem elegerunt, intellegimus, quam si errantes ab errore revoces. Cum enim errorum omnium animi sit infirmitas maior quam corporis,[84] maiorem certe illis gratiam habere debemus, qui nos ab aliquo errore, quam qui a quavis corporis infirmitate liberaverint.[85] Neque Te aliter Domino obtemperare posse videmus, qui semel quidem Petrum, Te vero semper, si illi cordis Tui aures libenter accomodaveris, admonet, ut conversus confirmes fratres Tuos, pro quibus sane Tua pastoralis cura maiori sollicitudine invigilare debet. Quoniam si hi ad[86] Te omnes tales non fuerint, quales esse oportet, nullam in ceteris inferioribus ordinibus propriarum regularum observantiam futuram suspicari non sine ratione possumus. Si vero tales sint, quales haec suprema dignitas expostulat, nulla ceterorum ordinum sollicitudo Beatitudini Tuae relinquitur; nam illis pro Te inferiorum ordinum curam, sollicitudinemque subeuntibus, nullus omnino erit, qui vel tantillum ab institutionum suarum semita aut temere audeat, aut impunis valeat aberrare.

Archiepiscoporum enim et episcoporum ordo, si, Te iubente, Cardinalibus ita subiiciatur, ut singulis annis, aut quolibet saltem triennio apud ipsos Cardinales rationem villicationis suae reddere episcopi omnes teneantur, et sub eorum iudicio, qui[87] aliter, quam Episcopum deceat, vixerint, et ministerium suum non impleverint, quique commissam sibi plebem non visitaverint, non verbo et exemplo recte vivere docuerint, dignitatis privatione puniri, et perpetuo carceri ad panem doloris comedendum emancipari timuerint, facile eveniet, ut illi, qui episcopali fulgent dignitate, episcopi etiam condignos mores habere studeant; et qui congaudent honore ministrationum, onera quoque portare non dissimulent.[88] Si itaque pro ignorantia, superstitione, ambitione, avaritia aliisque huiusmodi vitiis, quibus multos huius ordinis viros laborare non ambiguum est, vult Beatitudo Tua, Sanctissime Pater, his vitiis oppositas virtutes in hoc ordine inducere, optatque pietas Tua, ut omnes Ecclesiae tales episcopos habeant, quales esse oportere Episcopos Divinus nobis sermo demonstrat, sine crimine scilicet, non superbos, non iracundos, non vinolentos, non litigiosos, non percussores, non turpis lucri cupidos, sed irreprehensibiles, sobrios, continentes, ornatos, prudentes, pudicos, hospitales,

---

84   sit infirmitas maior quam corporis ED: sit infirmitas animusque corpore praestatior appareat MS

85   liberaverint MS: liberaverit ED

86   ad Te: ante MS, a Te ED

87   qui MS: an ED

88   congaudent...dissimulent MS: congaudet...recuset ED

[696] we feel that you could offer nothing more useful, nor do a greater favor to those who chose you as Pontiff, than to recall them from error when they stray. Since the source of all errors is an infirmity of the mind, and not of the body, we should be more grateful to those who free us from such errors than from some corporal infirmity. Nor do we see how you can otherwise obey the Lord, who warned Peter once, and who always warns you, if you willingly keep the ears of your heart open to him, to turn and strengthen the brethren, over whom, indeed, you should watch with still greater pastoral care and solicitude. If these are not always disposed to you as they should be, we foresee, not without good reason, that none of the inferior orders will keep its own rules. If however, they are such men as the supreme dignity of their office requires them to be, Your Holiness is left with no reason to worry about the other classes, for the cardinals will undertake for you the care of the lower orders, and no one will dare or be able to stray in the least from the path of their rule.

Indeed, let the order of archbishops and bishops be subject, at your command, to the cardinals, so that every year, or every three years at least, all bishops are obliged to give an account of their stewardship. If it turns out that, in the cardinals' judgment, they have lived otherwise than a bishop should, or that they have not fulfilled their ministry by visiting the people entrusted to them and teaching them by word and example how to live rightly, let them be punished with removal from office and life imprisonment, to eat the bread of sorrow. In this way those who enjoy the splendid office of bishop will also be eager to possess habits worthy of a bishop, and those who enjoy the privilege of ministry will not refuse to bear its burdens. And so, if Your Holiness is ready and willing, you can replace ignorance, superstition, ambition, avarice and other such vices, from which many men of this class are known to suffer, with the opposite virtues, so that all churches may have the kind of bishops required by the word of God (1 Tim 3:1-7), namely men without guilt, pride and anger, who are not given to wine or lawsuits, who are not violent or eager for gain, who are blameless, sober, self-controlled, respected, prudent, modest, hospitable,

[697] doctores, benignos, iustos, sanctos, divina praecepta et sacrae scripturae disciplinam amplectentes, qui possint Fideles in doctrina sana cohortari, et eos, qui contradicunt, arguere; oportet, ut credimus, Te ante omnia invigilare, ut, Te ecclesiam Dei moderante, nullus ad hanc dignitatem ambiendi sollicitudine, Principum gratia, importuna Tui vexatione, aut alia quavis non legitima ratione, sed sola vitae integritate, morum sanctitate, Divinarum Scripturarum doctrina ascendat. In monasterio, ait quidam, omnes recipiendi sunt, spe proficiendi et meliorandi; ad episcopatum vero non sunt admittendi, nisi qui antea eo ordine digni sunt; nisi enim quis[89] ad episcopatum veniens eas secum virtutes attulerit, quas habere episcopum oportet, quid de eo sperandum boni sit, non videmus; cum illos, qui mali antea sunt, dignitates non corrigere, sed depravare potius soleant.

Post haec[90] cura futura Tibi est, ut frequenter a Cardinalibus, aut a dignissimis integerrimisque familiarium Tuorum Episcopi visitentur, et ad eorum vitia cognoscenda clerus populusque illis commissus diligenter inquiratur, libenter audiatur, si in aliquo deliquerint, si neglegentius, quam episcopos deceat, munera sua impleverint, et tunc corrigantur, et si opus erit, ea, quam recte possidere neglexerunt, dignitate priventur; et pro criminum enormitate, si quae in illis apparuerint, gravius etiam plectantur. Discent profecto, qui a Te, aut a Tuis legatis frequentius sic visitentur et sollicite corrigantur, clericos, sacerdotes, et omnes, qui sub illis sunt et ipsi visitare, examinare atque corrigere, et quales illi sint, quibus manum imponere habeant, diligentius inquirere. In quo sane negotio multum profuturum sperare possumus, si Tu, Beatissime Pater, episcopis omnibus iusseris, ut nemini nisi bene nato riteque educato, nisi bona indole et[91] bonis moribus praedito, nisi pro aetate mediocriter literis instituto, minores ordines conferant; neminem nisi probatae virtutis atque doctrinae ad sacerdotalem dignitatem assumant, et cui insuper de officio aut beneficio, ex quo victui et vestitui necessaria habere possit, provisum sit, quod in Germaniae partibus fieri solitum est. Multos enim nunc sacerdotes videmus, qui misera,[92] qua premuntur, paupertate vitae, urgentibus necessitatibus, ad minus sacerdoti congrua negotia, ad illicitas quasque artes, ad turpissimam quamlibet vivendi rationem descendunt

---

89   quis MS: qui ED
90   post haec ED: sequens vero post hanc MS
91   bona indole et: bona indole aut MS, bonae indolis, nisi ED
92   misera MS: miseria ED

[697] able to teach, kindly, just, holy, and eager to embrace the precepts of God and the discipline of Scripture, and who can encourage the faithful in sound doctrine and refute those who contradict it. To accomplish this, however, we believe that Your Holiness must take special care, as you govern the Church, not to allow anyone to assume this office through ambitious conduct, through the patronage of princes, by importuning you or by some other illegitimate means; rather, he should obtain it only by the integrity of his life, the holiness of his conduct, and his learning in the Holy Scriptures. One man has said that all persons should be received into a monastery, with the hope that they will make progress and improve themselves there; only those should be admitted to the episcopacy, however, who are already worthy of the office.[53] For unless a new bishop brings with him the virtues that a bishop ought to have, we do not see what good we may expect from him, since those who are already bad tend not to be corrected, but rather become corrupted, when they enter high office.

Next, you will see to it that bishops are frequently visited by cardinals or by the worthiest and most honest of your friends. Let these seek out the bishops' faults by diligently questioning and gladly listening to the clergy and the people committed to them, to see if they have failed in any respect or fulfilled their duties too carelessly; let them be corrected on the spot and, if necessary, deprived of the office that they have failed to hold properly; and let them be punished even more severely if more grievous crimes appear. When bishops are more frequently visited and corrected by you or by your delegates, they will quickly learn to visit, examine, and correct the clergy, priests, and all who are below them, and to inquire more diligently into the character of the men on whom they must lay their hands in ordination. In this matter, we anticipate a great benefit, Holy Father, if you command all bishops to ordain to the minor orders only those who are well-born and properly brought up, of good character and good conduct, and reasonably well educated for their age; and let them receive into the order of the priesthood only those who are men of proven virtue and learning, and for whom due provision has been made regarding the office or benefice on which they will depend for food and clothing, as is the custom in German lands. Indeed we see many priests who, because of their wretched poverty and urgent need, take on work that is inappropriate for a priest, practice illicit arts of all sorts, or enter shameful occupations.

53   St. Bernard (1090-1153) to Pope Eugenius III in the treatise *De Consideratione* 4, 4, 11.

[698] et eorum fidei commissam populorum curam aut ignorantia implere nequeunt, aut aliis occupationibus distracti neglegunt, aut, quod deterius est, propria etiam pravitate eos corrumpunt, quos corrigere, atque ad meliora studia invitare debebant. Quae quidem non acciderent, si pastor et episcopus super eos invigilaret, si ignavos ac vecordes et vitiis obvolutos ad sacerdotium non admitteret; si quotannis aut etiam saepius in anno clericos suos episcopus visitaret, admoneret, argueret, increparet, corrigeretque. Legimus olim, quod ad sacerdotalem ordinem non admittebatur quispiam, nisi, praeter alia plura, omnes Prophetae psalmos memoriter teneret, et qui ex psalmorum numero aliquem memoriae non mandasset, difficillime a summo Pontifice ad Sacerdotium admittebatur; nunc vero miraculum reputatur, si quis ex sacerdotibus aut omnes, aut aliquos psalmos memoriae tenere reperiatur, cum et multi sint, qui neque legere illos commode valeant. Olim post monasterii disciplinam, diuturnamque probationem, ad Sacerdotalem dignitatem, ad maioris scilicet perfectionis gradum aliquis evocabatur; nunc autem quisquis ex sacerdotali ordine ad monasterium convertitur, multum profecisse existimatur, non quod in monasteriis sit nunc perfectior, quam olim fuerat disciplina, sed quia, qui perfectissimus esse in ecclesia sacerdotalis ordo solebat, paulatim ita defluxit, ut imperfectissimus paene omnium effectus sit, et plurimorum ex eo ordine vita turpior, quam laicorum seu saecularium hominum appareat. Haec autem omnia singulorum membrorum, singulorum scilicet ordinum infirmitates a Capite ipso, a summis scilicet pontificibus ortum habere facile quilibet intueri potest. Sunt enim sic haec ad invicem singula membra coniuncta capiti suo, omnia simul subiecta, ut qualem superiora membra mediis sanitatem, robur et decorem praestant, talem, quae media sunt, inferioribus subministrent, suprema vero illa talem omnino praestant, qualem ipsa a capite recipiunt; qualem pontifex circa Cardinalium vitam et disciplinam curam et sollicitudinem habet, talem illi circa episcoporum mores custodiunt, et qualem episcopi a superioribus suis curam recipiunt, talem his, qui sub eis sunt, clericis scilicet et sacerdotibus impendunt. Sic enim in hac ecclesiastica hierarchia ordo se habet, ut illo, qui supremam sedem tenet, languescente, inferiores omnes ordines aegrotare necesse sit; eo autem convalescente, singula paulatim

[698] Others, because they are ignorant or distracted by other business, cannot or will not fulfill their duty to care for the people committed to them, or worse still, corrupt with their own depravity those whom they ought to correct and attract to better pursuits. These things would not happen if a shepherd and bishop were watching over them, if he did not admit worthless, lazy, and vicious men to the priesthood, and if he visited his clergy once a year, or even more often, and admonished, reproved, scolded, and corrected them. We read that formerly no one was admitted to the priesthood unless, among other things, he knew all the Psalms by heart; and if a candidate had failed to memorize any of them, the Supreme Pontiff was most reluctant to accept him for the priesthood. Now, however, one thinks it miraculous to have found a priest who has memorized all or even some of the Psalms of the Prophet, since there are many who cannot even read them properly. In former times, one was called to the priestly dignity, which is a higher state of perfection, after training in a monastery and a lengthy probation. Now, however, anyone who turns from the priesthood to a monastery is thought to have made great progress—not because the current discipline of monasteries is greater than it once was, but because the priesthood, which was once considered the most perfect order in the church, has gradually declined to become virtually the most imperfect of all, and many in this class seem to live more disgracefully than laymen. All of the infirmities that exist in particular members, however, originate from the head, namely from the Supreme Pontiff, as anyone can see.[54] For these members are all joined to their head and subject to him in such a way that the kind of health, strength, and beauty that the superior members bring to those in the middle will be passed on by these in turn to the lower members, while the superior members will provide what they receive from the head. In the same way, the care that the Pontiff has for the life and discipline of the cardinals is the same that the latter will have for the conduct of bishops, and the care that the bishops receive from their superiors is the same that they will devote to the clergy and priests who are below them. This is how the Church's hierarchy operates, so that when the man who occupies the highest place languishes, all the inferior orders must do likewise; but when he recovers his strength, the various members,

---

54 Reform in "head and members" was already called for in the Council of Constance (1414-1418).

[699] membra, ea etiam, quae inferiora et infima sunt, convalescere soleant.

Quare, Sanctissime Pater, cum totius ecclesiastici Deo militantis exercitus salutem aut infirmitatem Tibi imputandam esse non ambigis, maxima Tibi vigilandi necessitas incumbit, ut a Te ante omnes, et a[93] domus Tuae familia, in quam omnes intuebuntur, rectae institutionis, sanctaeque conversationis exemplum omnes inferiores ordines accipere possint. Familiam autem domus Tuae, de qua dicere paene exciderat, omnes superiores, medios, inferioresque ordines[94] intuituros esse[95] diximus, quoniam Teipsum intueri non omnium est, et[96] qui in domo Tua versantur, ita eos aliud a Te non existimantur, ut qui illos intuebuntur, Te videre existimabunt, nam neque umbra figuram corporis, neque cera annuli imaginem expressius exprimunt, quam familiares domus principis vitam exprimere soleant.[97] Ex domo autem, sive recte sive perverse instituta sit, principis vita et disciplina in totam civitatem diffunditur, et ex civitate in universum eius imperium spargitur. Quare cum Te sanctissimis moribus ornatum, omniumque virtutum inaestimabili[98] pulchritudine decoratum videmus, talem futuram domus Tuae familiam credimus, et Cardinalium superiorem, Episcoporum medium, Clericorum ac Sacerdotum inferiorem ordinem cito similem videre speramus. Te enim pastoralis dignitatis regulam diligenter servante, et sedulam de omnibus sollicitudinem habente, reliqui certe ordines suas sunt institutiones servaturi, religiosorum maxime virorum et mulierum, quibus Tu[99], Beatissime Pater, speciali innatae caritatis Tuae praerogativa, maiori quodam amoris affectu devinctus es. Semper enim religiosos omnes ordines, dum in minoribus ageres, fovere, ornare, beneficiisque cumulare contendisti; unde in maximam spem bonorum religiosorum animas erexisti, postquam Te ad supremam dignitatem ascendisse intuentur, et veteris in religionem caritatis minime oblitum esse existimant, ac Tuo nutu statim universos religiosorum ordines reformandos expectant. Non enim minus, quam ceteri omnes, immo et multo fortasse magis a regularum observantia, a rectis patrum institutionibus singuli fratrum, et sanctimonialium monacharum ordines aberraverunt, et quamquam alii quidem magis, alii minus a recta semita declinaverint, nequaquam tamen dubium est, omnes non mediocriter declinasse, et paene inutiles factos esse.[100]

Tuum igitur erit, Beatissime

93   a MS: *om.* ED
94   ordines MS, *Barletta*: ordinis ED
95   intuituros esse: intuitu eos MS, intuituros eos ED
96   et MS: quomodo ED
97   existimantur: existimant MS, ED
98   inaestimabili: inextimabili MS, ED
99   Tu *Barletta*: Te MS, ED
100 alii quidem magis, alii minus...declinaverint *Barletta*: alios quidem minus, alios autem minus ...declinaveris MS; alios quidem minus, alios minus … declinaverint ED

[699] even those that are in lower positions or the lowest of all, tend to get better.

And so, Holy Father, as you are aware that the health or infirmity of the entire Church Militant of God must be attributed to you, you must show great vigilance, so that all the inferior orders will receive from you and from your household, toward which they all will be looking, an example of proper conduct and holy living. As for your household, which we had almost forgotten to mention, we said that all the orders of the church—lower, middle, and higher—will be looking toward it, since it is not possible for everyone to see you in person; for those who dwell in your house are not considered different from you, and those who see them will think that they see you. Indeed, the shadow does not more faithfully express the shape of the body, nor wax the image of the ring, than the members of a prince's household express the life of the prince. From the prince's house, whether it has been rightly or crookedly managed, his life and discipline spread to the whole city, and from the city it is diffused upon his entire realm. Thus, seeing that you are adorned with the holiest conduct and with the inestimable beauty of every virtue, we believe that your household will be adorned likewise, and we hope to see the superior order of Cardinals and the middle order of bishops and the lower order of clergy and priests follow suit. When you diligently keep the rule of your pastoral office and maintain a deep concern for all, the remaining classes will certainly keep their rules— especially the class of religious men and women, to which you, Holy Father, are joined by a greater bond of affection through a special prerogative of your innate charity. While you were involved in lesser ministries, you always sought to support, adorn, and lavishly benefit all religious orders; thus, you have raised the spirits of good religious men and women to the greatest hope, as they see that you have risen to the highest office. They are confident that you have not forgotten your former love of the religious life, and expect that you will immediately give the nod to a general reform of religious orders. No less than the rest, and perhaps even more, various orders of brothers and nuns have strayed from the observance of their rule and from the institutes of their founders; and while some have wandered further than others from the right path, there can be no doubt that all have strayed somewhat, and become practically useless.

Therefore, it is up to you,

[700] Pater, speciali quadam cura religiones omnes ad perfectissimam regularum suarum observantiam, et sanctam antiquiorem illam conversationem adducere. Quod si facere semel decreveris, nullum in hoc Beatitudo Tua laborem, nullam difficultatem sentiet, quoniam licet longius fortasse, quam reliquos ordines Ecclesiasticos, a sancta sua antiqua institutione monasticos ordines discessisse invenies, ceteris tamen faciliores ad qualemcumque correctionem atque emendationem recipiendam reperies; neque enim contradicere voluntati Tuae, neque mandata Tua spernere, neque correctionem ex pietatis Tuae manibus minus libenter suscipere audebunt,[101] immo quasi mollem ceram sese imperiis Tuis praestabunt, et ad qualemcumque eos formam deducere volueris, eam facillime ac libentissime suscipient. Tuum igitur est, Beatissime Pater, si recte existimamus, omnes religiosos ordines inspicere, omnes religiosorum virorum ac mulierum regulas, institutiones et vivendi rationes considerare; multae etenim sunt ab invicem diversae religiose vivendi institutiones, et cotidie nova aliqua resurgere videtur novae religionis forma, et omnis paene civitas, praeter communes, peculiarem habere videtur religionis ordinem, nullaque est sanctorum Patrum regula, sub qua non multae diversaeque militent religiosorum virorum et feminarum congregationes. Ut enim ex una ceterarum omnium coniecturam capiamus, sub unica beati Benedicti regula quamplures militant Monachorum ordines, et quilibet in semetipso minoris ac maioris observantiae divisionem experitur. Has Tu tantas tam varias multiplicesque regularum et institutionum diversitates considerans, et singulas, quales sint, linceis illis mentis Tuae oculis prospiciens, ante omnia ea, quae approbationem Apostolicae Sedis mereri videbuntur, si ante Te approbatae fuerint, confirmabis; sin minus, Tu primus approbare non dissimulabis. Sunt enim aliquae, quae recte institutae existimantur religiones, quibus, in quantum non adhuc ab Apostolica Sede approbatae videantur, non ita libenter simpliciores mentes acquiescunt. Quas autem minus recte institutas, et proinde minus dignas, ut Apostolicae auctoritatis[102] virtute confirmentur, existimabis, eas palam improbare, manifeste damnare, destruere, atque ad nihilum redigere Beatitudinem Tuam non pigebit. Sicut enim nihil omnino sanctius in universa ecclesia existimatur, quam rectae religionis institutio, ita nihil penitus detestabilius inter

---

101   audebunt MS: recusabunt ED
102   Apostolicae auctoritatis MS: Apostolicae Sedis et auctoritatis ED

[700] Holy Father, to take special care to lead every religious order to the perfect observance of its rule and to its ancient and holy manner of living. If you decide to do this, you will have no trouble or difficulty; for while you may find that the monastic orders have departed from their ancient ways for a longer period of time, you will see that they can be corrected and amended more easily. Indeed, they will not dare to oppose your will, spurn your mandates, or refuse correction from your kindly hands; rather, they will present themselves like soft wax to your precepts, and will easily and gladly assume any form to which you care to bring them. It is your task, Holy Father, if we have a right estimate of things, to inspect all the religious orders and to examine the rules, customs, and way of life of all religious men and women. For there are many diverse ways of organizing the religious life, and it seems that every day some new form arises, and that virtually every city has, in addition to the common forms, its own peculiar religious order; nor is there a single rule of the Holy Fathers that does not have many diverse groups of religious men and women living under it. To take one case as illustrative of all: under the single rule of St. Benedict live numerous orders of monks, and in each of these there is a division between greater and lesser observance. When you have surveyed these considerable and complex differences in rule and custom and have considered their relative merits with the keen insight of your mind, you will first confirm the rules that seem to merit the approval of the Apostolic See, if they have already been approved before your Pontificate; otherwise, you will not hesitate to approve them yourself. For there are some religious rules that are considered properly established, but, since they have not yet been approved by the Apostolic See, simpler minds are reluctant to assent to them. Those, however, which have not been rightly established and consequently are less worthy of confirmation by the Apostolic See, Your Holiness will promptly denounce and manifestly condemn, destroy, and annihilate. For just as there is nothing more sacred in the Church than the establishment of correct religious life, there is found among Christians nothing more detestable

[701] Christianos reperitur, quam perversa aliqua sub religionis nomine vivendi institutio.

Si quae vero earum erunt, quae bonis multis institutionibus perversum aliquod unum, aut non multa permixta habeant, eas Tu, Piissime religionum Pater, corrigere ac emendare, sicque postea approbare, potius quam destruere aut improbare non refugies, confirmandas a Te non solum, quae olim ab Apostolica sunt Sede approbatae, sed et quasdam alias recte institutas non ambigimus. Aliquas tamen improbandas esse credimus, quoniam perversas sub religionis nomine institutiones Sanctitatis Tuae rectitudo ecclesiam sanctam Dei contaminare non patietur. Nonnullas etiam corrigendas, atque Sapientiae Tuae iudicio in melius reformandas speramus. Quae autem sint approbatione, quae damnatione, quae reformatione dignae, dicere non audemus, ne in messem alienam falcem ponere voluisse temerario ausu videamur. Hoc unum tamen tacere non possumus, quasdam esse institutiones, quas sacri canones damnant, quas singulis annis in Cena Domini ecclesia improbat, atque anathematizat, sicut Beguinarum ordo, qui in Gallia viget, aut eorum, qui Fraticelli de Opinione appellantur, qui Sabaudiam Pedemontanamque regionem misere corrumpunt. Alias praeterea institutiones esse credimus, quas non Deo militandi gratia, sed ut per mille fallaciarum genera homines facilius decipiant, multi suscipiunt, qualis eorum existimatur, qui nudis pedibus, non velato capite, sacco induti, nulla certae institutionis norma per saecularium domos discurrunt; quos prudentissimus ille senex Hieronymus, post multas illorum fallacias atque perversos mores, quos recitat, tandem Satanae Apostolos vocat. Huiusmodi, Sanctissime Pater, institutiones, si quae sunt, quae haeresim sapiant, quae superstitionibus foedatae sint, quae non Deo, sed diabolo militare videantur, improbare atque destruere magnum pietatis opus existimabis. Si enim has quasi zizanias e Dominico agro evulseris, bonis insitionibus, rectarum scilicet institutionum religionibus uberiorem crescendi locum dabis, et a multis erroribus atque deceptionibus Christianam plebem liberabis.

Post haec illud statim mentis Tuae oculis occurret sub quarumcumque approbatissimarum regularum rectarum institutionum vexillo aliquos militare, qui quoniam eas ipsas regulas et institutiones servare nituntur, Observantes appellantur, aliquos vero, qui, quoniam praeter hoc, quod in unum conveniunt, aut

[701] than a twisted practice that goes by the name of religious living.

If, however, there are some rules that have one or a few perverse features mixed in with many good customs, we are confident that you, the kindly Father of all Religious, will not refuse to correct and amend these rules, and will afterwards approve them rather than abolish and condemn them; and this applies not only to rules that have already been approved by the Apostolic See, but also to others that have been rightly formulated. Some, however, will no doubt have to be rejected, for Your Holiness will not permit the twisted practices of some religious to contaminate God's Holy Church. We hope, as well, that some rules will be corrected and improved by your wise judgment. We dare not say, however, which ones are worthy of approval, condemnation, or reform, lest we seem too bold and to wish to reap in another's field. There is one thing, however, that we dare not pass over in silence. There are certain organizations that the Sacred Canons condemn, and which the Church anathematizes every year on Holy Thursday, such as the order of Beguines,[55] which flourishes in France, and the so-called *fraticelli della opinione*,[56] who sadly corrupt the region of Savoy and the Piedmont. We believe that there are many other modes of life that people take up not to serve God, but to trick men more easily through a thousand means of deception—such as the life of those who wander through the homes of laymen with bare feet and uncovered heads, dressed in sackcloth, and with no fixed rule of life, and whom that wise old man Jerome, having observed their many deceptions and perverse manners, which he enumerates, calls "Apostles of Satan." If there are any such institutes which have a heretical flavor or are fouled with superstition, and which appear to serve not God but the Devil, you will view it as your solemn duty to condemn and destroy them. If you pull these weeds from Lord's field, you will leave more fertile ground for a good sowing—that is, for religious orders with a proper rule of life—and you will free the Christian people from many errors and deceptions.

Next, your eyes would meet with the fact that there are some who serve under the banner of the most correct and tested rules and usages, and who, because they endeavor to keep these rules and usages, are called "observant," while there are others who, beyond the bare fact that they

---

55 The Beguines, along with the male counterparts, the Beghards, were condemned at the Council of Vienne (1311-1312). They were quasi-religious groups who lived a kinds of monastic life without ecclesiastical approval.

56 These were a renegade group of Franciscans, affirming absolute poverty for the order and lamenting what they saw as corruption within the church. They also claimed that the papacy had come to an end in 1323. The group ceased to exist by Roman decree in 1466.

[702] nihil aliud sanctarum regularum ac institutionum observant, aut potiora omittunt, Conventualium sibi nomen reservant. Quam Tu singularum fere regularum divisionem, et alterius partis perversae consuetudinis abusum depravationemque non ferens, omnes, qui Conventuales appellantur, ad propriarum regularum exactiorem observationem diligentissime reducere conaberis, ut hoc Conventualitatis nomen penitus destruatur. Quod facillime fiet, si in Conventualium monasteriis neminem posse religionem profiteri imperabis, ut omnes religiosorum virorum ac mulierum congregationes Observantes merito valeant appellari. Vanum enim esset de Observantiae nomine sibi blandiri aut gloriari, nisi rebus ipsis per veram exactissimam perfectamque sanctarum regularum ac institutionum observantiam condignum nomen inveniretur. Quod facilius fiet, Beatissime Pontifex, si, Te sub anathematis poena iubente, nullus monachorum quovis modo professus religionem extra claustrum, et extra monasterium, ac seorsum a congregatione valeat habitare, sed quisquis exire monasterium suum, et congregationem relinquere audebit, hic etiam monasticum aut religiosum, quem sumpserat habitum, deponere cogatur, sitque irregularis, ac excommunicatus, et saecularibus potestatibus subditus; si, Te imperante, sanctimoniales omnes sic intra monasteria sua restringantur, ut non solum nullam exeundi facultatem habeant, sed neque videant ipsae quempiam[103], neque ab aliquo videantur, nimiaque illis cum viris alloquendi libertas auferatur; si omnes religiosorum ordines, quemadmodum iam a nostra Camaldulensi religione incepisti, ad reformationem invitabis, et quae singularum religionum Patres in suis conciliis congregati pro bono religionis suae recte instituerint, Apostolicae auctoritatis plenitudine confirmanda decreveris. Existimandum enim est singulos proprias infirmitates efficacius omnibus sentire, et quae illis opportuna sint remedia, intellegere; si tam monachi quam sanctimoniales religiosique omnes penitus, quocumque nomine censeantur, ad episcoporum subiectionem, ut non multo ante haec tempora esse solebant, Te instituente, revertantur, non quod in electionibus praelatorum aut in temporalium rerum administrationibus se intromittere possint episcopi, sed ut quotiens illis visum fuerit, monasteria per se solos, et non per alios vicarios visitare, errantesque corrigere, et ad veram regularum observantiam

---

103   quempiam MS: quidpiam ED

live together,

[702] observe none of their holy rules and customs, or else they omit the more important ones; these have the name "conventual." Since you, however, will tolerate neither the division of individual rules nor the abuse and depravation involved in a second, deformed way of living, you will carefully endeavor to bring those who are called conventual to the more exact observance of their rule, so that the name itself is abolished. You will accomplish this more easily if you declare that no one may take vows in conventual monasteries; thus, all congregations of religious men and women will deservedly be called observant. Indeed, it would be pointless to glory or boast in the name "observant," unless the name should be equal to the facts, through a truly exact and perfect observance of the holy rule and customs. This is more likely to happen, Holy Father, if you command, on pain of excommunication, that no monk who has made any kind of religious profession may live beyond the cloister and monastery apart from his community, and that whoever dares to leave his monastery and community shall be compelled to give up the monastic or religious habit and will be considered irregular, excommunicate, and subject to the secular authorities; if you command that all nuns be restricted to their monasteries, not only that they may not leave, but also that they may not see anyone or be seen by anyone, and that excessive freedom to speak with men may be taken away from them; if you invite all religious orders, just as you invited our own order of Camaldoli, to reform themselves, and if you confirm with the fullness of Apostolic authority the measures which the superiors of the various orders, in conference with their advisors, will have decreed for the good of their way of life—for one must suppose that individual orders are more aware of their own infirmities and better understand which remedies are appropriate; if you command that all monks, nuns, and religious of every kind be subject, as they were not long ago, to the authority of bishops—not so that bishops may interfere in the election of superiors or the administration of temporal affairs, but that they, whenever it seems appropriate, may visit monasteries in person, and not through vicars, and may be able to correct those which are in error

[703] adducere valeant; quod monachi ipsi, quibus subesse, potius quam praeesse, proprium est, patientissime libentissimeque suscipient, si viderint prius episcopos tales esse, quales illos esse oportet, qui aliis recte vivendi viam exemplo et doctrina demonstrent.

Neque enim alia de causa factam credimus subtractionem, exemptionemque hanc Abbatum et monachorum ac religiosorum ordinum ab episcoporum potestate, quam olim, cum ipsa fieri coepisset a sancto viro Bernardo, neque decere, neque licere, neque postremo expedire apud Eugenium Pontificem maximum multi conquerebantur, nunc non tantum licitam ac decentem, sed et utillimam et optimam experimur, nisi quod ea tempestate illi, qui episcopis subiiciebantur, pastores se habere non[104] sentiebant. Hac autem temporum, immo rerum omnium depravatione rapacissimos lupos pro pastoribus illi se habere, misere experiuntur, qui episcopis subiecti sunt. Unde cum subiiciendos episcopis monachos atque alios religiosos dicimus, ut ad perfectam regularum observantiam eos reducant, episcopos prius tales esse oportere intellegimus, ut ipsi propriam episcopi atque pastoris regulam observare didicerint; aliter enim non prodesse, sed obesse plurimum religiosis ordinibus possent; sanius enim est nullis quam lupis gregem committere. Haec aliquaque huiusmodi, quae partim ad extirpationem ignorantiae, superstitionis, dissensionis, ambitionis, avaritiaeque a religiosorum animis opportuna iam diximus, partim consulto pertransimus, quoniam, quae Tibi notissima sunt, longioribus persequi minus decet; quae, si Tu, Beatissime Pater, facienda studueris, fierique mandaveris, facillime omni labe vitiorum purgata, religiosorum omnium ordines ad sanctam conversationem, ac ad perfectam sanctarum regularum et institutionum observantiam redibunt, et quales fuisse in initiis suis monachorum et ceterorum religiosorum virorum[105] et mulierum ordines legimus tales in hoc saeculorum fine sub Leone X, Pontifice Maximo intuebimur.

Sic sane omnibus Religiosorum hominum vitiis expurgatis, sanctaque in singulis propriae institutionis observantia renovata, sicut nunc ex religiosorum hominum vitiis quasi ex propriis fontibus multi vitiorum rivuli in Christianam plebem scaturiunt, sic ex melioribus religiosorum studiis virtutes in plebem virentes exsurgent; talem enim semper plebem vidimus, quales illi religiosi sunt, qui plebi adhaerent, ita ut si religionis vitia expurgaveris, eodem certamine saecularium

---

104   non: *om*. MS, ED
105   virorum MS, *Barletta: om*. ED

[703] and to bring them back to the true observance of their rule. The monks themselves, whose proper role is to be subjects, rather than superiors, will accept this more patiently and willingly, if they first perceive that their bishops are the kind of men they should be, showing by example and teaching how one ought to live.

Indeed, we think that the exemption of abbots, monks, and religious orders from the power of bishops—about which many complained at the time to the great Pontiff Eugenius, who first granted this privilege to St. Bernard, saying that it was neither fitting, licit, nor expedient, although it has now proved to be very good and useful—came about because those who were subject to bishops did not believe that they really had shepherds.[57] Now the times and indeed all things have declined to the point that, sadly, they feel that they have not shepherds, but ravenous wolves, instead. And so, when we say that monks and other religious should be subject to bishops, so that the latter will bring them back to the perfect observance of their rule, we understand that bishops must first be the kind that have learned to observe their own rule as pastors and bishops. Otherwise, they will not help, but greatly hinder religious orders, since it is better to commit the flock to no one at all than to entrust it to wolves. If you undertake these and similar measures for the removal of ignorance, superstition, dissension, ambition, and avarice from the souls of religious—which we have stated in part and deliberately omitted in part, since it is not proper to discuss at length matters which are already well known to you—all religious orders will easily return to a holy way of living and the perfect observance of their rule and customs, purged from all stain of vice, and we shall see such orders of monks and religious men and women in these latter days under the Supreme Pontiff, Leo X, as there were in the days of their founding.

Thus, when you have cleaned up all the vices of religious and renewed the holy observance of each particular rule, virtues derived from the best religious shall well up and flourish among the people, just as vices, all trickling from their own sources, currently gush up among them. Indeed, we see that the people are always like the religious who minister to them, so that if you eradicate the vices of the religious,

---

57   The exemption or independence of monasteries from the local bishop was in exis-
      tence already at the time of Gregory the Great who insisted that monasteries should
      not be subject to bishops. And Bernard in *De Consideratione* virtually argues against
      exemption, while Peter the Venerable argued for it, at least for the Cluniacs.

[704] vitia expurgasse videberis. Si autem praeter maiora apertioraque peccata, quae a sacris tam ecclesiasticis, quam civilibus legibus,
divinisque praeceptis prohibita ac damnata sunt, quaedam alia
non tam peccata, quam peccatorum occasiones a Christiana plebe
abstuleris, non solum perfectos religiosorum omnium ordines, sed
etiam sanctam plebem habere poteris. Quae autem illa sint, quae
occasionem peccandi populis praestent, ut ex infinitis paene quaedam
dicamus, iuramenta ante alia peccandi occasionem dare credimus.
Quoniam dum saepius iuramus, peierare aliquando contingit. Unde
Christianis populis profuturum existimamus, si nemo in iudicio, aut
extra iudicium possit ad iurandum vocari, sine expressa episcopi sui
concessione, qui et nemini iurare concedat, nisi prius et homines,
vitam ac mores, et causam, in qua quisque iurare debeat, diligenter
cognoverit; si ab omnibus collegiis, consiliis, congregationibusque
saecularium virorum ita haec iuramenta prohibeas, ut nulla sit lex,
quae sub poena periurii custodiri praecipiatur,[106] neque ad aliquid
sub sacramenti lege possint ullo modo saeculares adstringi. Multa
enim sunt collegia, multi senatus, qui leges suas sub sacramento
iurisiurandi observandas proponunt, quae tamen minime observari
consueverunt, et quod leve aliquando peccatum erat non observari,
pro iurisiurandi obligatione mortale crimen efficitur.

Ludus praeterea cartarum, taxillorumque, et omnia ludorum genera maximas praebent peccandi occasiones; per haec enim lucrandi
cupiditas, fallaciarum genera multa, irae, blasphemiae, inimicitiaeque
oriuntur, et quod horum non levius est, furandi aviditas crescit. Cum
enim quis per lucrum proprias amisit pecunias, alienas furari omnino ac rapere stimulatur; unde si ludos omnes a Christianis populis
auferri iusseris, multae omnino tollentur peccandi occasiones. Sunt
enim, qui minori quodam corporis, praesentisque vitae detrimento
ab iis, quae animae perditionem aeternam operantur, cavere, bonum
esse existimant, et hos, qui aut cartis ludere aut aleis audent, dextera
mutilari; eos vero, qui horum ludorum instrumenta conficiunt, poena
capitis, si non destiterint, vellent puniri. Nos haec, quae occasionem
delinquendi praestant, omnino prohibenda censemus; quae vero poena praevaricantibus sit statuenda, non facile audemus definire.

Sed et quaedam sunt sancta ecclesiae praecepta, quae non propterea,
quod ipsa

---

106   praecipiatur: praecipiat MS, ED

[704] you will seem to have eliminated those of lay people in the same contest. If, however, you free the Christian people not only from the greater and more obvious sins, which have been condemned and prohibited by both ecclesiastical and civil law and by divine commandment, but also from other faults that are not so much sins as the occasions of sin, you will have perfected not merely the various religious orders, but the Christian people as well. What are these things that cause an occasion of sin to the people? The list is practically endless, but we will sketch just a few and begin by saying that oaths provide the greatest occasion for sinning. For when we swear oaths too frequently, it sometimes happens that we swear falsely. Thus, we think it would be beneficial to the Christian people if no one is invited to take an oath either in court or outside it without the express permission of the bishop, who, for his part, will not permit anyone to swear an oath until he has carefully investigated the persons involved, their life and character, and the facts of the case in which the oath is to be taken; and if you banish oaths from all associations, councils, and congregations of laymen, so that there is no rule which must be kept under penalty of perjury, and that laymen cannot be bound to anything by means of an oath. For there are many councils and many associations that require observance of their rules under the form of an oath that is hardly ever respected, and what would have been a venial sin is rendered mortal by the obligation of an oath.

Next, cards, dice and other games present great occasions for sinning, since they give rise to greed, various forms of cheating, anger, blasphemy, and hostility, and—what is just as bad—they increase the temptation to steal. For when someone has lost his own money through gaming, he is tempted to steal or seize another's. Thus, if you would prohibit all gaming among the Christian people, many occasions of sin would be eliminated. Some think that we should guard against the agents of eternal perdition with a lesser form of corporal and temporal punishment—for example, by punishing anyone who dares to play with cards or dice with the amputation of his right hand.[58] Those, however, who make the instruments of these games should be executed if they refuse to stop. As for us, we agree that things that provide an occasion of sin should be prohibited; what the penalty for deliberate transgressors should be, we would not presume to say.

There are also some precepts of the Church that provide many occasions of sin,

58   This radical suggestion might be influenced by Mark 9:44, Matt 18:8

[705] non recti in se aliquid habeant, sed quoniam non observantes
peccato subiiciunt, perversa autem quadam consuetudine, quae temporum iniuria iam inolevit, a pluribus minus observantur, ideo plurimorum peccatorum occasiones habere videntur; quae quidem cum
Divina praecepta non sint, quae immutari ab hominibus non possunt
(ius enim Divinum ex hominum iudicio non pendet) sed de positivo
iure censet ecclesia, scilicet potius quam immediata Dei praecepta, et
proinde immutari propter populorum salutem non dedecet; propterea
sicut multae religiosorum institutiones habent, ut nullam obligent
ad culpam, sed solum ad poenam, ita si in ecclesiis, vel omnibus vel
quibusdam praeceptis intellegendum statueris, multa certe a populorum multitudine peccata resecabis; inter ea autem, quae huiusmodi
sunt, quadragesimalis abstinentia atque ieiunium esse manifestissime
cognoscitur; dum enim abstinentia a carnibus, ac ieiunare sub mortalis
peccati poena praecipitur, multi autem sunt,[107] qui a carnibus non se
abstinent, plures, qui non ieiunant, omnis fere Christianus populus hoc
peccatorum laqueo irretitur. Unde quidam sic illud de ieiunio praeceptum moderandum censent; quadragesimale et vigiliarum indicere[108]
ieiunium volunt; non autem sub mortalis peccati poena, sed ut libenter
observetur, ieiunantibus plena peccatorum remissio offeratur; sine
ieiunio autem ab esu carnium se abstinentibus, dimidiae peccatorum
suorum partis indulgentia concedatur. Quomodo autem sint haec
moderanda et alia huiusmodi praecepta, ut neque nimia indulgentia
peccandi libertatem praebere videatur, neque dum ad mortale peccatum obligant, quae ad salutem instituta sunt, ad damnationem esse
videantur, Tuae solius sapientiae munus esse censemus.

Alium praeterea a diabolo paratum laqueum videre nobis videtur, qui
multas saecularium hominum animas capit. Mos enim in plurimis
locis pessimus, ut nos credimus, inolevit; contrahentes enim inter se
saeculares viri pro debito excommunicari se posse statuunt, nisi statuto
tempore solverint; quod, si recte sentimus, idem est, quod in forma camerae obligari, et cum minus possint, quae promittunt, debito tempore
exsolvere, excommunicationis poenam incurrentes, pro temporalibus
negotiis aeternam salutem amittunt. Unde Sanctitatis Tuae pietatem
haec passuram[109] non credimus, sed statues potius, Beatissime Pater, ut
nullus, qui clericus non sit, possit aliquo modo

---

107   sunt: sint MS, ED
108   indicere *Barletta*: indicari MS, indicare ED
109   passuram MS: passura ED

[705] not because there is anything wrong with the precepts, but because they bind those who do not observe them to sin, and through a perverse and growing habit, many people fail to keep them. Since they are not divine precepts, which cannot be changed—for the law of God does not depend on the judgment of men—the Church counts them as positive law, rather than unmediated commands of God; thus, they are subject to change for the good of the people. You would eliminate many sins among the people if you were to state clearly that some or all of the precepts observed in churches, like many customs in religious houses, do not incur fault, but only a penalty. Among these, the Lenten fast and abstinence are clear examples. For when abstinence and fasting are commanded under pain of mortal sin, there are many who do not abstain from meat, and more who do not fast, and almost the entire Christian people is caught in the net of sin. Accordingly, some think that the precept of fasting should be modified; they would impose the fast in Lent and on vigils, but not on pain of mortal sin, and would encourage voluntary observance with a plenary indulgence; for those who only abstain from eating meat, an indulgence applied to half of their sins might be offered. Precisely how these and other precepts should be moderated, so that an excessive laxity does not seem to grant license to sin, and that obligations under pain of mortal sin, which were created for the sake of salvation, do not appear to be the cause of damnation, we leave to your wisdom to decide.

There appears to be another snare prepared by the Devil, which captures the souls of many laymen. A bad custom, in our opinion, has arisen in many places, whereby laymen making contracts stipulate that they may be excommunicated for a debt, if they fail to pay it on time. This, if we are not mistaken, is the same as to be obligated *in forma Camerae*,[59] and when they are unable to pay the debt as promised and incur a penalty of excommunication, they lose not their temporal business but their eternal salvation. We are certain that Your Holiness will not tolerate this, but will declare that no one who is not a member of the clergy

---

59   A loan contract *in forma Camerae* would include the provision that an overdue debt would be transferred to the *Camera Apostolica*, the Holy See's own treasury. That seems to imply for Giustiniani that the debtor would eventually be excommunicated and hence lose eternal life.

[706] neque in forma Camerae se obligare, neque pro debito aliquo excommunicari.

Praebent multas viris delinquendi occasiones lasciviores mulieres. Dum enim et fuco et cerussa faciem pingunt, dum discoopertis crinibus in aliquibus locis procedunt, dum ad Missarum celebritates, ad divinum audiendum verbum permixtae viris mulieres, et viri mulieribus conveniunt, magna et paene inevitabilia animarum incendia praeparantur. Quare si fucis omnibus uti mulieres prohibeantur, si velato capite incedere praecipiantur, si in ecclesiis semper mulieres seorsum a viris, et viri a mulieribus esse statuantur, quod antiquae legis praeceptum est, ut usque ad praesentem diem ab Hebraeis custoditur, ut ecclesiarum anterior pars mulierum, posterior virorum sit, multa peccatorum incitamenta et fomenta destruentur.

Sed et illud abominatione plenum esse videtur, quod cum olim meretricibus unus tantum in occultioribus civitatis partibus locus concederetur, nunc passim per omnes vicos et plateas habitare, maxime in ea, in qua Tu resides, Urbe permittatur. Quae impia indulgentia multa milia animarum pessime perdit; dum et mulieres hoc pacto minus per verecundiam coercentur, et viris occasio peccandi ubique parata eos saepius peccare invitat, et iuniores adolescentulae malarum feminarum, quas ubique videre possunt, exemplo, ad quascumque turpitudines incitantur. Hoc tam magnum malum auferre volens Tu, Beatissime Pater, cui non maximarum modo rerum, sed minimarum etiam cura incumbit, et pessimas feminas in aliquo civitatis cuiusque angulo relegandas curabis, et illos, qui alibi in civitate domum illis ad habitandum concesserint, gravissime puniendos esse statueris. Communia haec omnibus Christianorum civitatibus satis futura esse remedia contra hoc letale malum existimamus. Romae autem, quae gravius turpi hucusque foedissima deformitate laborat, maiora efficacioraque sunt remedia excogitanda. Non enim facile potest perversa consuetudo, peccandique impunitas, quae in Urbe praevaluit, auferri; in ea enim nulla est adeo frequentata via, in qua non plures meretrices inhabitent. Horret animus cogitare sacratum palatium tuum meretricibus circumdatum ita, ut neque Tu e domo pedem efferre possis, neque aliquis sedem Tuam adire, cui mille meretricum una spectacula non sint intuenda. Eam semitam, qua Tu sacratissimum Christi corpus sanctis manibus deferre soles, quinam, nisi

[706] may obligate himself *in forma Camerae* or be excommunicated for a debt.

Another occasion of sin is provided by lascivious women. For when they paint their faces with makeup and lipstick and go about in some places with heads uncovered, and when men and women come to celebrate Mass and hear the word of God all mixed together, great and practically unavoidable fires are kindled in their souls. Thus, if women are forbidden to use any kind of makeup and are required to go about with their heads veiled, and if men and women are kept separate in church—which was the rule in the old law, observed even now by the Hebrews, so that the exterior part of churches is reserved for women, and the interior for men—many a stimulus and incitement to sin will be eliminated.

Here appears yet one more abomination: formerly one place was allowed to prostitutes in a rather obscure district of a city, but now they are permitted to live anywhere in all the streets and wards, especially in that City where you reside. This impious concession ruins many thousands of souls, since women are accordingly less inhibited by shame, and men are more often tempted to sin by the opportunities that are constantly presented to them, and young girls are seduced to the foulest behavior by the example the of the bad women they can see everywhere. You will want to abolish this great evil, Holy Father, since it falls to you to care not only for the greatest things but also for the least; thus, you will see to it that the worst women are relegated to some corner of every city and will decree that those who give them a home elsewhere in the city should be punished most severely. We think that these remedies will ordinarily be sufficient to combat this deadly vice in Christian cities. In Rome, however, which has suffered more seriously from this foul and disgusting deformity, better and more efficacious remedies must be devised. The perverse habits and license to sin that have prevailed in the City will not easily be removed, since there is no street so populous that a number of prostitutes do not live there. One shudders to think that your palace is surrounded by such women, so that you cannot set foot outside, nor can anyone approach your throne, without encountering the spectacle of a thousand prostitutes. Who indeed lives on that very street where you are accustomed to carry the Holy Body of Christ,

[707] turpissimae meretrices inhabitant? Eoque deventum est,
ut palam media die per Urbis frequentissima loca Curiales ipsas
meretrices in equis suis deferre non erubescant. Audiveramus olim;
haec nec[110] credere potuissemus, nisi his oculis et haec vidissemus,
et turpiora, quae pudor referre prohibet. Effecta est iam Roma, quae
civitas regia sacerdotalisque esse solebat, turpissimum foedissi-
mumque lupanar, ita ut ex sacerdotibus, et iis, qui in maioribus sunt
dignitatibus constituti, non unam, sed plurimas concubinas habere,
easque ex ecclesiae redditibus delicatissimis cibis pascere, pretiosis-
que indumentis vestire nullus sit pudor. Haec, si Tu non vides, quae
in oculis tuis fiunt, nescimus, quomodo episcopi munus adimpleas; si
vides et dissimulas, timendum est, quod cum bona Sanctitatis Tuae
venia dixerimus, ne Heli sacerdotis poenam incurras. Excita, Pie
Pater, rectitudinis Tuae zelum, et turpia haec et foetida, quae universum fere orbem ad indignationem commoverent, ex Urbe expelle, aut
saltem longe a palatio Tuo remove. Dum enim haec permittuntur,
mirum non est, si apud Christianas nationes Romana Curia non
ea, quae decet, veneratione habetur.[111] Quis enim has turpitudines
audiens potest eos, qui haec faciunt, aut fieri permittunt, ullo modo
venerari? Sed unde digressi sumus, revertentes, his, quae diximus,
Beatissime Pater, multa similia esse credimus, quae Christianae plebi
plurimas peccandi occasiones praestare videntur; quae a Te corri-
genda esse non minus optamus, quam speramus; dimittimus autem
plura recensere, quoniam Sapientiae Tuae omnia notissima esse non
ambigimus, et haec pauca exempli potius gratia diximus, quam quod
haec ipsa Te latere ullo modo suspicati simus.

Christianae Reipublicae membris omnibus languentibus, Te, Beatissime Pater, singulis pro singulorum infirmitate remedia excogitare
atque praeparare (sicut iam diximus) dubitare non possumus. Sed et
praeter peculiaria[112] singulorum membrorum medicamenta, quaedam
etiam universalia omnibus simul corporis huius membris salutaria, ac
multum omnibus profutura perquisisse atque iam advenisse Sanctitatem Tuam existimamus; inter quae primum fortasse locum tenet
illud unum, sine quo nulla religio, nullus ordo, nulla congregatio, nulla
ecclesia rectae conversationis, sanctaeve alicuius institutionis regulam
custodire diutius potest; sine quo neque pars huius Christianae Reipublicae ulla, neque tota ipsa Fidelium congregatio

---

110   nec *Barletta*: ne MS, ED
111   veneratione habetur MS: venerationem habeat ED
112   peculiaria *Barletta*: peculiara MS, peculiarem ED

[707] but meretricious women? It has gotten to the point that members of the Curia are not ashamed to convey prostitutes in broad daylight through the busiest parts of the City. We had heard this once, and would not have believed it had we not seen it with our own eyes, along with sights even more shameful, which modesty prevents us from relating. Rome, once a royal and priestly city, has now become a foul and disgusting brothel, so that among priests and those who enjoy high office there is no shame in having not one, but several concubines, and to provide them with delicacies and fine clothing from ecclesiastical revenues. If you do not see these things, which are in plain sight, we do not know how you can fulfill the role of bishop; if you see them and look the other way, we should fear, if Your Holiness will pardon us for saying so, that you will incur the punishment of Eli the priest.[60] Stir up, Good Father, your righteous zeal, and expel this filth, which arouses the indignation of practically the entire world, or at least banish it far from your palace. While these things are permitted, it is not surprising that the Roman Curia does not receive due respect from Christian nations; for what man who hears of this disgrace can respect those who do these things or allow them to be done? But to return to the point of our discourse, Holy Father, we believe that there are many similar occasions of sin for the Christian people, which we both wish and hope that Your Holiness will correct. We will not list any more of them, since we know that they are all well known to you, and we have mentioned these few only to give examples, rather than because we thought they had escaped your attention.

When all the members of the Christian Commonwealth are languishing, we cannot doubt that you, Holy Father, will devise and prepare remedies for the infirmities of each; but in addition to the medicines proper for each of the members, Your Holiness has no doubt sought and discovered others, which are applicable to all the members of this body and will help them all a great deal. The first of these is something without which no religious community, no order, no congregation, and no church

---

60 The reference is to the priest Eli in 1 Sam 2-4. The story of the death of Eli's sons is told in 1 Sam 4:11, a death probably because of their sins in 1 Sam 2:12-26. Eli himself dies in 1 Sam 4:12-18.

[708] proprium robur, et proprium decorem servare diutius valet.
Hoc autem est frequens Conciliorum celebratio. Te igitur, si omnia
sanctae ecclesiae membra iuvare atque fovere desideras, hoc potissimum statuere decet, ut omnis religionis ordo, omnis religiosorum
congregatio frequenter Patrum, qui in eo ordine sunt, concilium,
quod ipsi Capitulum vocant, studeat advocare atque celebrare; ut
omnis episcopus eorum, qui sub se sunt, clericorum ac presbyterorum
et sacerdotum omnium synodum saepius advocet, in qua cum Dei
timore de ordinis sui reformatione, atque de recta populorum institutione quisquis sollicitus sit; ut ad Metropolitanum episcopum ceteri
sub eo constituti episcopi, cum sacerdotum suorum senioribus, atque
praestantioribus, quotannis ad synodum metropoliticum celebran-
dam statuto die occurrant. Quibus episcopalibus, aut Metropolitanis
conciliis saepius, aut semper aliquis ex Cardinalium numero, aut[113]
familiarium Tuorum probatissimus vir Tuo nomine assistat atque
praesideat. Ut illud, quod tanto perfectius esse credimus, quanto
commune est universali Ecclesiae, custodiatur, ut scilicet universalia
totius Ecclesiae Concilia non solum quolibet decennio, sed omni
quinquennio celebrentur; sine his enim stare Ecclesiam Dei non posse
experientia didicimus; nihil enim aliud ex optima atque perfectissima,
ecclesiam Dei ad eum, in quo nunc est, miserrimum statum deduxit,
nisi huiusmodi Conciliorum omissio.

In universali autem Concilio, si de totius Ecclesiae unitate, si de singularum ecclesiarum reformatione agendum sit, non videmus, cur, qui
Christiano nomine censentur, et illi, qui magis, quam reliqui omnes,
reformatione indigent, nimirum Graeci homines, atque sex aliae
Christianorum Nationes ad hoc Concilium non advocentur? Quantum enim legimus, universalia Concilia cum celebrari priscis temporibus solebant, non ex Italia, aut ex Europa solum, sed ex universo
orbe Patres advocabantur; unde et oecumenica vocata esse censemus.
Quem si morem, qui Apostolicam sedem tenuerunt, studuissent servare, non esset Romana Ecclesia, quae caput cunctarum Ecclesiarum
est, iam nobilissimis membris suis viduata, neque essent aliae tam
clarae ac praestantes Africae et Asiae Ecclesiae a Romana omnium
Ecclesiarum matre divisae, et his, qui Romae degunt, incognitae.

Tibi vero Beatissime Pater, qui a Domino ad Ecclesiarum omnium
sollicitudinem habendam advocatus, universis Ecclesiis praepositus es,

---

113   aut *Barletta*: aut ex MS, ED

[708] can long preserve its rule of life and holy observance, and without which no part of the Christian Commonwealth or the whole gathering of faithful can long maintain its strength and splendor: the frequent meeting of councils. And so, if you desire to help and foster all the members of our Holy Church, you will see fit to declare that every religious order and congregation should frequently convoke a council—what they call a "chapter"—of the fathers who belong to it; that every bishop should more frequently convene a synod of the clergy, elders and priests who are below him, in which every member may attend with the fear of God to the reformation of his own order and the proper formation of the people; that the metropolitan bishop should assemble all the other bishops established under him, along with their senior and more important priests, at a metropolitan synod on a certain day every year, and that the diocesan and metropolitan synods should often or always be attended and presided over by a cardinal or a trusted associate of yours, acting in your name; that the custom, which we regard as superior because it affects the whole Church, should be established of convening a council of the entire Church not merely every decade, but every five years; for without such councils, as we have learned from experience, the Church of God cannot stand, nor has anything reduced God's Church from an excellent and perfect condition to its present wretched state so much as the omission of these councils.

If a general council should take up the issue of the reformation of particular churches, we do not see why those who are called Christians and who particularly need reform, especially the Greeks and the six other Christian nations, should not be invited.[61] From what we have read, when general councils were convened in the early days of the Church, the fathers were summoned not only from Italy and Europe but from all over the world, and for this reason these councils were called "ecumenical."[62] If those who occupied the Apostolic See had endeavored to preserve this custom, the Roman Church, which is the head of all churches, would not be deprived of her noblest members, nor would the other illustrious churches of Africa and Asia be divided from the Roman Church, the mother of them all, so that they are not even known to those who live in Rome.

This is your task, Holy Father, whom the Lord has called to care for all churches

---

61 Greeks were present at both the Second Council of Lyons (1274) and the Council of Florence (1439-1445). Both attempts at reunion failed to be accepted by the Greek populace. The Great Schism between the East and the West is traditionally dated to 1054. It began with mutual excommunications.

62 The word comes from the Greek, and refers to the entire "inhabited world."

[709] opus incumbit, ut quemadmodum nobilissimae illae Ecclesiae per incuriam, socordiamque aliquorum, qui sedem hanc Romanam tenuerunt, ab ipsa Romana Ecclesia ita divisae sunt, ut vix aliqua earum memoria reservetur, ita sapientia sollicitudineque Tua hae ipsae Ecclesiae capiti suo, Romano scilicet Pontifici, coniungantur, uniantur, ac in manifestiorem cognitionem eorum, qui Europam incolunt, redire incipiant. Quod si non omnes simul statim ad unitatem atque subiectionem Romanae Ecclesiae reducere poteris, maxime nisi prius Infidelium, et Mahumetanorum hominum genus deleveris, quod quasi inter Te et illas paries a Diabolo constructus eas longe retinet, satis futurum esse credimus, quod sicut paulatim per multorum annorum tempora haec divisio facta est, ita paulatim per alicuius temporis curriculum ad unitatem redire, modo una, modo alia, incipiat; neque nunc parum erit, si tot iam ante annis dimissam penitus, nuperrime autem in lucem revocatam Conciliorum consuetudinem stabilire decreveris, et[114] universale Concilium, quod apud Lateranum celebrare Iulius coepit, et Tu prosequi non destitisti, perfici curabis, si illud non ad aliud, quam ad Ecclesiae veram unitatem atque reformationem celebrari statueris; si ad Concilium illi advocentur potius, qui zelo fidei nihil veritati praeponere audent, quam illi, qui sublimioribus blandiri atque adulare consueverunt; si iis, qui in eo fuerint, loquendi omnis penitus libertas tradatur, et veritas ita suscipiatur, ut fallaciis et adulationibus nullus in eo locus esse videatur; si non veteri illo proverbio: Veritas odium, adulatio amicitiam, sed potius adulatio indignationem, veritas gratiam pariat. Si tale, Beatissime Pater, Concilium celebrare statueris, facillime fiet, ut in eo, et singulorum membrorum Christianae Reipublicae, et universae Ecclesiae saluberrima remedia Domini benignitate, administrante Te, et libenter saniora consilia recipiente, inveniantur, quibus ad veram sanitatem ac perfectum decorem languida diu, et turpitudinibus multis foedata haec Christi sponsa reducatur, ut qualem a[115] Salomone descriptam in Canticis Canticorum legimus, talem ipsam his oculis sine ruga et sine macula totam pulcherrimam et totam decoram intueamur.

In hoc autem Concilio nihil fortasse Beatitudini Tuae magis curae erit, quam exortum sub Iulii pontificatu schisma, quemadmodum coepisti, iam penitus sedare, atque singula divisa membra ad caritatis

---

114   et *Barletta:* ut MS, ED
115   a MS: in ED

[709] and who has placed you at the head of them all. Just as these noble churches have been divided from the Church of Rome through the carelessness and idleness of some who occupied the Roman See, so that scarcely any memory of them remains, let them be joined and united through your wisdom and solicitude to the Church, their head, and to the Roman Pontiff, and let them be better known by those who live in Europe. If, however, you cannot bring them all at once to the unity and authority of the Roman Church, especially without first destroying the race of Infidels and Muslims, which, like a wall constructed by the Devil between you and them, keeps them far away, we think it will be sufficient if first one, and then another church returns in the course of time to unity, just as this division occurred gradually over many years. Nor will it be a small thing, if you decide to normalize the custom of holding councils, which was abolished for so many years before, but has recently been brought back to light; if you establish that the Lateran Council, which Julius began and which you have continued and will bring to conclusion, has no other object than the unity and reform of the Church; if you invite to the Council men who, with zeal for the Faith, prefer nothing to the truth, rather than those who like to please and flatter their superiors; if complete freedom of speech is allowed in the Council, and the truth is accepted, so that there seems to be no place for deception and flattery; if, in contrast to the old proverb, "truth breeds enmity, but flattery breeds friendship,"[63] you see to it that flattery breeds indignation, and truth, favor. If you decide to hold such a council, Holy Father, you will find salutary remedies for each of the members of the Christian Commonwealth, thanks to the Lord's goodness and your administration and willingness to accept better counsels, so that the Spouse of Christ, who has been ill for too long and soiled by many vices, may be restored to true health and perfect beauty; and that, just as we find her described in the Canticle of Solomon, we may see her before our eyes, all beautiful and fair, without wrinkle or spot (Eph 5:27).[64]

In this Council, then, nothing may be more important for Your Holiness than to heal, as you have begun to do, the schism that occurred during the pontificate of Julius and to bring back the separated members to the bond of charity.

---

63 Cicero, *De Amicitia* 24, 89, cites the play *Andria* 68 written by Terence (190-160, B.C.E.).

64 Giustiniani writes, as did many Christian writers, as if the Song of Songs (Cant 4:7) were written about the Christian church.

[710] unitatem ducere. Quid enim boni in Ecclesia esse possit, si caritatis perfecta unio desit, non videmus; propterea sapientiam Tuam ante omnia curaturam credimus, ut ad imitationem illius Domini, qui omnes a se recedentes benigne advocat, revertentes laete suscipit, eos, qui quavis ratione ab ecclesia recesserunt, illa, qua maxime praestas, benignitate advocare non cesses, reversos autem non secus ac filios tractes, et eos, qui posthac reverti voluerint, laeto animo ac serena fronte suscipias, non quantum erraverint, sed quantum Tibi eorum, ecclesiaeque salus curae esse debeat, respiciens; neque enim pius ille de Evangelio pater filium prodigum ad se revertentem, quod omnia bona sua dissipaverat, arguit, sed potius quod filius erat, magno gaudio suscepit, celebreque laetitiae convivium parari iussit. Qui enim examinare praeteritam culpam intendit, hic non parcere ac misereri, sed potius vindictam retribuere velle videtur; qui namque magnanime parcit, ille non errasse etiam eum, cui parcit, cupit videri. In hoc autem toto schismatis negotio, quod magni quidem momenti est, et Iulio, qui ante Te beati Petri sedem tenuit, multas sollicitudines pariebat, nullus Tibi labor futurus est, cum Deus, qui omnia in hoc pontificatu Tuo mirabiliter operatur, ita ut verissime nunc dicere possint, qui videre redemptionem Israel expectant; Magnificavit Dominus facere nobiscum, ipse, Te hoc nec procurante, nec cogitante fortasse, et quasi dormiente, ipsos schismatis auctores his proximis diebus, praeter omnium expectationem, in Tua posuit potestate, et eorum animos ita ad Tui reverentiam, atque Ecclesiae caritatem convertit, ut magis a Iulio, quam a Pontificis persona, magis ab eo uno homine, quam ab ecclesia dissensisse ostendere multis argumentis conati sint. Et Tu, qui pii parentis erga omnes affectum geris, hos ipsos schismatis auctores, Pontificis auctoritate undequaque servata, ad pristinam dignitatem restituisti; pulcherrimum certe facinus, et pontifice maximo dignum; uno namque eodemque[116] die poenitentibus magnanime pepercisti, divisa a Capite nobilissima membra omni cum dignitate ad unitatem reduxisti, oves, quae perierant, invenisti, et ad gregem Domini propriis fere humeris reportasti, et perfectum certe pii parentis, pontificis maximi, optimique[117] pastoris munus implevisti. Cum vero ipsa Dei providentia hos duos totius schismatis principes ad te adduxisse videatur, et illi non corpore tantum, sed animo et

---

116   eodemque *Barletta*: eodem MS, ED
117   optimique MS: *om.* ED

[710] Indeed, we do not see what good there can be in the Church if it lacks the perfect union of charity. Thus, we are confident that Your Holiness—in imitation of our Lord, who kindly summons all who desert him and joyfully takes them back—will be certain above all to recall without ceasing and with the greatest charity those who have left the Church for whatever reason, to treat those who return no differently than sons, and to receive with joy and serenity all who want to return hereafter, not considering how much they have strayed, but how much you must care for their well-being and that of the Church. When the prodigal son returned, the kindly father of the Gospel did not scold him because he had squandered all his goods, but rather received him with great joy because he was his son, and he prepared a great feast of celebration (Luke 15:11-32). Whoever troubles to examine a bygone fault appears not sparing and merciful, but rather intent on revenge, since one who generously spares another prefers that the latter should not even seem to have erred. This matter of schism, which is very important and which caused Julius, who occupied the See of St. Peter before you, no little concern, will be no trouble for you. For God, who is wonderfully arranging everything in your pontificate, so that those who await the redemption to Israel can truly say, "The Lord has done great things for us" (Ps 126:3), has placed the very authors of this schism in your power these last few days, to the surprise of all, without any thought or effort on your part, as if you were sleeping, and has moved their souls to revere you and to love the Church, so that they have tried to show by various arguments that they dissented from Julius rather than from the Pontiff as such, and from that one man, rather than from the whole Church. You, in turn, with the affections of a kindly parent toward all, have restored these schismatics, without prejudice to the authority of the Pontiff, to their former dignity.[65] This is a splendid accomplishment and worthy of a great Pontiff. For in a single day you generously spared the penitent and restored those noble members, once divided from the Church, to unity with all due respect; you found sheep that had strayed and carried them back to the flock of the Lord, and thus perfectly fulfilled the role of a kindly parent, a Supreme Pontiff, and a good shepherd. Since, however, the very providence of God seems to have brought the two leaders of the schism to you, and since they have given themselves not only in body, but also in mind and will,

---

65 Cardinals Bernardino Caravajal and Frederico Sanseverino had joined with other dissidents to form the schismatic council of Pisa in September 1511. Leo X
welcomed them back to the unity and authority of Rome in June 1513, and the
renegade synod of Pisa was disbanded.

[711] voluntate, in quibus nulla potestatis Tuae vis extenditur, sponte sese ad unitatem caritatis, ad subiectionis reverentiam obtulerint; quid aliud sperare nunc possumus, quam horum exemplo reliquos omnes schismaticos iamiam Tuae subiectos esse voluntati? Qua quidem in re, si fuerit Tibi a Domino reliquos etiam conciliandi oblata occasio, Tu eam nequaquam spernes, ut vera Ecclesiae pace atque unitate reddita, magno harum sollicitudinum onere liberatus, ad Ecclesiae sanctae reformationem maiori cura, liberiorique animo vacare possis. Reliquos igitur schismaticos, Beatissime Pater, quos pro innata benignitatis Tuae observantia, pro pastorali, quam geris, omnium cura, etiam retrocedentes revocare, ac repugnantes amare debes, cum sese ultro revertentes obtulerint, et oboedire potius Tibi, quam repugnare ullo modo paratos esse confessi fuerint, suscipere ne differas. Aliter enim, nec fratrum Tuorum salutem amare, neque Ecclesiae unitatem, neque ea, quae unitati coniuncta sunt, bona diligere, calumniari poteris.

Vera autem atque perfecta reddita Ecclesiae unitate, tunc ad reformationem Romanae curiae omnes mentis Tuae vires extendere debebis. Ad quam perfecte instruendam tria Tibi potissimum, praeter ea, quae dicta sunt, necessaria existimamus. Primum quidem, ut Sapientiae Tuae oculos, nulla rerum magnitudine, nulla consuetudinis, immo perversae abusionis causa perstringi aut obcaecari patiaris; sed et praesentem Ecclesiae statum, ne ruinam ac desolationem potius dicamus, intuens, et in profundum vulneris eius aciem dirigens, Ecclesiam ipsam Dei magna reformatione egere in animo statuas, eamque Tibi, non sicut est, possidendam, sed reformandam a Deo traditam, sine haesitatione arbitreris, atque pro reformatione eius multo magis quam pro quavis alia re Tibi laborandum esse statuere velis. Nisi enim laborare Ecclesiam credideris, nisi Tibi quasi medico[118] ad sanandam traditam credas, nisi diligenter salutem eius curare statuas, nihil est magni, quod sperare Christiana abs Te Respublica possit; nihil est momenti alicuius, quod Tu praestare valeas.

Si vero haec, quae diximus, semel susceperis ac statueris, Secundum, quod non minus necessarium credimus, est, ut non tantum, quales illi nunc sint, qui sub Te Ecclesiae sanctae moderamina tenent, respicias, sed potius quales illi futuri sint, qui a Te ad huiusmodi regenda munera eligendi sunt, sancta intentionis perspicacia, sancta mentis

[712] virtute intuearis. Vinea enim haec Domini, quae pro uvae dul-

---

118   medico MS, *Barletta*: medio ED

[711] upon which no force of yours is applied, to the unity of charity and respectful subjection, should we not hope that all the other schismatics, following their example, have already been subject to your will? In this matter, if the Lord provides an opportunity to reconcile the rest, you will in no way spurn it; thus, when true peace and unity have been restored to the Church and you have been freed from the great burden of these concerns, you will be able to devote yourself with greater attention and a less distracted mind to the reform of the Church. Therefore, Holy Father, when the other schismatics—whom, in keeping with your innate kindness and pastoral care for all, you should call back and love even when they pull away and oppose you—spontaneously offer themselves and say that they are prepared to obey you rather than oppose you, do not hesitate to receive them. Otherwise, you may be accused of not caring for the well-being of your brothers, the unity of the Church, and the good things that come with unity.

When you have restored true and perfect unity to the Roman Church, you will be obliged to devote all of your mind's energy to the reformation of the Roman Curia. To accomplish this perfectly, we believe three things, apart from what has been said already, are necessary. The first is not to allow your eyes to be distracted or blinded by the greatness of your affairs or by any custom—or should we say, abuse. Rather, looking straight at the present state of the Church, not to say its ruin and desolation, and investigating the depth of its wound, you must determine that the Church of God herself is in great need of reformation, and that she has been entrusted to you not to be possessed as she is, but to be reformed. You should make this judgment without hesitation and happily reckon that you must work harder for her reformation than for any other thing. For unless you accept that the Church is in trouble, and unless you believe that she has been entrusted to you for healing as to a physician, the Christian Commonwealth can hope for nothing great from you, and there is nothing worthwhile you can provide.

Once you have determined and undertaken the tasks we have mentioned, however, the second thing, which we believe is no less necessary, is not only to consider what sort of people currently govern the Church under you, but also to ponder with holy discernment and strength of mind what sort of men should be chosen for these duties in the future.

cedine, fellis parit amaritudinem, et venenum aspidum insanabile, non tantum est veterum vitium curatione in meliorem formam vertenda, quantum novis optimis surculis positis penitus innovanda; minor enim labor futurus est, novas teneriores vites alere, quae dulces afferant fructus, quam veterum amaritudinem in dulcedinem commutare. Tibi praesertim, qui ea diei hora, eo aetatis Tuae flore, ad colendam Domini vineam advocatus es, ut quos modo humiles surculos plantare incipies, eosdem altissimas vites videre possis, fructusque ex laboribus tuis desideratissimos abundantissimosque suscipere: cum enim vetera quaeque[119] paulatim deficiant, si nova Tu a veteribus diversa statuere decreveris, non post multum temporis fiet, pro veteribus novis semper crescentibus, ut tota innovata Ecclesiae forma appareat. Et qualem Tu Tibi ipsi illam facere proposueris, talem Te videre continget. Summo etiam desiderio Te omnes Italiae partes, omnes Christianas regiones iam perquirere credimus, et quoscumque viros moribus doctrinaque praeditos invenies, eos in mentis Tuae arcano seu aliquo etiam quasi catalogo describere censemus, ut cum aliquis ex iis, qui modo Ecclesiae gubernacula tenent, decesserit,[120] semper in promptu habeas, quem loco eius subrogare debeas, sique paulatim his, quos ex universa Christiana Republica elegeris, sanctam Ecclesiam Dei committes, fiet quam cito, ut recedentibus veteribus, nova sint omnia.

In hac autem electione, in hac electorum a Te promotione, atque in omni Pontificatus Tui munere non eos Te audire velle consiliarios credimus, qui blandiri, qui adulare, simulare atque dissimulare studeant, quales fere omnes futuros illos existimamus, qui a Te aut dignitatem, aut beneficium, aut propriam gratiam aliquam sibi reportare cupiunt; hi enim propriis affectibus devincti, dum illis inserviunt, raro veritatem propriae commoditati, aut propriis desideriis anteponunt. Sed illis potius aures a Te sunt accommodandae, qui non, quae sua sunt, sed quae Domini Iesu Christi quaerere soleant, qui nihil a Te nisi commune omnium bonum aut postulare statuant, aut recipere sint parati, qui usque adeo non seipsos magis, quam Ecclesiae sanctae integritatem diligant, ut pro communi Christianorum bono morti etiam,[121] si opus sit, se adiicere non recusent. Tales, qui sincere, nulla propria affectione ducti, veritatem ante omnia

---

119   quaeque MS: quaequam ED
120   decesserit MS, *Barletta*: decesserint ED
121   morti etiam MS: morti, et ED; et morti *Barletta*

[712] This vineyard of the Lord, which instead of the sweetness of the grape furnishes the bitterness of gall and the incurable venom of asps (Deut 32:32-33), does not so much need to be improved by care for the old vines, as it needs to be completely renewed by planting new and better shoots. Indeed, it will be less work to feed new and tender vines, that they may bear sweet fruit, than to change the bitterness of the old vines into sweetness. This holds true for you especially, who have been called at this hour of the day, in the very flowering of your life, to cultivate the Lord's vineyard, that you may see the humble shoots you have planted become towering vines and may gather the long-desired and abundant fruits of your labors. If, then, when all the old things gradually fail, you have decided to establish new and different things in their place, the new will soon grow in place of the old, and a totally new form of the Church will appear, and you will see exactly the kind of Church that you have decided to make her. We know that you have inquired with the keenest interest throughout all parts of Italy and all Christian lands, and we gather that you are noting in the secret catalog of your mind, as it were, any men you find endowed with character and learning, so that when one of the current governors of the Church should die you will always have someone to put in his place. In this way you will gradually commit God's Holy Church to those you have chosen from the whole Christian Commonwealth; the old will very soon pass away, and all will be new.[66]

In making this choice and in promoting those you have chosen, and indeed in every task of your pontificate, we are confident that you will not listen to those who want to flatter, praise, pretend, and dissimulate. Such are all who want to obtain from you some rank, benefice, or personal favor; for being overcome by their own passions, they become slaves to these and rarely place the truth before their own convenience and desires. Rather, you should listen carefully to those who, instead of their own interest, seek that of the Lord Jesus Christ, who will ask for and are prepared to receive from you nothing but the common good of all, and who, finally, do not love themselves more than the integrity of our Holy Church and would not refuse even to die, if necessary, for the common good of Christians. If you will listen to men who desire with sincerity and from no personal motives

---

66 Giustiniani elsewhere also quotes this from the hymn *Sacris Solemniis* which Thomas Aquinas wrote for the feast of Corpus Christi, "recedant vetera, nova sint omnia." This echoes Rev 21:5, "I make all things new."

[713] colere cupiant, si audire statueris, nullae blanditiae animi Tui
virtutem emollire, nullae adulationes mentis Tuae aciem perstringere
poterunt. Sed Te sapientissime excogitante, et his, qui ad aures Tuas
loquuntur, recta animi Tui consilia non corrumpentibus, sed potius confirmantibus, eveniet certe, dum Tuum potius quam aliorum
consilium suscipies, dum illud, quod proverbio dici solet, eos qui im-
perant, ab aulicis semper vendi atque decipi, evitabis; ut quod vix fieri
nunc posse existimatur, statim ab omnibus factum esse conspiciatur,
novaque quasi de Caelo veniens ornata viro suo sponsa sancta appa-
rebit Ecclesia. Maximam vero in electionibus ac promotionibus hoc
pontificatus Tui initio Te habere velle rationem iudicamus, quoniam
omni dubio procul qualis futura sit sub Te Christi Ecclesia, qualis
Pontificatus Tui cursus, in his initiis quasi in quodam speculo universi intuebuntur, et omnes iam, qui tam propria commoda quaerunt,
quam qui communem utilitatem desiderant, tam mali scilicet quam
boni, ad hoc unum intentissime respiciunt, quales scilicet Tibi eligere,
quales promovere viros incipias, ut inde argumentum capere possint
eorum, quae aut illi propria, aut isti communia bona sperare valeant.
Magni certe momenti totiusque rei pondus hoc est; in quamcumque
enim partem haec primo libra inclinare coeperit, in eam perquam
certissime[122] tota deverget Ecclesia.

Tertium post haec, quod maxime omnium ad perfectam Ecclesiae
reformationem necessarium credimus, est, ut quae sive a sanctis
civilibus et ecclesiasticis legibus recte decreta sunt, sive quae Tu in
universali hoc Lateranensi Concilio, aut alio quovis modo decreveris
atque statueris, custodiri atque observari inviolabiliter facias, im-
punisque nullus sanctarum institutionum praevaricator permittatur;
aliter sanius certe est nihil statuere, quam statuta permittere, ut minus observentur; et nihil sane prodest ea sapientia, quae recte novit
excogitare, si illa iustitia desit, quae excogitata faciat custodiri.

Tria haec, quae diximus, quaeque etiam Te cotidie excogitare credimus, ad totius Ecclesiae reformationem, quamquam alia minus certe
necessaria deesse possint, satis sunt futura. Nam si Tu ad hanc reformationem toto animo respexeris, si ad hoc opus invigilare decreveris
non deerunt sapientiae Tuae optima ad ipsam aggrediendam consilia.
Si vero diligentissimorum, quorum consilia audias, considerabis, si
quos ad Tecum regendam Ecclesiam suscipias,

---

122   perquam certissime MS, *Barletta*: per quam certissima ED

[713] to cultivate the truth above all things, no flattery will bind your understanding. Instead, when you ponder everything wisely and the words that come to your ears do not corrupt, but rather confirm the counsels of your mind, and when you take your own advice rather than others' and avoid the proverbial situation in which rulers are sold and deceived by their courtiers,[67] surely we shall all witness that which no one thought possible, and a new Church will appear as if coming from heaven, like a bride all adorned for her husband (Rev 21:2). We assume that you want to give the most careful thought to the men chosen and promoted in the beginning of your Pontificate; for without a doubt the kind of Church we will have under your leadership and during your pontificate will appear in these beginnings, as in a mirror. All people, both those who seek their own advantage and those who desire the common good, both the bad and the good, are watching to see what kind of men you will first choose and promote, so that they may get an idea of the good things, either for themselves or in common, that they may hope for. This is very important—indeed, it is the whole matter, for in whatever direction the balance first seems to incline, the entire Church is surely bound to follow.

After these, the third thing that we consider especially necessary for the reform of the whole Church is that the decrees of civil and ecclesiastical law, or those which you have established in the Lateran Council or in any other way, be inviolably kept and observed, and that no one be allowed to break these holy ordinances with impunity. For it would be better to make no laws than to allow them not to be observed, and surely nothing good comes from the wisdom that thinks aright without the justice that causes those thoughts to be respected.

The three items that we have mentioned, and which we suppose are in your thoughts every day, will be sufficient for the reform of the entire church, even if other things, which are surely less important, are lacking. If you give this reform all your attention and determine to keep a close watch on it, you will not be lacking in good advice for handling it. And if you consider which are the diligent men whose advice you will heed and whom you will choose to rule the Church with you,

---

67   Seneca (10 BCE-65 CE) wrote this in his play called *Hippolytus* or *Phaedra*, 982.

[714] intuearis, non deerunt Tibi auxilia, quibus suffultus rem ipsam pro votis perficere possis. Si postremo, quae a sanctis Patribus decreta iam sunt, aut deinceps a Te statuentur, observari curabis, perfectioni firmitatem tantam adiicies, ut nulla perversitatis vis sanctam valeat amplius Ecclesiam conturbare, sed Petro et Paulo, qui Ecclesiae Romanae maximam semper curam habuerunt, intercedentibus, votis Tuis,[123] immo bonorum omnium, Deus ipse et Dominus Iesus Christus ita propitius aderit, ut sicut in Caelis ipso regente una est Beatorum omnium Ecclesia, sic etiam in terris unam sub Te humanarum creaturarum omnium Iesu Christo servientium Ecclesiam intuebimur, ad instar illius caelestis Ierusalem, pacis ac iustitiae plenam, in qua nullum vitium, sed perfectarum omnium virtutum plenitudo inhabitabit, cui Tu, Beatissime Pontifex, qui Christi vices geris in terris, dux, princeps et pastor, custos, solusque moderator assistes.

[Pars VI]

Hoc est, Sanctissime Pater, Ecclesiae Dei curam habere, iura Ecclesiae tueri; Ecclesiam enim regere nihil aliud est, quam humanarum creaturarum omnium gubernationem recipere; hoc est beati Petri domum, quam destructam, desolatamque, ac totam paene solo miserabiliter aequatam accepisti, reparare et erigere, ut in sanctum vivis ex lapidibus aedificium ad caelum usque consurgat. Haec quidem magni animi, magnae prudentiae, magnaeque sanctitatis opera sunt, et quae maximum atque magnanimum pontificem decent, quaeque etiam illum possint veris laudibus, ac solida gloria ad Caelum extollere, et caelestis aeternaeque felicitatis participem facere. Qui autem putant, quod pretiosarum in conspectu Domini animarum cura neglecta, terrenum Ecclesiae imperium aut tueri aut augere, atque in hoc uno omnes curas et sollicitudines ponere, magnanimi pontificis sit, illi certe non rerum naturas considerant, non recta iudicant ratione, sed perversa quadam consuetudine obcaecati, rerumque visibilium ac praesentium nimio amore devincti[124] falluntur quam maxime, dum caducis et vanis bonis perpetua ac vera bona praeponere nequeunt, dum Ecclesiam sanctam Dei, non Fidelium congregationem, sed terrenum aliquod imperium putant, dum Pontificis curae et fidei, non animarum salutem, sed terrenarum rerum administrationem[125] commissam existimant, et illum, qui in terris est dignissimus Dei vicarius, et divinis solum atque aeternis rebus intentus esse deberet, vilissimum

---

123 Tuis MS: Tus ED
124 devincti MS, *Barletta*: devicti ED
125 administrationem MS, *Barletta*: administrationum ED

[714] you will not lack the support needed to accomplish your plans. Finally, if you see to it that the decrees of the Holy Fathers and those which you yourself shall make are observed, you will add strength to perfection, such that no perversity will ever again trouble our Holy Church, and through the intercession of Saints Peter and Paul, who have always had the greatest care for the Church of Rome, our Lord and God Jesus Christ will answer your prayers and those of all good men, so that just as there is one Church of all the blest under his rule in heaven, we shall see on earth one Church of all creatures serving Jesus Christ under your direction, in the likeness of that heavenly Jerusalem, full of peace and justice, in which no vice, but rather the fullness of virtues will dwell, and over which you, Holy Father, who are Christ's vicar on earth, will be the one leader, prince, shepherd, guardian, and governor.

[Part VI]

This, Holy Father, is what it means to have the care of the God's Church and to safeguard her rights; for to rule the Church is nothing other than to accept the governance of all human creation. It is to repair and erect the House of Peter, which you have received destroyed and desolate and practically leveled to the ground, that it may rise to heaven as a holy edifice of living stones (1 Pet 2:5). These are works requiring magnanimity, great prudence, and sanctity, and which befit a great and magnanimous Pontiff, and which can raise him with true praise and enduring glory to heaven and make him a sharer in eternal and heavenly bliss. Those, however, who think that the mark of a magnanimous Pontiff is to neglect the care of souls, which are precious in the sight of God, and to guard or increase the worldly power of the Church and to put all one's care and solicitude into this alone, surely misunderstand the nature of things and fail to use right judgment. Rather, they are blinded by perverse custom and deceived by an excessive love of visible and present things, since they are unable to prefer lasting and true goods to empty and transitory ones, and they think that the holy Church of God is not a congregation of faithful, but a kind of worldly empire, and they suppose that the administration of worldly things, rather than salvation of souls, has been entrusted to the care and good faith of the Pontiff, and they make the worthy vicar of Christ, who ought to be intent upon divine and eternal things alone,

[715] terrenarum divitiarum negotiatorem faciunt. Quod si quis obdurato ita sit corde atque obcaecata mente, ut nihil aliud esse Ecclesiam Dei, quam civitates, regna atque imperia terrena arbitretur, ac dignissimum ac magnanimum illum vocare pontificem velit, qui haec ipsa Ecclesiae bona aut tueri, aut ex tyrannorum manibus vindicare invigilet atque laboret, nonne dementiae atque insaniae proximum est, illum magnanimum atque potentissimum pontificem credere, atque communi omnium voce acclamare, qui magna regna, magna Ecclesiae imperia ab impiis tyrannis inique possideri permittat, neque ad ea consideranda, nedum vindicanda, aciem armatorum virorum, sed neque oculorum convertat, ad quasdam autem sarcinulas colligendas totus occupetur, omnes pontificalis dignitatis vires auctoritatemque exerceat, nescio quomodo non videat, quomodo pontifici maximo, et ei pontifici, qui pro magnanimo velit haberi, indecens atque indignum sit, cum universus orbis terrarum sub pontificis positus sit potestate, minutias quasdam atque exiguas portiones ipsius creditae sibi universitatis diligentius quaerere? Si vero ad temporale Ecclesiae imperium augendum spectes, numquid Te animo et virtute Alexandro minorem sentis, cui unus non sufficit orbis? Numquid ullum unquam Romanum Principem Te maiorem fuisse existimas? Et tamen olim Romanis Pontificibus orbis serviebat universus. Numquid Te Urbano, aut Iulianum fratrem Tuum Balduino aut Gottifredo conferre timebimus, qui Ierosolymam et alia circumiacentia loca, expugnatis Infidelibus, Christiano adiecere imperio? An propria haec istorum hominum virtute facta existimas, an Domini auxilio perfecta? Si de humana virtute haec evenisse sentimus, de Tua, quae magna certe est, et omni maior existimatione, cur talia et his maiora sperare non possumus? Si de divino auxilio procedunt; quid est, unde Sanctitati[126] Tuae divinum defuturum auxilium suspicari valeamus, cum Tu sis super mortales omnes moribus optimis praeditus, virtutibus praeclarissimis ornatus, religionis zelo et pietatis fervore succensus, et maxima erga Deum et homines caritate plenus? Numquid sic affecto deesse unquam divinae clementiae munus potest?

Aggredere, Beatissime Pater, aggredere opus, ad quod a Domino vocatus es, et haec omnia, quae diximus, quae nobis magna videntur, in propriae virtutis conscientia, Te nequaquam maiora, existima, et de Divini auxilii confidentia ea

---

126 Sanctitati MS, *Barletta*: Sanctitatis ED

[715] a vile merchant of riches. But even if there is someone so hard of heart and blinded in mind as to think that the Church of God is nothing but cities, worldly kingdoms, and empires, and whose idea of a worthy and magnanimous Pontiff is one who takes care and works hard to preserve these goods or to wrest them from the hands of tyrants, wouldn't it be next to madness and insanity to consider one a great and powerful Pontiff and to give him common acclaim, if he should permit great kingdoms and empires of the Church to be unjustly possessed by impious tyrants, and should fail to direct not only his troops, but even his attention to consider—not to say, avenge—these matters, and if he should be entirely occupied and exercise all the power and authority of the Pontifical office to collect sacks of money, and should somehow fail to see that it is unbecoming and unworthy of a Pontiff, especially one who wishes to be considered great, to be diligent about some small and insignificant portions of his trust, when the entire world has been placed in his power? If you look to increasing the temporal power of the Church, do you feel inferior in virtue and courage to Alexander, for whom one world was not enough?[68] Do you think that any Roman emperor was greater than yourself? And yet the whole world once served the Roman Pontiff. Shall we hesitate to compare you to Urban,[69] and your brother Julian to Baldwin or Godfrey,[70] who besieged the Infidels and added Jerusalem and its surrounding areas to the Christian empire? Do you think that these things were accomplished by the virtue of those men, or done with the help of the Lord? If we suppose that they were accomplished by human strength, why can we not hope for such things, and greater still, from your virtue, which is beyond all calculation? If they proceed from divine help, why should we think that divine assistance will be lacking to Your Holiness, when you are endowed with character beyond all other men and adorned with the most illustrious virtues, when you are aflame with religious zeal and fervent piety and filled with the greatest love for God and men? Can the gift of divine mercy ever be lacking to one who is so affected?

Begin, Holy Father! Begin the work to which God has called you, and consider the things that we have been discussing, which seem great to us, in the knowledge of our own strength, by no means too much for you; and with confidence in God's help,

---

68   It is said that Alexander the Great (356-323 BCE) was disappointed, having conquered eastern lands, that there were no more worlds to conquer.

69   Pope Urban II (1088-1099) called for the First Crusade in 1095.

70   Baldwin (1058-1118) and Godfrey (1060-1100) were brothers. Both were among the leaders of the First Crusade. After the conquest of Jerusalem (1099), Godfrey became the first Ruler of Jerusalem and was succeeded by Baldwin, the first King of Jerusalem.

[716] certe non solum minora quam[127] nobis apparent, sed parva et levia et ad conficiendum faciliora iudica; aggredere iam opus, quod nisi incipere pigeat, nunquam incepisse poenitebit; perficies enim, si semel inceperis, facilius omnia, quam sperare aut optare potuisses. Id nos existimare ea faciunt, quae in Te a Domino mirabiliter sunt operata. An sperare aliquis aut optare unquam potuisset, Te ex captivitate ad libertatem, ab exilio in patriam, ea quae vidimus, facile reverti? An Tibi aliquis ita affectus est, ut Te trigesimum septimum annum agentem, ac iuniore aetate, his adhuc florentibus annis, praeter temporum consuetudinem, ad Apostolicae dignitatis sublimitatem ascendere, aut sperare, aut optare ausus esset, et tamen, cum ceteris paene fratribus[128] omnibus Tuis Cardinalibus minor aetate sis, quasi alterum Iosephum adoraverunt te fratres Tui, et quasi alius David, qui fratrum suorum minimus fuit, a Domino electus es, ita ut vere ad Te dicere possit Dominus: Posui adiutorium in potente, et exaltavi electum de plebe mea, inveni Leonem servum meum, oleo sancto meo unxi eum. Lege, Beatissime Pater, quae sequuntur, et vide, si non ille, qui haec mirabiliter in Te operatus est, adhuc mirabilia promittat: Manus, ait, mea auxiliabitur ei, et brachium meum confortabit eum; et ut magna cum fiducia inter cetera, quae a Te perficienda sunt opera, ad Infidelium expugnationem accederes, de illis victoriam promittere Tibi non dissimulavit, dicens: Concidam a facie ipsius inimicos eius, et odientes eum in fugam convertam. Vide, si non hoc iam praestare ipse abundantius voluit, quam aliquis Tibi optare potuisset. Quis enim Tibi tanta caritate devinctus est, ut optare aut sperare unquam potuisset, in his Pontificatus Tui auspiciis, schismatis auctores in Tua devenire potestate; reges ac Christianorum omnium Principes a Tua pendere voluntate? Quae quidem omnia Divinae in Te propensionis magna sunt argumenta. Non est igitur, unde haec ipsa, quae tam magna, tam ardua[129] prima facie videbantur, exigua, leviaque ac facilia Tibi non appareant. Qui si et de virtute Tua (nisi humilius quam ceteri omnes de Te sentire didicisses) confidere satis posses, quique in arduissimis semper rebus Domini auxilium Tibi adfuisse expertus es, eundem semper Tibi affuturum, non est cur sperare non debeas.[130]

Aggredere igitur Iudaeos, et Idololatras convertere, Mahumetanos aut ad fidem aut ad interitum

---

127   minora quam MS: maiora, quae ED
128   fratribus MS: patribus ED
129   ardua MS, *Barletta*: ardue ED
130   debeas MS, *Barletta*: debeas? ED

[716] esteem them not only less than they seem to us, but small and light and easy to accomplish. Begin the work now, which you will never regret having begun unless you are slow to begin it; for once you begin, you will finish everything more easily than one could have hoped or wished. We are inclined to believe this by the great things that the Lord has already accomplished in you. Could anyone have hoped that you would easily return from captivity to freedom and from exile to your own country, as we have seen?[71] Is anyone so fond of you that he dared hope or wish that you would rise to the Apostolic Office at the age of thirty-seven, much younger than is customary, in the very prime of life? Nevertheless, even though you are younger than practically all your brother cardinals, your brethren knelt before you like a second Joseph,[72] and like David,[73] who was smaller than all his brothers, you were chosen by the Lord, so that he could truly say to you, "I have laid help upon one that is mighty, and have exalted one chosen out of my people; I have found Leo my servant, with my holy oil I have anointed him" (Ps 89:20).[74] Read what follows, Holy Father, and see whether the one who has accomplished these wonders in you promises yet more wonderful things: "My hand shall help him, and my arm shall strengthen him" (Ps 89:21). That you might undertake, among other tasks, the conquest of the Infidels with great confidence, he promised you victory in no uncertain terms, saying, "I will cut down his enemies before his face, and them that hate him I will put to flight" (Ps 89:23). See then, whether God desired to grant you more than anyone could have wished. For who is so bound by affection to you that that he could ever have hoped or wished that, in the very beginnings of your pontificate, the authors of schism would come into your power, and that the kings and princes of all Christian nations would await your good pleasure? These are all great evidences of God's favor toward you. There is no reason why you should not regard these tasks, which at first glance seemed so great and difficult, as small, trifling, and easy. Having sufficient confidence in your own virtue—unless you have learned to hold a lower opinion of yourself than everyone else—and having already experienced the constant presence of God's help in the most difficult matters, there is no reason not to hope that he will always be at your side.

And so, boldly undertake the conversion of Jews and idolaters; bring the Muslims to the Faith, or to destruction;

---

71   The Medici family, who had risen in power in Florence during the fifteenth century, were expelled from the city 1494-1512. The future Leo X was nineteen years old at the time of the expulsion.

72   Joseph was sold into slavery by his brothers, Gen 37:27-28, but reunited with them in Gen 45:15.

73   The prophet Samuel passed over the other seven sons of Jesse to anoint David, the youngest (I Sam 16:10-13).

74   Giustiniani replaces the name David in the psalm text with Leo.

[717] deducere, Christiani nominis populos omnes Romanae Ecclesiae potestati subiicere, et quasi capiti suo membra coniungere, a fidelibus omnibus Ecclesiae filiis vitia evellere, virtutes plantare, Ecclesiam Christi et numero et virtute Credentium et spiritualium rerum
imperio augere. In quibus tamen conficiendis, si pro experienda animi Tui fortitudine, contradictiones, difficultatesque aliquas insurgere
Deus optimus rerum moderator permittet, Tu, Beatissime Pater, qui
non cedere malis usu iam didicisti, contra omnia, quae adversari votis
Tuis videbuntur, audentior ibis; sciens, quoniam opera, quae secundum fidei pietatem fiunt, contradictionem sustinere solent; omnes
enim, qui pie volunt vivere in Christo, persecutiones patiuntur, et vita
hominis militia est super terram. Quod pietatis Divinae dispensatione fieri non ambigimus; qui enim nos gloria et honore coronare vult,
his contradictionibus atque difficultatibus non opprimi quidem, sed
exerceri permittit; quoniam coronari minime dignus videri potest,
nisi qui legitime certaverit. Quae Tu, Sanctissime Pater, optime intellegens, et quaecumque oppugnationes insurgent, in his perficiendis
non ad opprimendam, sed ad exercitandam virtutem Tuam, non ad
diminuendum laborum Tuorum fructum, sed ad mercedem augen-
dam permitti cognoscens, tamquam strenuissimus miles laeto animo
excipies. Solent enim, qui magnanimitate pollent, in hac spirituali
terrenaque militia, ad declarandam virtutis suae praestantiam fortem
atque ardentem, potius quam ignavum[131] aut desidem adversarium
optare; ubi enim maior pugna, et difficilior expugnatio, ibi et virtutis
apertior est declaratio, et non recedentibus victoria laetior, mercesque
copiosior certa fide promittitur.

Haec tamen omnia cum Tu perfeceris, cum et alia assecutus a
Domino, et maiora fueris, quae nec nos cogitare possumus, neque Tu
optare fortasse audes, tunc illud, quod perfectionis multum plus habere certissimum est, quasi ultimum comoediae actum Tibi perficere
superest; quod pastoralis officii ac muneris postremum esse beatissimus Gregorius affirmat. Hoc autem est, ut postquam et recte vivens,
et alios omnes recte vivere docens, haec omnia confeceris, Tu
        temetipsum consideres, ne magnitudo virtutis occasionem
perditionis praebeat; et qui universum orbem deviceris, Temetipsum
per veram humilitatem, quae perfectior est victoria, et triumphi spe-
cies magnificentior, vincere satagas, non de

---

131 ignavum MS, *Barletta*: ignarum ED

[717] subject all Christians the power of the Roman Church, and join them as members to their head; eradicate the vices of the faithful sons and daughters of the Church and plant virtues instead; increase the Church of Christ in the number and virtue of the faithful and in spiritual power. But if God, the great ruler of all things, permits that some contradictions and difficulties should arise in the accomplishment of these tasks to test your fortitude, you, Holy Father, who have learned by experience not to yield to evils, will go more boldly to face everything that seems to oppose your plans, knowing that works done from a motive of piety tend to carry the burden of opposition. All men who wish to live devoutly in Christ endure persecutions, and the life of man is that of a soldier on this earth. We have no doubt that this happens by God's kindly dispensation; for since he desires to crown us with glory and honor, he permits contradictions and difficulties—not, indeed, to overwhelm us, but to develop our strength, because only one who has legitimately entered the contest deserves to be crowned the victor. Since you, Holy Father, clearly understand this and recognize that any attacks which arise are permitted not to overwhelm, but to exercise your virtue, you will face them joyfully, like a sturdy soldier. Magnanimous individuals, in order to show their outstanding virtue in this spiritual and earthly campaign, prefer a brave and earnest adversary to a foolish and lazy one, since a greater battle and a more difficult victory are more obvious demonstrations of virtue; and those who do not withdraw from the contest are promised greater joy in victory and a more ample reward.

When you have accomplished all this and have succeeded in still other and greater commissions from the Lord, which we cannot even imagine and which, perhaps, you dare not hope for, there remains one thing, which is surely the most perfect of all, for you to do as the final act of your comedy. This is the final task of the pastoral office and duty, as St. Gregory affirms. After accomplishing all these things, while living well and teaching others to do so, you must attend to yourself, lest the greatness of your virtue present an occasion for being lost; after conquering the whole world, you must strive to conquer yourself with true humility, which is the more complete victory and the more illustrious triumph.

[718] iis, quae feceris, gloriam quaerens, sed de iis, quae omiseris, rationem reddere pertimescens[132]; immo et in iis, quae feceris, non Te auctorem, sed ministrum, ac Domini illius instrumentum cognoscas, qui pro sapientiae potentiaeque suae immensitate et vilioribus saepe et minus idoneis instrumentis mirabilia solet operari. Memineris, quale Tibi sit a Domino concessum ministerium, et dices cum Paulo: Si evangelizavero, si haec omnia perfecero, non est mihi gloria, sed necessitas ita faciendi incubuit; et secundum Domini Iesu Christi praeceptum, cum haec et [719] alia omnia, quae ipse Dominus praecepit, impleveris, dices: Servi inutiles sumus, quod debuimus facere, hoc fecimus; neque propterea mercedem aut gratiam a Domino expostulare audebis, quia ea feceris, quae imperavit, sed potius misericordiae eius confidens, Te totum miserationibus eius committes; omnes enim cum peccaverimus, omnes misericordia eius egemus.

Haec sunt, Beatissime Pater, quae dicere debuimus. Tu nobis quaesumus, vestigia pedum Tuorum devoto corde osculantibus, benedictionis Apostolicae munus impartire.

---

132   pertimescens *Barletta*: pertimescas MS, ED

[718] You must not seek glory from the things you have done, but should fear to give an accounting for what you have omitted; indeed, you should not consider yourself the author of your deeds, but rather the minister and instrument of the Lord, who in the immensity of his wisdom and power likes to work wonders through lowly and less suitable instruments. Remember the ministry that the Lord has entrusted to you, and say with Paul: "For if I preach the Gospel, if I have accomplished all these things, it is no glory to me, for a necessity lies upon me" (1 Cor 9:16); and, according to the precept of Jesus Christ, when you have done these and [719] all the other things that the Lord has commanded, say, "We are unprofitable servants; we have done that which we ought to do" (Luke 17:10). Nor will you dare to require a reward or favor from the Lord, because you have done what he commanded; rather, trusting in his mercy, you will commit yourself entirely to his goodness; for since we all have sinned, we all require his mercy.

These, Holy Father, are the things we had to say. Devoutly kissing your footsteps, we beseech you to impart your Apostolic blessing.

INDEX